PIMLICO

160

CHINA

Arthur Cotterell combines a career in education and training after school with an extensive interest in other civilizations. His previous books include *The Minoan World*, *A Dictionary of World Mythology*, *The Penguin Encyclopedia of Ancient Civilizations*, *The First Emperor*, *East Asia: From Chinese Predominance to the Rise of the Pacific Rim*, *Origins of European Civilization* and *The Penguin Encyclopedia of Classical Civilizations*. He is currently at work on *The Pimlico Dictionary of Classical Civilizations*.

CHINA

A History

———

ARTHUR COTTERELL

PIMLICO

PIMLICO
An imprint of Random House
20 Vauxhall Bridge Road, London SW1V 2SA

Random House Australia (Pty) Ltd
20 Alfred Street, Milsons Point, Sydney
New South Wales 2061, Australia

Random House New Zealand Ltd
18 Poland Road, Glenfield
Auckland 10, New Zealand

Random House South Africa (Pty) Ltd
PO Box 337, Bergvlei, South Africa

Random House UK Ltd Reg. No. 954009

First published by John Murray 1988
First published with revisions by Mentor 1990
Pimlico edition 1995

13 15 17 19 20 18 16 14

Printed and bound in Great Britain by
Mackays of Chatham plc, Chatham, Kent

Papers used by Random House UK Limited are
natural, recyclable products made from wood
grown in sustainable forests. The manufacturing
processes conform to the environmental regulations
of the country of origin

ISBN 0-7126-6251-0

To Alan

CONTENTS

Contents

ACKNOWLEDGMENTS

The author wishes to acknowledge the assistance provided by the Chinese authorities in inviting him to visit Shaanxi province in 1980. He is also grateful for permission to use photographs of the terracotta army in this book. Closer to home, he is indebted to his wife for assistance with translation from the Chinese and to his son for several of the line drawings. Figure 86 is reproduced by kind permission of the Bibliothèque Nationale, Paris.

PREFACE

The Oldest Surviving Civilisation

When in 960 the first Song emperor Tai Zu was reuniting China after a brief period of disunity, possibly connected with the invention of gunpowder, one of the regional rulers begged for independence. Without a moment for hesitation the emperor asked, "What wrong have your people done to be excluded from the Empire?" It was inconceivable that any province should seek to isolate itself: the imperial boundaries enclosed the Greece and Rome of East Asia, China was the civilised world.

A not dissimilar conviction was held by the scholar and would-be reformer Kang Youwei, who still hoped as late as 1908 that national recovery could be achieved under the tottering Qing dynasty. What changed his mind was the murder that year of Guang Xu, the emperor whom he had advised during the abortive Hundred Days of Reform in 1898. Although the despair of Kang Youwei marked a watershed in Chinese attitudes towards an imperial system of government, it did not represent any abandonment of belief in the central importance of the civilisation itself. Traumatic as the collapse of China was in the late nineteenth and early twentieth centuries, when foreign nations brought the full impact of modern technology to bear, few Chinese ever doubted the survival of their country as a great power. This belief may account in part for the imperviousness of China to

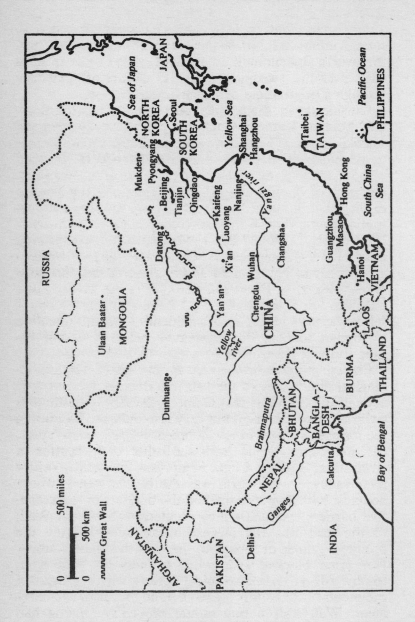

Fig. I China, showing present-day boundaries

modernisation before the foundation in 1912 of the Republic.

Japan, by contrast, had always been more open to foreign influences, borrowing heavily from imperial China for over a millennium: its method of self-defence after 1868 was the sweeping away of inefficient feudalism through a programme of selective westernisation.

Outside Japan, the colonial port cities—Calcutta, Bombay, Madras, Karachi, Colombo, Singapore, Batavia and Manila—created westernised Asian élites, for whom national independence was a goal that could be pursued without apology or a sense of contradiction. Not so in Shanghai or Tianjin, despite the interest of Kang Youwei in the institutions of the Treaty Ports, the international trading centres which were forced upon China from 1842. In contrast to colonial India, where foreign rule fostered a national consciousness as well as tolerance of western approaches to government and administration, the presence of assertive European enclaves in the Treaty Ports only sharpened the traditional Chinese tendency towards self-sufficient and self-absorbed identity. The intervention of foreign soldiers was impressive only because of the superiority of their arms.

Chinese attitudes have a very ancient origin. The archaeological discoveries of the last two decades are not only enough to remind us that China is the oldest continuous civilisation in existence, but they also indicate that during the formative stages of development it was a world apart, cut off geographically from the other early centres of civilisation. Ancient China comprised the fertile Yellow river valley: to the north was the barren steppe whose nomadic inhabitants compelled the building of the defensive barriers eventually incorporated in the Great Wall; to the east was the largest ocean in which lay the primitive islands of Japan; to the west the highest mountain system blocked trade routes to India and West Asia; southwards were semi-tropical forests where groups of rudimentary cultivators lagged behind in cultural achievement. Well over a millennium of civilised living had passed before the Chinese realised in the Former Han period (206 BC–AD 9) that there were any other civilisations. We can still catch something of the amazement of the envoy Zhang Qian when he returned to Chang'an, the capital, in 126 BC and reported that in what is now Afghanistan there were "cities, mansions and houses as in China."

Even then the difficult overland journey via the oasis towns of Central Asia kept outside contact down to the bare minimum, though foreign merchants carried along the Silk Road, as this caravan route became known, the greatest Chinese import before modern times—Buddhism. The fact that this Indian belief arrived so late in China, penetrating all parts of the country only towards the end of the fourth century, helps to explain why it failed to dislodge Confucianism as the state religion. While the struggle for spiritual eminence was fiercely contested and accompanied by scenes of mass fervour, the strength of the rational, sceptical mould of Confucian philosophy prevailed. The Buddhist church was brought by the Tang emperors (618–906) within the compass of the state, a Bureau of National Sacrifice being established in 694 to scrutinise the ordination of monks and nuns. The Chinese political tradition that took for granted strong central authority, embodied in the emperor as the Son of Heaven, was too firmly rooted for Buddhist evangelists to alter permanently either the social or the spiritual landscape.

Notions about divine approval of the throne, the so-called Mandate of Heaven *(tian ming)*, predate the unification of China in 221 BC and ultimately derive from the ritual observances practised by the Shang kings, who ruled the Yellow river valley and surrounding areas from about 1650 till 1027 BC. A closely knit kinship group, the Shang nobles traced their descent through their chief member, the king, from the supreme deity, Shang Di, the founder-ancestor of their people and the ruler of the natural world. Our knowledge of the sacrifices offered by the reigning king in order to gain divine goodwill comes from the ideographic script which almost certainly evolved out of the practice of reading oracles from the shape of

Fig. 2 Four ancient ideograms from Shang inscriptions relating to settlement: *(l-r)* the first means city, and shows a man kneeling in submission beneath an earthen enclosure; the second refers to worship in the ancestral temple—the hand beneath is offering the smell of cooked meat to the sacred niche from whence spiritual influence was thought to emanate; in the third an aristocratic residence is depicted on its earthen platform; and the last represents the city wall, the earthen defences of a Shang settlement

the cracks made by scorching animal bones and tortoise shells. Shang religion was, in effect, an elevation of ancestor worship, a practice distinguishing Chinese culture from prehistoric times. So powerful, however, has been sentiment over such rituals that in 1916 general Yuan Shikai chose to signal the conversion of his presidency into a dynasty by donning imperial costume at the celebration of the New Year. To thwart this warlord's pretensions the exiled Kang Youwei wrote to provincial governors urging them to remain neutral in the ensuing civil war, even though this meant that free scope was given to the republicans led by Dr Sun Yatsen.

That it should have been a scholar who attempted to rally support for the throne during the final decline of the empire is hardly surprising. The proposed reforms of Kang Youwei can be seen as the tail-end of a tradition of state service stretching back to the lifetime of Confucius himself. When in the sixth century BC this great teacher tried to deal with the abuses prevalent amongst the numerous feudal states, Confucius placed emphasis on loyalty to principles not factions, and argued that only through

benevolence and propriety could a ruler lead his subjects
to perfect lives. The character for propriety *(li)* tells us
exactly what Confucius had in mind, since the strokes
represent a vessel containing precious objects as a sacrifice
to the ancestral spirits. The rite of ancestor worship thus
became the focus of a moral code in which proper social
relations were clearly defined: the loyalty a minister owed
to a prince was the same as that owed to a father by a
son.

Under the empire (which lasted, with interruptions,
from 221 BC till 1912) administrative requirements allowed the service rendered by the scholar-bureaucrat to
be a reality as well as an ideal. Confucian scholars connected with the landowning class were one of the twin
pillars of imperial society: the other was the great multitude of peasant-farmers, no longer tied to a feudal lord
but liable to taxation, labour on public works, and military service. The low social position of merchants—a
prevailing feature in Chinese history—was the natural
outcome of economic development down to 221 BC because princes had always assumed most of the responsibility for industry and water-control works. Metallurgy
tended to be under state supervision, as in Shang times
when foundries and workshops were first set up close by
cities, but the blocking of all avenues of social advancement to merchants was the really effective curb since it
prevented the sons of successful traders from becoming
officials. A poor scholar without an official position would
prefer farming to trade as a means of livelihood, lest he
spoil any future opportunity of a civil service career.
Fully aware of the role of education in sustaining the
traditional order, Mao Zedong said he had hated Confucius from his boyhood. Because of his interest in the
Chinese countryside, however, Mao Zedong was the first
Communist leader to appreciate the revolutionary dynamic inherent in the agrarian revolts which had punctu-
ated imperial history. Before anyone else he understood
that in China, unlike the West, political control was
strongest in the urban areas.

"The police know all that is going on," noted Father

Amiot of eighteenth-century Beijing, "even inside the palaces of princes. They keep exact registers of the inhabitants in every house." Above all, the French Jesuit was impressed by the way in which the city's numerous inhabitants were steered along "the path of order and duty without arrests, without harsh actions, the police seeming hardly to interfere at all". Perhaps ignorant of the unusual extent of censorship under the foreign Qing dynasty, Father Amiot was still correct in contrasting the orderliness of the Chinese capital with life in its European contemporaries. Whereas in Europe major cities have tended to expand from a nucleus such as a marketplace or a cathedral, in China there has always been a more deliberate pattern of foundation. The Chinese use the same word, *cheng,* for a city and a city wall, revealing a very deep-rooted veneration of encircling walls. In the records of the Ministry of Works it is stated that when at the beginning of the fifteenth century the Ming emperor Yong Le decided to establish his residence at Beijing, he first built "a wall around the capital which was forty *li* long and pierced by nine gates". Although the rigidity of town planning was often relaxed, as a result of population growth or enforced movement during barbarian invasion or a weak dynasty, the Chinese city never succeeded through trade and industry in becoming sufficiently independent to challenge established political, legal and religious ideals. It was never a centre of social change.

The very Chinese sense of unity, of belonging to a civilisation rather than to a state or a nation, was fostered by the early development of the city. Long before unification by the Qin dynasty in 221 BC there were concentrations of ancient cities on the loess plains of northern China. This fine soil, windblown from the Mongolian desert in the last Ice Age, literally shaped the origins of China, since its fertility when watered led to state interest in the benefits to be derived from water-control works. Philosophically the king preserved the prosperity of the people by maintaining good relations with the heavenly powers, but along the riverbank his officers oversaw the extensive conservancy schemes upon which agricultural prosperity depended. Increased output sustained a large population in high densities and accentuated the division between the steppe and the sown lands. That the ancient Chinese came to equate civilisation with walled settlements surrounded by fields given over to intensive agriculture was only natural and must explain how they absorbed the less advanced cultivators who lived to the south. Yet the hilly terrain of much of southern China has permitted the survival of a great number of subcultures and different dialects, in contrast with the northern provinces where almost everyone now speaks Mandarin, as it is named after the former lingua franca of the imperial officials.

The standardisation of the written script, some time before 210 BC, at the behest of Qin Shi Huangdi, the First Sovereign Emperor, was a contributory factor towards national integration. Even more, the centralised bureaucracy he established in place of the feudal administrations his armies overthrew in 221 BC proved to be the basis of the most durable framework for social order ever invented, as the latterday efforts of Kang Youwei to salvage its remains early this century dramatically bear witness. Into the imperial bureaucracy were recruited scholars, especially after examinations in the seventh century became the principal means of qualification: their scale of values differed profoundly from that of merchants, thereby confirming the influence of the state over economic activity. Equally the power of the brush proved stronger than the sword, despite the Chinese invention of both the crossbow (before 450 BC) and the gun (in the thirteenth century). While China has suffered its fair share of war, more indeed than most other countries this century, it never accepted the necessity of a powerful military class. On the contrary the low esteem accorded to the armed forces is evident in the saying: "A good man is not made from a soldier, nor fine furniture from rotten wood". At any rate it helps to explain the somewhat ambivalent feelings of the colonial inhabitants of Hong Kong towards the British royal family, whose male members on official occasions invariably dress in military uniform.

This unique attitude towards the military is probably due to Chinese inventiveness. Early production of cast iron and steel provided efficient hoes, ploughshares, picks and axes: it allowed effective tillage by a small number of peasant-farmers, so reducing feudal bonds. Slavery was never a significant feature of Chinese civilisation after 1000 BC, in striking contrast to Greece and Rome. Imperial unification was intertwined with technical advance, but the ability of a dynasty to endure was also related to the acquiescence of the governed and the means by which they could effect political changes. It happened in China that offensive weapons were always superior, the crossbow before the lifetime of Christ having already ruled out an armoured domination like that of the medieval knight in the West. For this reason Mencius (372–288 BC), the greatest disciple of Confucius, could reasonably argue the right of the people to take up arms against tyrannical government.

Although the People's Republic currently lays claim to a large area of the China Sea, the historical fact remains that the Chinese never used their nautical skills to gain possessions overseas. Nor did they seek to expand their landward borders by unnecessary conquest: the Great Wall epitomised a state of mind which regarded defensive measures as a necessary evil. "An army is kept for a thousand days to be used on one," went an old saying. How advanced were Chinese vessels, for instance, can be seen by a comparison with those of the Portuguese explorers. Had Vasco da Gama rounded the Cape of Good Hope seventy years earlier, he would have found his own craft of 300 tonnes sailing alongside a Chinese fleet with ships of 1500 tonnes under the command of grand eunuch Zheng He. What the Portuguese adventurer actually encountered was an empty Indian Ocean, since after 1433 the Ming emperors discouraged maritime activities and ran down the imperial fleet, a policy of indifference to sea power which eventually exposed China to the unchecked depredations of European navies. The emptiness of the eastern seas gave the Portuguese, the Spaniards, the Dutch and finally the English the false impression that they were the first explorers to reach the area. Nowadays we know that the eastern Pacific, the China Sea and the Indian Ocean were Chinese lakes until the mid-fifteenth century.

Another difference between the ocean reconnaissance of the Chinese and the Portuguese concerns treatment of the peoples they met. Instead of pillaging the coastline, slaving, seeking to establish colonies and monopolise international trade, the Chinese fleets engaged in an elaborate series of diplomatic missions, exchanging gifts with distant kings from whom they were content to accept merely formal recognition of the overlordship of the Son of Heaven. There was neither the intolerance of other religious beliefs nor the search for material wealth, in the form of a fabulous city such as El Dorado, which were characteristic of the Portuguese expeditions. Sobering indeed is the statistic of 1 million slaves transported from Angola to the New World during the sixteenth century.

The Chinese distaste for organised war has a parallel in the traditional emphasis placed on clan and family. The ideal of four generations living beneath one roof reflected a belief in the value of custom, in a society largely unaffected by matters of state. The point is made in the famous interview between Confucius and the Duke of She, elder statesman of semibarbarian Chu. The duke argued that an individual's first loyalty was owed to the state, but the philosopher maintained it was to the family. "Among us there are those who are so upright", said the duke, "that if his father steals a sheep, the son will testify against him." To which Confucius replied, "Among us the upright act quite differently. The son shields the father, and the father shields the son: this we consider to be uprightness." An offshoot of large families and clans were secret societies, associations for mutual protection in disturbed times. Often republican in temper during the nineteenth century, the secret societies of today have largely forfeited their role and, in some cases, they have turned to crime.

The strength and resilience of the family has undoubtedly sustained Chinese culture during the periods of crisis; it has also ensured in nearly every case of conquest that foreign rulers have been absorbed and sinicised. Very different to the Germanic invasion of the western provinces of Rome was the Tartar partition of China (317–589), when most of the lands to the north of the Yangzi river passed into the hands of barbarian tribesmen from the steppes. Sinicisation of the invaders of north China eventually led a Tuoba Wei emperor to issue a decree prohibiting the use of the Tartar language, costume, and customs. Everyone had become Chinese. There was nothing like the collapse of the Latin West, where barbarian inroads destroyed the ancient civilisation with the exception of tiny pockets hidden away behind monastery walls, and a definite lowering of social conditions occurred, in which the Germanic peoples lost both their own culture and that of the world they had won. Unlike China, the western provinces of the Roman empire were not populated by large numbers of people who partook of the cultural tradition, and, besides, there was an enormous slave class.

The amazing absorptive power of Chinese culture has encouraged some observers to label it as unchanging. In reality there were large-scale internal transformations and constant movements of the imperial boundaries: these alterations are not always perceived clearly for the reason that they were slow in comparison with the rush of events in the twentieth century. Yet even the policies of the Tuoba Wei dynasty can be seen as the foundation of the brilliant Tang renaissance which made China the largest, most populous, and most tolerant country in the world. To the Tuoba Wei emperor Xiao Wen Di the Chinese owed the reform of the tax system, the re-introduction of salaries to officials, the re-creation of the militia, and not least the revision of land tenure. The tendency to overt concentration of ownership was arrested as the throne reasserted its authority to be the true custodian of the soil.

Present-day Chinese are aware of past greatness, though

there remains something of a love-hate relationship with the splendours of imperial and pre-imperial history. Mao Zedong was quite typical when he told the people not to dismiss the past but make it serve the present. Only then would China be able to "separate all the rotten things of the ancient feudal ruling class from the fine ancient popular culture that is more or less democratic and revolutionary in character". Where the past is at its most fascinating is in the amazing discoveries of archaeology, which since the founding of the People's Republic in 1949 has been given a degree of official support unmatched in the modern world. The 1973 Chinese Exhibition in London was the showcase of the People's Republic, since not a few of the pieces on display, including the jade funeral suit of the Han princess Dou Wan, had been excavated during the Great Proletarian Cultural Revolution. However, the most impressive archaeological find was made only in 1974, when peasant-farmers sinking a series of wells at Mount Li in Shaanxi province unearthed a section of a life-sized terracotta army buried close to the mound marking the tomb of Qin Shi Huangdi, the unifier of China. Over 7000 figures are estimated to be in the four chambers that have only been in part explored.

During the summer of 1980, at the time that bronze chariots were also discovered, the author was fortunate enough to be invited to visit the excavations at Mount Li. It was in conversation with the archaeologists there that a difference in attitude towards history became so apparent. No sense of urgency prevailed on the site, where magnificent pieces of sculptured terracotta were being patiently restored and exhibited in the positions they were found. There were no immediate plans to open the tomb mound itself, and Yang Chen Ching, the site curator, joked that its excavator might well be his own grandson. This deliberate slowness rests on a profound awareness of cultural continuity, on an intimate connection with the past. The individual portraiture of the soldiers in the terracotta army, Yang Chen Ching suggested, was a celebration of China's unification in that all the varying physical features of its various peoples were represented.

What he did not need to add was that they still inhabit the country and fully expect to do so forever. Belonging to the oldest surviving civilisation justifies such confidence, especially in the context of the spectacular Chinese recovery following the end of the Second World War, and makes any study of China impossible without reference to its ancient origins.

PART I

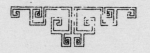

PRE-IMPERIAL CHINA

1

THE EMERGENCE OF CIVILISATION

Prehistory, Shang and Early Zhou (earliest times till 771 BC)

THE BEGINNINGS OF CHINESE CULTURE

Today archaeology is confirming the view expressed in Chinese myth about the remote origins of settlement in the country. Since the discovery of Peking Man at Zhoukuodian in the 1920s, there have been innumerable finds relating to the prehistoric period, which ended during the seventeenth century BC with the foundation of the Shang dynasty.

Excavation at Zhoukuodian had yielded evidence of forty individuals by 1938, when the operations of the Imperial Japanese Army made the site dangerous. Though these fossil fragments were lost in the hostilities, detailed study had already identified Peking Man as an advanced hominid whose limbs and trunk were of ordinary proportions. In 1959 the cave at Zhoukuodian was reopened and newly excavated materials shed light on a band of hunters and food gatherers which thrived there some 500,000 years ago. A tool-maker with the knowledge of fire, Peking Man had a varied diet of edible leaves, nuts, and roots, plus meat from the animals which roamed the locality—deer, antelope, sheep, horses, pigs, buffaloes, cats, rhinoceroses, camels and sabre-toothed tigers. In

1963 an older cousin was found at Lantian, about sixty kilometres south-east of Xi'an, the capital of Shaanxi province. Living some 600,000 years ago, Lantian Man had a thicker skull and more pronounced jaws, clear indications of an earlier stage of human evolution. The cranial capacity is 780 cc compared with the 850–1300 cc of Peking Man, and the 1350 cc of ourselves. The most primitive hominid so far discovered, however, is Yuanmou Man, who existed in Yunnan province over 1.7 million years ago. Possible use of fire is suggested by the presence of ashes and charred bones near the place where the fossil teeth of Yuanmou Man were unearthed.

All these early hominids were dependent upon nature's bounty. As hunters and food gatherers, they had to be mobile in order to follow the seasonal changes of natural resources and therefore little time was available for the development of culture. They also had to cope with the alterations in natural conditions brought about by glaciation: Peking Man endured two long periods of cold dry weather as well as one short warm and moist period without biological change. Not until a relatively recent date, within the last 10,000 years, were the ancestors of the Chinese people ready for a settled way of life based on agriculture. At present the earliest village site is five kilometres east of Xi'an at Banpo and dated between 4700 and 4200 BC; it is representative of at least 400 known settlements located on the loess terraces of the Wei river valley.

The domestication of plants and animals enabled people to remain in one locality and multiply. As in Mesopotamia and Egypt, the invention of food production was rightly looked upon as a cultural turning point. Chinese legend says that Shennong introduced agriculture by fashioning wooden implements and cultivating plants, whose seeds fell from the mouth of a red bird. He made pottery too. Besides being the inventor of agriculture, Shennong was regarded as the original herbalist who investigated the medicinal properties of plants, including tea. Endowed with a transparent stomach, he was able to observe the effects upon his body of all that he ate and drank, and learned that tea thoroughly cleaned out his intestines. Thoroughly Chinese as this interest in food as a preventative medicine is, the drinking of beverages made from the native tea plant appears to have begun only in the Spring and Autumn period (770–481 BC).

At the end of the Ice Age a layer of loess was deposited over a large area of north China, in some places nearly 100 metres deep. Blown from the semi-arid steppe, the yellow soil is easy to work and self-fertilizing if well watered, thus rendering primitive slash-and-burn methods of cultivation unnecessary. On this rich land, along the middle Yellow and Wei river valleys, the first settled culture developed in the fifth millennium BC: it is called Yangshao after the village in Henan province where in 1921 the initial identification occurred. The excavations at Banpo since 1952 afford a glimpse of what life was like in a Yangshao village of between 500 and 600 inhabitants. Enclosed by a circular ditch, six metres in depth, the settlement area was extensive, almost 50,000 square metres: or three and a half times the size of Jarmo in northwestern Iraq, where about 7000 BC a population estimated at 150 offers one of the earliest proofs for the mastery of tillage and animal husbandry. Remains of implements at Banpo include hoes, spades, cutters and digging sticks, while grinding stones show that the chief crop, millet, was prepared and preserved in the form of flour. The most important domesticated animal was the pig, but bones unearthed indicate that hunting and fishing supplemented the village diet. How crucial rivers and streams were can be seen not only from the abundance of fishing tackle on the site but also in the frequent use of stylised fish for the decoration of pottery. More than half a million pieces of pottery have been recovered, some 1000 of which are sufficiently well preserved to display the achievements of Yangshao ceramics. Whereas a fine-grained ware with geometric designs in black, red and brown was reserved for ritual purposes, impressed coarse grey vessels met daily needs. The latter were decorated with cord, mat or basket impressions.

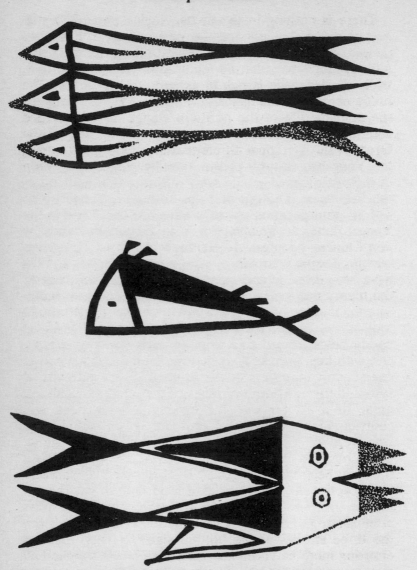

Fig. 3 Fish designs are particularly abundant on Yangshao pottery recovered from the Wei river valley, Shaanxi province. Here the earliest farmers in China used the rivers and streams to irrigate their fields as well as add to their diet

There is nothing in the archaeological record to suggest that the Chinese, or the proto-Chinese Yangshao people, ever passed through a pastoral phase. Milk and milk products have hardly featured in the Chinese diet, while the language is rich in agricultural metaphor. The fundamental division historically always has been between the nomadic life of the northern steppe and the settled communities of farmers to the south of the line of the Great Wall. A gradual differentiation was at work during the Yangshao cultural phase, as millet became the crop of the north and rice held sway in the central and southern provinces. Though rice was known at Yangshao itself, its domestication seems to have been achieved in the Yangzi delta, an area inhabited in prehistoric times by non-Chinese peoples. At Hemudu, south of Hangzhou bay in Zhejiang province, rice remains found in 1978 have been dated to approximately 4000 BC, which negates the theory that rice was imported into China from India. The inhabitants of the prehistoric settlement at Hemudu took advantage of natural swamps, or created artificial paddy fields, in order to raise an early-ripening subspecies with long grains. Thus the one food crop destined to overshadow all others in the future Chinese agricultural system derived from the fringes of the Yangshao cultural area. In a similar way the invaluable soya bean was contributed in the seventh century BC by the Turkic Jong, who were asked to send large quantities to north China. Quite possibly cultivated first on the Manchurian plains, the soya bean was recognised by the ancient Chinese to be exceptionally nutritious as a food and an enrichment for the soil. The character for the soya bean, *shu*, draws attention to the nitrogenbearing nodules of its root, since the three strokes at the bottom signify plenty. Besides ensuring more balanced harvests, soya beans supplied all classes of the population with cheap protein as well as vitamins and, once the method of extraction was perfected, a useful source of oil.

The loess soil at Banpo assisted the building of dwellings, most of which were semi-subterranean. It is easily shaped for fire holes and storage pits, as well as shelves,

Fig. 4 Banpo village was defended by a ditch some six metres in depth. This Yangshao site is situated a few kilometres to the south of Xi'an, capital of Shaanxi province

seats and bed platforms. During the final stage of occupation there may have been as many as 100 houses, judging from the excavated portion of the site. Twenty-four late houses, along with 160 storage pits, are fully dug and presently on display inside a permanent building. Also visible are the foundations of a huge longhouse (20 by 12.5 metres), which was divided by partition walls into separate rooms with hearths. House floors were usually plastered, while reed roofs supported by wooden posts surmounted low wattle-and-daub walls. Outside the defensive ditch there was a cemetery, containing 130 adult burials, and a pottery with no fewer than six kilns, in one of which were found unfired pots.

The pattern of subdivision into dwelling area, kiln centre, and cemetery recurs throughout Yangshao village sites. Shared burial grounds are also in evidence, but however many villages were involved the deceased are always laid to rest close together in neat rows. The custom of sharing cemeteries during the later phase of Yangshao culture shows that population pressure had caused the growth of a feeling of community wider than the individual village. It shows, too, that there existed a sense of lineage strong enough to require the burial of the dead in ancestral ground. Belief in an after-life is indicated by the placing of food and utensils in graves, so we may surmise that here are the dim beginnings of ancestor worship, which is attested unequivocally during the following Longshan cultural phase. Argument continues about the nature of Yangshao society, however. Chinese archaeologists have analysed a number of unusual graves as examples of matrilineal burial practice: they find special significance in the grave of a little girl at Banpo which yields rich funerary gifts besides the vestiges of a wooden coffin. That the leader of the village was female cannot be determined with assurance from the archaeological survey of the site, but evidence from legends concerning the tribal origins of the historical Zhou people would support the prevalence of matriarchy in remote times. According to *The Book of Odes (Shijing)*, collected not later than the sixth century BC, the Zhou descended from Jiang Yuan, who "prayed she might no longer be childless. She trod on the big toe of Heaven's footprint and thereby attained her desire."

Equally uncertain are the antecedents of Yangshao culture, now generally recognised as the genesis of Chinese culture because of the permanent influence its self-sustaining agriculture exerted over the tribes who subsequently came to regard themselves as the Chinese people. Physically the inhabitants of Yangshao villages resemble the present-day Chinese of the southern provinces, but this is not unreasonable when it is recalled how, during the imperial era, nomadic invasion turned north China into a melting pot. Yet even from Zhou times, when literary sources become more available, it is obvious that the criterion for defining membership in the Chinese world was awareness of a common cultural heritage rather than ethnic affinity. "King Wen," Mencius could say openly in the fourth century BC, "was a barbarian," when he laid the foundation of the Zhou conquest of Shang. He came to be regarded by the Chinese as a sage-king through the contribution made by his successors to the civilisation itself. The prehistoric Chinese, then, were never a homogeneous people and the growth of the original cultural area established in Yangshao times came through the gradual adoption of a standard way of life by separate groups. Of central importance was the development of a religion focused primarily on male-ancestor worship.

Before Yangshao culture had run its course, another
culture emerged called Longshan after the type-site of
Chengziyai in Shangdong province, where it was discovered in 1929 near to Longshan or "Dragon Mountain".
Chengziyai's rectangular ramparts of rammed earth indeed anticipate the long tradition of walled cities about
to be inaugurated by the Shang; furthermore, the settlement area they enclosed was over five times larger than
that within the defensive ditch at Banpo. Other resem-
blances with later times include divination techniques,
pottery shapes and, interestingly, a number of potters'
signs which are similar to characters found in Shang
oracle inscriptions. Either an evolution of Yangshao culture or a distinct eastern tradition with connections leading north-eastwards into eastern Siberia, Longshan is
essentially characterised by its advanced pottery, a thin,
highly polished ware, either grey or black, which shows
signs of having been made on a wheel. This culture
flourished until the start of the Bronze Age sometime
after 1800 BC, and its remains are found beneath those of
the Shang in Henan province, the seat of that dynasty.
But its infiuence was very widespread during the third
millennium BC, when notable material progress was being
made in several different areas. While the Henan Longshan
was ancestral to Shang civilisation (with its cities, metallurgy, writing and elaborate art), the same culture in
Shaanxi province also underlay the future Zhou dynasty,
in Shandong province the famous state of Qi, and in the
Yangzi delta the rising powers of Yue and Wu.

Funerary gifts in Longshan cemeteries reflect both increasing social differences and the cult of male-ancestor
worship. From Shaanxi province comes the earliest ce-
ramic phallic symbol, dated to the first quarter of the
third millennium BC. Its association with ritual can be
deduced from the etymology of *zu*, the character for
ancestor, which is simply a depiction of a phallus. The
rise of a patrilineal society was connected probably with
the expansion of the Longshan cultural area in that migration led to conflicts favouring the authority of the
warrior. Certainly Sima Qian (145–90 or 79 BC), who

wrote the first general history of China, thought that the accession of Huang Di, the celebrated Yellow Emperor, was the result of his military successes against warlike tribesmen. The earliest mortal ruler, Huang Di is supposed to have been enthroned in 2697 BC. He was looked upon as the founder of governmental institutions. Some traditions credit him with the invention of the magnetic compass and coined money, which replaced cowrie shells as the medium of exchange, and his wife is said to have excelled in household skills and sericulture, though we are aware of the raising of silk worms even in the Yangshao period.

Closely related to the cult of ancestor worship was divination from the cracks that develop in scorched animal bones, usually the shoulder blades of sheep, cattle, and pigs, but sometimes deer. After 1300 BC divination became elaborately standardised, when the Shang not only expertly treated bones and tortoise shells in advance but also inscribed on them the questions asked of the ancestral spirits and sometimes the answers received. Questions put by the Shang aristocrats touched on matters of state as well as family affairs. Uniquely Chinese, this oracle method predates any other known in ancient civilisations, its closest rival being the examination of the liver of sacrificed animals by Babylonian priests around 2000 BC.

THE XIA DYNASTY (BEFORE 1650 BC)

The size of the rectangular enclosure at Chengziyai hints at a stratified society in which its occupants held some kind of sway over the smaller settlements in the immediate vicinity. The strong walls, eight metres wide at their base, could have acted also as a refuge for these villages in troubled times. Such an interpretation would square with Chinese legends about the start of dynastic rule towards the close of the third millennium BC. The earliest of the Three Dynasties *(san tai)* before imperial unification took place in 221 BC was believed to have been the

Xia: it was followed by the Shang, then the Zhou, the longest-enduring dynasty in Chinese history. Prior to the establishment of Xia power, the throne was not passed on to the next ruler according to birth, each successor being chosen by merit. Possibly this tradition recalls dimly some arrangement whereby a confederation of tribes elected a paramount chief to lead them against outside attackers. However, the moral predilection of Chinese historians may have caused them to conclude that formerly an ideal system determined selection on the basis of a candidate's outstanding qualities alone. Thus "able and virtuous Yao united the black-haired people and brought harmony to the land". Flood control was brought about by the "excellent Shun, who deepened the rivers", but to their minister Yu (2205–2197 BC) went the privilege of founding the Xia dynasty.

Legend attributes the elevation of Yu's kinsmen to his achievement in containing the Great Deluge. Thirteen years Yu spent "mastering the waters" without once returning home to see his wife and children. By means of extensive water-control works, he brought "water benefits" to the people—floods ceased and fields were irrigated—and by organising labour on a massive scale in order to achieve his goal he would have laid the basis of feudalism. That the ancient Chinese associated Yu with hydraulic conservancy, though major schemes occur only from the fifth century BC onwards, must mean that the appreciation of its political importance is very old. The fact that in imperial times irrigation channels, reservoirs, and drainage schemes were built mostly as public works linked them closely with the fortunes of the ruling house. Just as flood or drought could be read as divine disapproval, so slowness in mounting adequate relief measures inevitably encouraged peasant rebellion. As a minister was to advise the Han emperor Wu Di (140–87 BC), the absence of a state grain reserve left the throne vulnerable in the event of famine or an unexpected campaign. Agriculture thus needed to be sustained through the maintenance of extensive water-control works.

While large-scale undertakings are quite late, it seems

unlikely that nothing was done in the loess areas prior to the Chang river scheme of northern Henan province, which we know the state of Wei started in 424 BC. Prince Huan of Qi (685–643 BC) is said to have thrown up dykes along the lower reaches of the Yellow river in order to concentrate the nine streams of previous delta into one. The undertaking ended of course in failure, not least because the supposed wisdom of Yu was forgotten: he had always dug the channels deep and kept the dykes low, conducting the torrent naturally to the sea. Attunement to the rhythm of nature was considered vital, its perfect expression being the Yin/Yang theory, which envisaged two interacting forces, not in conflict but existing together in a precarious balance that if disturbed would bring disasters to mankind. This perception of natural forces could have arisen only in loess country, where a sudden downpour or a burst embankment might drastically alter the landscape.

Of the Xia dynasty there is so far no conclusive trace, though Chinese archaeologists are busily searching for representative artefacts in the Longshan levels immediately preceding the emergence of Shang civilisation. Reassessment of finds at Erlitou in Henan province may well result in the identification of a Xia phase there. The site was dug between 1959 and 1964, with impressive finds leading to speculation that perhaps it was Po, the capital of the first Shang ruler, Tang. Excavations were resumed in the 1970s and work continues today. Moreover, the accuracy of Chinese record-keeping makes it foolhardy to dismiss the Xia dynasty as mythical. A royal genealogy preserves the names of seventeen monarchs who all together reigned for nearly 500 years, and it is remembered that when in 1027 BC the Zhou toppled the Shang seven principalities of Xia fame were restored. The last Xia king is said to have been the tyrannical and cruel Jie, whom Tang overthrew with the support of celestial aid. "Because of his arrogance," said the chief minister of Tang, "Heaven viewed him with disapprobation, caused our Shang to receive the Mandate, and employed Your Majesty to stir up the people."

Fig. 5 Shang ideograms found in bronze inscriptions relating to war. Clockwise, the top left shows the presentation of a banner to an ancestral spirit; then a chariot; in the bottom right a drummer signifies an advance, while the final one reveals how a halberd was swung from a speeding chariot

SHANG CIVILISATION (c.1650–1027 BC)

The legendary cruelty of Jie is minor in comparison with that practised by Di Xin, the last Shang king. But as the vices of both rulers are described as being almost the same, we should guard against a tendency among Chinese authors to explain a change of dynasty in terms of virtue sweeping aside corruption. Ancient historians perceived events as moving in cycles, whereby a new cycle began when a new hero-sage toppled the worthless tyrant of the old house and set up a new rule. Whatever the truth behind the savage deeds of Jie, tradition is unanimous in its praise for the just overthrow of the unworthy ruler by Tang, who was endowed "with valour and prudence to serve as a sign and a direction to the myriad regions and to continue the old ways of Yu".

The event is supposed to have taken place in 1766 BC. Tang's own reign was noted for its military exploits and the attention paid to domestic affairs. Efficient government coupled with the promotion of increased agricultural output, upon which, during campaigns, he could support his army, now equipped with the chariot, gave supremacy to the new Shang dynasty. The period which he inaugurated marks the emergence of civilisation in China, as the Shang distinguished themselves not only in handicrafts and technology; they introduced stone carving, bronze-casting, chariot warfare, writing, systematised oracle-taking, urban palaces, kingship, nobility, massive public works, an accurate calendar, a pantheon of deities, organised ancestor worship, and great tombs replete with treasure and sacrificial victims. The horse-drawn chariot alone may have been a borrowing, since its construction was very similar to the model developed long before in West Asia. Yet above all else, the Shang gave to ancient China a centralised realm that was capable of embracing the tribal groups living north of the Yangzi river. They facilitated a historical process by which the coalescence of various regional Longshan cultures brought about the birth of Chinese civilisation.

The core of the kingdom was that part of Henan province where the higher ground declines into the floodplain of the Yellow river. Despite the tentative identification of Erlitou with Po, there are other sites contending for the honour of being the capital of Tang. Across the Lo river from Erlitou stands modern Yanshi, since 1958 the subject also of archaeological investigation. Remains of early Shang buildings are known to exist in fourteen places in and around the town. Perhaps as important is Kaoyai, a site to the south with evidence of continuous occupation from the Yangshao period, through the Longshan, to Shang times. Current opinion in the People's Republic, nonetheless, favours the extensive site of Erlitou, which is raised slightly above the surrounding land. In 1975 the outline of a palace was reported, along with house floors, storage pits, kilns, pottery water-pipes, bronze-casting moulds, crucibles, stone and bone. The palace foundation, comprising an earthen platform 108 by 100 metres, is the oldest known and once boasted rectangular timber-framed buildings, whose main columns rested on pieces of stone placed at the bottom of post-holes. In general the architectural features of the plan are identical with those of the palaces of kings and lords in later historical ages. Very eminent Shang people must have lived at Erlitou, although there is no positive proof that they were of royal blood.

Survey of the site indicates that a major complex existed there in the sixteenth century BC, somewhat after the ancient Chinese calculation for the start of the dynasty. But earlier settlement levels than the palace one have been dated to shortly before 2000 BC, and these are currently under scrutiny for Xia remains. The earliest bronzes discovered in China come from them, thin-walled sparsely decorated vessels fired with the aid of moulds. Parallels with Longshan pottery shapes support the view that the practice of metallurgy was an indigenous invention, springing from advances in kiln design. But the greatest concentration of bronzes is found at Anyang, the final capital of the Shang kings.

Before Great Shang (as Anyang was called in oracle inscriptions) became the capital about 1400 BC the seat of government had already been moved six times. One of these capitals is now thought to be sited at Zhengzhou, the administrative centre of Henan province. Discovered in 1950, the Shang ruins are still being excavated and studied; they are tentatively identified as Ao, the second Shang capital established by the tenth ruler, Zhong Ding. Whereas Po served as the royal headquarters for nearly two centuries, the choice of Zhong Ding satisfied only himself and his brother, who succeeded him. After twenty-six years the next king is credited with the removal of the capital across the Yellow river to an unspecified place called Xiang.

The rectangular city wall of Ao, built by the same method as employed at Chengziyai, extends for over 7000 metres and encloses an area of 3.2 square kilometres. A maximum width at the base of 36 metres and a height of slightly under 10 metres for the surviving sections of the wall leave one in no doubt that the defences were originally very substantial. The estimate of labour required for construction—10,000 men working for eighteen years—brings into focus the great power wielded by the Shang

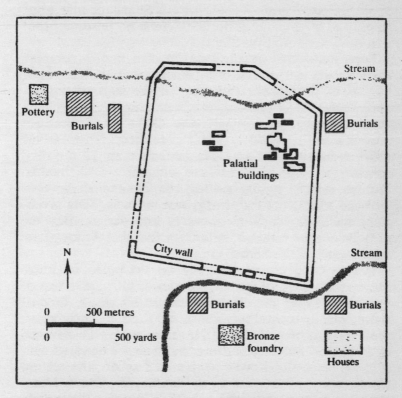

Fig. 6 Shang dynasty remains at Zhengzhou, Henan province. The site is tentatively identified with the second capital, known in the Histories as Ao. So far no gateways have been excavated

kings, who like their bronze-age peers in West Asia and the Mediterranean, were able to dominate the peasantry through the exercise of a metal monopoly.

The enclosure at Zhengzhou was an aristocratic stronghold, in which ceremony and administration could take place safe from the common gaze. At one stage it would seem that burials as well as dwellings were considered appropriate, though until the whole site and its surroundings have been fully explored any generalisation about funerary practices must be tempered with caution.

By the concession of land within the defences, no less than by conferring distant territories on the nobility, the Shang king was able to secure loyalty and keep a sharp eye on his most powerful subjects. The palace buildings themselves are located in the north-eastern portion of the enclosure, their outlines described on earthen platforms by large floors and post-holes. The means of wall construction was rammed earth, a Longshan inheritance. Wooden shuttering was used, dry earth being rammed till solid; then, the shuttering would be removed and the process repeated at a higher level. Bamboo or another wooden material might be placed between each layer to absorb moisture. Earthen walls have determined the two characteristic features of Chinese architecture—that walls were not usually weight-bearing and that buildings were furnished with generously overhanging eaves. They were very suited to north China, a region troubled by frequent earthquakes; the remains of the city wall of Ao show that repairs were often needed.

A representative palatial building, found in 1977, is nine roomed with pillared corridors. Stone pillar bases were placed in the earth foundation, and from ash deposits it can be assumed that pillars, cross beams and ridgepoles were made of wood; in the same way as the Egyptians had recourse to the Levant, so the Shang probably imported the longer pieces of timber needed in construction from the forests of Shaanxi. The entire structure was finished with finely plastered earthen walls and the double-eave construction of the thatch roof ensured protection from the worst of summer heat. As no trace of

Fig. 7 A reconstruction of the palatial building excavated in 1977 at Zhengzhou, Henan province. Dating from the sixteenth century BC, it was probably used by courtiers of the Shang king

clay or baked tile has been found, the roof can have been covered only with vegetable material.

Its excavators believe the purpose of the building was practical, the cool interior offering accommodation for either royal concubines or high officials attending upon the king. Later in Anyang it is likely that some of the ceremonial buildings had a second storey. During the laying of foundations both human beings and animals were ritually killed and interred, in Zhengzhou a ditch below one palatial floor containing about 100 human skulls, mostly sawn off across the eyebrow and the ear. The nearest equivalent at Erlitou would be burials of victims with heads or parts of the limbs missing. These finds reveal a highly stratified society in which slaves or prisoners of war, possibly both, could be used in religious ceremonies and even as raw material for bone manufacture. Human sacrifice lingered on after the fall of Anyang in 1027 BC, but declined before the humanist teaching of Confucius and his followers. In the first century BC a Han prince was severely punished for forcing slave musicians to follow him into death: his lands were confiscated and his son disinherited by the emperor.

Two other kinds of buildings existed at Zhengzhou, both without the earthen ramparts. First, there are the homes of ordinary people, still semi-subterranean with floors as much as 2.7 metres below ground-level. The earthen steps down into these simple dwellings and those giving access to the terraces on which stood the houses of the nobles must have determined the everyday usage for visiting and movement: the Shang Chinese said "ascend and descent" for "come and go". The second kind of building, likewise underground, is connected with economic activity. Some of these functioned as storage pits, others as workshops for potters, bone-makers and bronze-smiths. One bronze foundry, south of the ramparts, has preserved moulds for both ritual vessels and weapons of war, pottery crucibles, charcoal, and lumps of melted metal.

Although three pieces of inscribed oracle bone have been recovered at Zhengzhou, it is argued that they were introduced from Anyang, which Pan Geng selected as the final Shang capital. The prime source for the written language, the site of Great Shang at Xiaotun village near present-day Anyang was excavated from 1928 to 1937 and after 1950, revealing enormous royal tombs, palatial buildings, and deposits of oracle bones.

Recorded in the *Book of History (Shu Ching)*, a collection of documents edited during the fourth century BC, are the difficulties faced by Pan Geng when he wished to move the capital. As these chapters are held to be authentic by modern scholars, the words of the king are quoted at length. Speaking firstly to the most senior members of his court, he countered their resistance thus:

> Our king Zu Yi came and fixed on Geng for his capital. He did so from a deep concern for our people, because he would not have them all die where they cannot help one another to preserve their lives. I have consulted the tortoise shell and obtained the reply: "This is no place to live." When former kings had any important business they paid reverent attention to the commands of Heaven. In a case like this they were not tardy; they did not linger in the same city forever. If we do not follow the example of old, we shall be refusing to acknowledge that Heaven is making an end to our dynasty. How small is our respect for the ways of

former kings! As a felled tree puts forth new shoots, so Heaven will decree us renewed strength in a new city. The great inheritance of the past will be continued and tranquillity fill the four quarters of our realm.

Separately he charged his nobles with stirring up trouble amongst "the multitudes through alarming and shallow speeches", a grievous crime he pointed out considering how their own ancestors shared in the sacrifices offered to former kings. Unless they treated the ruler, the One Man, with sufficient honour and loyalty, there would be inevitable punishments and afflictions laid on the Shang by an outraged Heaven. In order to ram home this point, as well as broadcast his views more widely, Pan Geng then addressed the multitudes, who were "charged to take no liberties in the royal courtyard and obey the royal commands". He told the people of the reasons for the removal, stressing the calamity which the founder ancestor of the dynasty would surely inflict on the existing capital, and let it be understood that nothing would affect his "unchangeable purpose".

Having won the day by direct speech, Pan Geng transferred everyone across the Yellow river to Great Shang, where he instructed his officials to "care for the lives of the people so that the new city would be a lasting settlement". The story is interesting for several reasons. Obvious are the threats of the priest-king to invoke the royal ancestral spirits to punish dissidents, yet the strength of Pan Geng's conviction of impending disaster without a change of location cannot be denied; he genuinely believed that only his "great anxiety" stood between the Shang and their ruin. Again it was Heaven which had given the crucial sign via the cracks on the tortoise shell. How could a king ignore so dire a warning? "When great disasters came down from Heaven," Pan Geng said, "the former rulers did not fondly remain in their place. What they did was with a view to the people's advantage, and therefore each of them moved the capital." This solicitude for the welfare of the ordinary people, even more

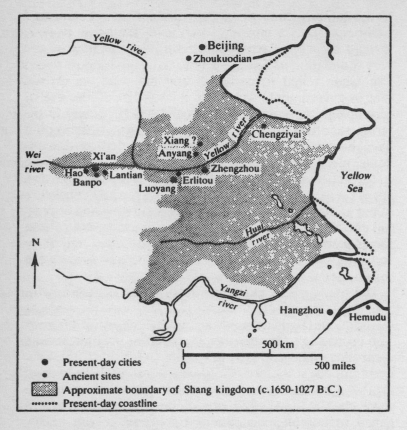

Fig. 8 Earliest China

the face-to-face explanation they received in the royal
courtyard, jars with the notion of Shang society being
based entirely on slavery, which is the view presently
favoured in the People's Republic.

Controversy turns on the translation of the character
zhong in oracle inscriptions. Were the *zhong*, "the multitudes", a vast class of slaves under the control of royal
officials, or were they the Shang people below noble
rank? Oracle texts reveal that they cultivated fields belonging to the king and the nobility, participated in royal
hunts, formed a sizeable element in the army, and undertook garrison duties. Some inscriptions testify eloquently

to the fatherly concern of the ruler for their health and well-being, plus a nagging worry over their loss in war. Instead of being slaves, "the multitudes" appear as the very foundation of Shang society, the people upon whom Pan Geng relied to construct and maintain his chosen seat of government. An oracle relates that on the eve of a campaign the commander-in-chief led his *zhong* in offering sacrifices to a royal ancestral spirit, which could have happened only if they were regarded as descendants, albeit distant ones of the tribal founder. But there is textual evidence for the keeping of both male and female slaves in Shang times, the largest group consisting of war captives from the non-Chinese peoples living beyond the northern and western frontiers of the kingdom. These slaves worked in royal and noble households, either as servants, grooms or gardeners, and from their ranks were drawn those destined for sacrifice.

The existence of numerous male slaves contrasts with contemporary practice among the Mycenaeans, whose warlike sovereigns dominated much of mainland Greece. The bronze-age Mycenaeans also lived in fortified towns, controlled trade and industry, rode to battle in chariots, and built royal tombs. Baked-clay writing tablets, found at Pylos in the south-western Peloponnese, show the slave class to have been predominantly female and engaged in humble occupations on behalf of the palace authorities. Their children lived with them, but no mention is made of their husbands. This arrangement must have prevailed for the reason that after a slave raid it was easier to slay the men and to take captive only the women and children. The origin of most of the slaves was recorded as Asia Minor, though whether the palace of Pylos recruited these women through raids of its own or relied on slave markets run by Mycenaeans settled on islands in the Aegean there is no way of telling. This is very different from the situation in Shang China, where the servile status of large numbers of men could be readily ascertained by a special hair braid they were compelled to wear.

The greatest service these men were called upon to

render their masters took place in the grave pits of royal tombs near Anyang. One such place of sacrifice boasts human remains on all four of its approach ramps: seventy-three skulls were distributed in rows along them, while the southern ramp had fifty-nine headless skeletons grouped together. The cemetery, sited a few kilometres to the north-west of the main Shang settlement, includes eleven royal graves and 1222 lesser interments. The twelfth king who ruled Great Shang did not require burial, since he was burned to death when the city fell to the Zhou invaders. Oriented north/south, the royal tombs each possess four ramps shaped like a cross, the longest measuring 30 metres; they climb from a central grave pit, which is often 10 metres or more below ground-level. In the grave pit smaller depressions were filled usually with sacrificial remains, human beings and dogs accompanied by bronze daggers, before a wooden chamber was constructed for the deceased king. Once the body and its funerary offerings had been safely stowed inside the chamber a roof was added, additional goods were placed on

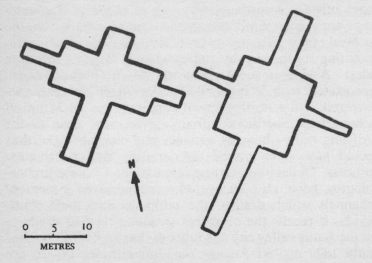

N

0   5   10

METRES

Fig. 9 Typical plans of the Anyang royal tombs, north-west of the Shang palatial complex. They were not pillaged when the dynasty fell in 1027 BC the ramps, further human sacrifice occurred, and then earth was poured in and beaten solid layer by layer. Tomb finds are rich: stone sculpture, carved jade, bronze cauldrons and weapons, pottery, bone carvings and decorative shells.

The scientific precision with which Great Shang was excavated from the start made certain that not only was the existence of the Shang dynasty accepted as a historical fact but in addition the site has furnished us with indispensable information concerning Shang civilisation. The data given in oracle inscriptions alone illuminates Chinese traditions, as we have seen from the discussion of the Pan Geng chapters of the *Book of History:* it is hoped that further decipherment of the 5000 characters used by Shang scribes will prove no less valuable. Though the main centre of archaeological research is now in the vicinity of Zhengzhou, the fundamental importance of Anyang is unlikely to be challenged. The size of the palace complex is great, despite encroachment by a river on its eastern side. The central group of twenty-one extensive halls seems to have been placed in relation to each other in accordance with an overall plan. The buildings are arranged in three rows on a north/south axis, the central row consisting of three large rooms and five gates pointing south. Nearby stands what is thought to be an altar. A similar square platform of compressed earth, associated with a big building, has been recently discovered in the north-western corner of the enclosure at Zhengzhou. Sacrificial burials are located close to the Anyang gates—humans, animals and chariots—and they could have been placed there during the construction process. Under the earthen foundations Chinese archaeologists have also uncovered a complicated system of channels which drained the buildings and their courtyards. It recalls the obsessive attention paid to drainage in the Indus valley city of Mohenjo-daro, which flourished until 1800 BC. At Anyang the drains, however, do not embrace the entire settlement but are restricted to the centre which may have served as the ancestral temples of the royal family. Another ceremonial section, to the south-

Fig. 10 A fragment of an oracle bone found at Anyang. Some scholars regard the site as the Shang equivalent of Delphi, a place given over to oracle-taking

west of the central halls, was almost certainly a sacrificial altar.

The absence of a surrounding wall, and the scattered pattern of service areas such as bronze foundries, stone and bone workshops, and pottery kilns, has caused some scholars to doubt that Great Shang was a capital city at all. They have termed the Anyang site a Chinese Delphi, whose purpose was principally oracle-taking. Because little excavation has been done outside the cemetery and the palace, no overall picture of the site is currently available upon which to form a final judgement. Possibly the last royal seat of government was so vast and its garrison forces so concentrated that a rampart was thought to be unnecessary. On the other hand, the destruction of Great Shang in 1027 BC could have been made easier by its apparently sprawling layout. That year Wu razed the city to the ground.

The fall of the Shang dynasty is blamed on the way-wardness of Di Xin, the last Shang king. He was so infatuated with the outstanding beauty of Dan Ji that he neglected his duties and indulged in all kinds of perverted pleasures. Around her ornate chamber, decked out with the precious stones from the royal treasury, he heaped up mounds of meat, hanging dried joints on all the trees, filled a pond with wine until they could row a boat on it, while naked men and women would appear at the beat of a drum and drink up the liquor like cattle. It has been plausibly shown that this is a garbled and unfriendly account of a religious festival dedicated to fertility gods. Yet both Di Xin and Dan Ji are said to have delighted in hurting others to such an extent that at last they alienated the nobility. Dan Ji devised two new instruments with which to punish those who accorded the throne inade-quate respect. One was called "the heater" and consisted of a piece of metal, made redhot in a fire, which accused persons were obliged to grasp with their hands. The other was a metal pole, greased all over, and placed above a pit of burning charcoal. The victim had to walk across the pole and when his feet slipped and he fell into the flames, Dan Ji would burst out laughing. This was known as "roasting". As intolerant of opposition was Di Xin when he gave vent to an uncontrollable rage against his uncle Pi Kan. Prince Pi Kan had decided that the state of affairs was grave enough to risk death in reprov-ing the king. Consumed by anger, Di Xin exclaimed, "I hear the heart of a sage has seven holes," and had Pi Kan cut open in order to see if he were one.

Such actions pleased few. "The commoners complained and some of the nobles broke away." Significantly, the Histories say "the Senior and Junior Ritualists of Shang went to Zhou, carrying their ritual and musical parapher-nalia. Thereupon Wu, lord of Zhou, led his followers in a war against Di Xin." The defection of the experts in ritual would have been regarded as tantamount to a public declaration that the Mandate of Heaven no longer resided with the Shang kings. The invading host of Zhou was confronted by the royal army in the wilds of Mu, presumably to the west of Anyang, but the ensuing battle surprised Di Xin, for "those in the Shang front ranks turned their spears and attacked those behind until they fled". The stratagem would have been the work of nobles secretly in contact with Wu. As his enemies approached the capital, Di Xin "climbed the Deer Platform, put on his precious jade robes, and went into a fire to his death". The charred corpse was duly pierced with three arrows and the severed head hung at the top of a flag pole.

ANCIENT RELIGION

Behind the funeral megalomania of the Shang kings, entirely familiar in the Bronze Age, stood a body of religious ideas and cultic practices which were later transformed by Confucianism into the state religion of China. For the continuity of the Shang and Early Zhou eras with the remainder of Chinese history down till the abolition of the empire in 1912 lies in the rites of ancestor worship performed by a priest-king. Even at the end of the nineteenth century European visitors noted how the Qing, the last dynasty to rule China, zealously protected its own mausoleums with a permanent garrison of troops so as to remain on good terms with the spirits of deceased emperors.

Shang religion was bound up with divine justification of the Shang state. It was believed that Shang Di, the high god of Heaven, conferred benefits on his descendants in the way of good harvests and victories on the battlefield, and that through divination the advice of the king's immediate ancestors could be sought on the actions most pleasing to the supreme deity. Hence the worry of Pan Geng lest his people dally in an unlucky capital. By the reign of Di Xin there were few days in the year when the ruler was not occupied with one sacrifice or another that he had to offer to his ancestral spirits. It was from these rituals that he should have obtained answers to the problems which beset him, at least until his ritual experts absconded to Zhou. At its height, therefore, the Shang monarchy rested on a constant communion between the living and the dead.

All earthly power emanated from the One Man, the king who was Son of Heaven; only he possessed the authority to ask for the ancestral blessings, or counter the ancestral curses, which affected society. Political power was inextricably linked with spiritual power, and the ruler by his harmonious relation with the spiritual realm, ensured the welfare of the state—a concept that became in Confucian theory the basis of the right to enforce obedience. The unworthiness of a monarch would always be reflected in the attitude of Heaven, just as "the earth shook" and "rivers dried up" during the last years of both Jie and Di Xin. In this context later imperial interest in seismology is readily explained; the scientist Zhang Heng devised for the palace the first known practical seismograph about AD 130.

In order to consult the ancestral spirits about the future two methods of divination were employed by the Zhou, since they added the drawing of lots to the scorching of bones and tortoise shells. But the questions they asked were the same as those of the Shang. From the Anyang oracle inscriptions (*jiaguwen*) it can be seen that a persistent query to the female ancestral spirits concerned the pregnancies of royal wives and concubines: the rulers always wished to ascertain the sex of unborn infants. In asking about the sex of a forthcoming royal infant, the word "good" was used to denote a boy and the phrase "not good" to denote a girl. The Shang desire for male descendants is further reflected in the etymology of the character for grandson (*sun*), which consists of a boy on the left and a silk thread on the right, symbolising an unbroken line of descent.

In the *Book of Odes (Shijing)*, which describes feudal life from the late eleventh to the middle of the sixth century BC, good fortune is to have plenty of sons and

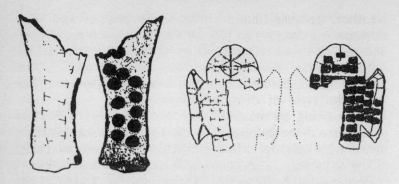

Fig. 11 Examples of Early Zhou oracle-taking in the form of a scorched cattle bone and tortoise shell, discovered during the late 1970s in Fufeng district, on the upper reaches of the Wei river, Shaanxi province. The depressions were drilled to facilitate cracking

grandsons. The Zhou earnestly besought that "such filial sons were never lacking", not least because, as Mencius said in the fourth century BC, the most unfilial deed was to produce no male descendants. With the passing away of the feudal courts through imperial unification in 221 BC, ancestor worship ceased to be the preserve of a ruling aristocracy and gradually permeated every class of society. At last the humblest peasant perceived himself as a member of an extended kinship group, which encompassed the dead, the living, and the yet to be born. He was not only grateful to his ancestors for what his own family enjoyed, but was responsible to them for improving the lot of the next generation: his efforts were directed at lineage enhancement, never individual salvation. Although formal ancestor worship is now nearly a thing of the past, the Chinese preoccupation with male heirs is by no means over, as the authorities in the People's Republic have learned during the recent "One Child Family is Good" campaign.

Intercession was the royal prerogative when the chief elements were involved. It is recorded in the Histories that Tang, "cutting his hair and clipping his nails", successfully sacrificed in order to end a long spell of dry weather, because Shang Di heard his prayers and sent rain-making dragons to refresh the land. Both the Shang and the Zhou perceived their societies as a mirror of the feudalism they believed that they encountered in the natural world. Mountains and rivers had bestowed upon them the style of duke or count, their investiture by Heaven being an assumed fact. Even as the One Man promulgated the calendar, so Shang Di was believed to instruct his celestial officials to arrange the proper cycle of the seasons.

Perhaps the unity of the Shang and the Early Zhou eras is best judged in the bronze vessels employed for ancestor worship. Their splendour and variety bear witness to the elaborate preparations that were made for these ceremonies. The idea of feeding the dead, however, was a widespread prehistoric legacy and not peculiarly Chinese. On the edge of Hades, the *Odyssey* tells us Odysseus performed similar rites to attract the shade of the seer Teiresias. Having "cut the throats of sheep over a trench so that the dark blood poured in", the adventurer "sat on guard, sword in hand, and prevented any feckless ghosts from approaching the blood before Teiresias came." But in ancient China the inability of the ancestral spirits to "eat blood" *(xieshi)* because of their descendants' political impotence was looked upon as a very serious matter. That is why, after the Shang deposition of the Xia dynasty, arrangements were put in hand for the maintenance of sacrifices to the deceased members of the Xia royal clan, and after the Zhou conquest of Shang, one of the surviving Shang princes was invested with the fief of Song.

For the cooking of food there were the *ding,* a tripod cauldron with a round shape (one discovered at Anyang stands 1.33 metres high and weighs 900 kg); the *li,* another tripod cauldron, but with a more bulbous appearance and hollow legs; the *xian,* a steamer, in which a lower part, like an enlarged *li,* is surmounted by another vessel with a perforated base (a common form in Longshan ceramics and, indeed, so characteristic of Chinese culture are these bronzes that the Shang sign for sacrifice is a drawing of a *xian*); and the *gui*, a container that recalls a pottery bowl. For wine, there was the *chun*, a tall jar, sometimes square in shape, and highly decorated by Zhou craftsmen; the *lei*, a later version of the *gui*; the *guang*, a wine mixer, often cast as a monster, with the blunted horns of a sacrificial victim: the *zhi*, a small container with a lid; the *yu*, round, with a small base, a lid and a handle: the *fangyi*, square, with a steep roof-like lid and a nob on top; the *jue*, a tripod libation cup, whose beak-like spout and handle make it the most striking bronze the Shang cast; the *gu*, a tall and slender goblet; and the *jia*, a tripod vessel, with a handle. For water, there was the *pan*, a basin used for ablutions; the *he*, a kettlelike pourer, with three or four legs and a spout; and the *yi*, another pourer that rested on either legs or a base.

A change in the style of decoration can be observed

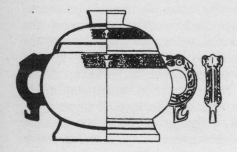

Fig. 12 A bronze ritual vessel (*gui*) from an Early Zhou tomb at Yongningbao, Shaanxi province. Unearthed in 1980, this bronze formed part of a large deposit which included some fine bells. A section of its inscription is shown

after 1027 BC, the year of Wu's accession. Early Zhou bronzes are even slightly less fine than late Shang examples, but not for long, and the relatively easy transition to the ceremonial vessels of the new royal house lends weight to the argument that regards the Zhou people as having an advanced bronze-using culture of their own. If the fugitive Shang experts in ritual stayed in the service of Wu, as the texts imply they did, then it may be assumed that the ceremonies performed by the Son of Heaven continued without interruption. The *Book of History* is quite emphatic about the transfer of the Mandate: it states that Wu "presented a burnt offering to Heaven and worshipped towards the hills and rivers, solemnly announcing the successful completion of the war". To all intents and purposes the ritual remained the same, especially as the Zhou adopted the Shang name for Heaven. Expedient as this decision was, the Zhou rulers could not shake off entirely a feeling of insecurity. They invested the supreme deity with greater power, more universal qualities, but an apprehensiveness is still evident in the *Book of Odes*. Although Shang Di's bounty sustains "the multitudes", the peace it brings is only preserved by unrelenting human effort. "To begin well is common, to end well rare indeed." Paradoxically the longest-lasting dynasty in Chinese history, the Zhou did witness the breakdown of the feudal order from the eighth century BC onwards, as the political system that was expressed in the ritual bronzes weakened and disintegrated amid the bitter feuds of noble houses, each daring to claim the legitimacy of an individual heavenly mandate.

Worship of the Earth was also a duty reserved initially for the ruler. The nobles propitiated other agrarian deities, such as the soil god Houtu and Houji, the god of grain. The earthen altar platforms at Zhengzhou and Anyang were built probably for royal ceremonies intended to aid harvests. Emperors maintained the cult until the present century, the would-be dynasty Yuan Shikai making the last sacrifice in 1916. They also turned the first furrow of the spring ploughing. This ceremony, the *yengji*, had a tremendous fascination for eighteenth-century European philosophers, to whom it appeared a perfect token of the solicitude of a ruler for his people. So much so that in 1756 Louis XV, at the suggestion of the encyclopaedist Quesnay made through La Pompadour, followed the benevolent example of the Chinese emperors and enacted what had become a hallowed Confucian rite.

Beneath the nobility existed "the multitudes", the craftsmen dwelling close to the cities and the peasant-farmers still using stone implements. These people would have been excluded from the ancestral cult, although under arms they played some kind of subordinate role in rituals devised to obtain victory. Cut off from the services of the learned diviners and ritualists who resided in the great households, the ordinary people had to rely on adepts versed in sympathetic magic. These sorcerers *(wu),* male and female, eased the lot of the hard-pressed tillers of the soil by placating malignant spirits and invoking aid from those more kindly disposed. Details of an early ceremony of exposure survive; it suggests that the drops of sweat shed by the sorcerer, dancing within a circle under the blazing sun, were expected to induce drops of rain. The psychic powers of the *wu* also enabled contact to be made with the departed, though their abilities in this direction were apparently ignored by the palace. In opposition to Confucian ethics, Daoism drew upon the primitive strength of these thaumaturges, whose shamanism was later reinforced by invaders from the northern steppes, and in the process the philosophy of Lao Zi (born 604 BC) and his followers was eventually subsumed in Daoist religion. During the crisis which overtook the early empire after AD 220 Daoism gave solace to the peasantry as an indigenous religion of personal salvation. The hold the chthonic deities of the countryside had over the minds of "the multitudes" was already evident at the beginning of the Shang dynasty, when Tang in vain tried to change the title of the god of the soil.

EARLY ZHOU (1027–771 BC)

The Zhou royal house claimed descent from Houji, "he who rules the millet", while another leading clan traced its first ancestor to his mother Jiang Yuan. Both of these clans, which intermarried with each other, are known to have derived their names from tributaries of the Wei river, the core area of Yangshao culture. Possibly a firmer economic base there and a residue of semi-barbarous vigour in arms combined to replace the Shang kingdom with the Zhou, notwithstanding the traditional version of the just usurpation of Wu. Since the first certain date of Chinese chronology is 841 BC, when rebellion against a Zhou king led to a regency that can be dated with accuracy, there are several possibilities for the end of Shang civilisation. For the sake of simplicity the traditional date of 1027 BC is accepted as the capture of Anyang.

In spite of the general hatred felt towards the last Shang king it was not until after Wu's death that the Zhou house was effectively founded. The person responsible for this event was his younger brother Tan, duke of Zhou, who acted as regent during the minority of the new king. Well acquainted with the Shang nobility from his many years as a young man at the Shang court, this elder statesman has received great praise for the wisdom of his government. Looking back on these early years from the growing confusion of the Spring and Autumn period, many scholars, the philosopher Confucius among them, regarded this age as a lost ideal. Tan suppressed a rebellion, drew up laws, established a central bureaucracy, organised schools throughout the realm, and showed proper respect for the fallen house by arranging for the continuation of ancestral sacrifices. His most conciliatory gesture was finding employment for Shang officials, a precedent that during subsequent changes of dynasty freed scholars from any slavish devotion to a royal lineage.

Eight objects of Zhou government are itemised in Wu's proclamation, recorded in the *Book of History:* "first food; then, wealth and articles of convenience; third, sacrifices; fourth, public works; fifth, instruction; sixth, the punishment of crime; seventh, courtesy owed to guests; and finally, the army". These governmental aims must have guided Tan, who was so energetic that he could hardly take a bath without rushing forth in the middle of it, holding his long wet hair in his hand, to consult some official on matters of state. But what appealed most to later generations was the tact with which he instructed the young king in his duties. Although he was the ruler's uncle, the majesty of his person demanded that Tan show the utmost reverence to the boy on the throne. How was he to correct what was wrong in the royal mind without any transgression of court etiquette? He hit on a very Chinese expedient, the moral instruction of another person, his own son. Tan used to lecture him in the presence of the king upon what was expected of him when he became a duke, and whenever the king did any wrong he had his son whipped as though he were the guilty party.

A relative backwardness may have inclined the first Zhou leaders to a policy of assimilation, though in the subjugation of the populous eastern plain the Zhou brought the feudal system to full maturity. Princes and royal kinsmen were installed as lords of the lower reaches of the Yellow river, their authority at the start maintained by garrisons of Zhou warriors. These vassals owed allegiance to the king, who styled himself Son of Heaven as in Shang times.

The nobility was divided into grades: duke, count and baron; the gentry, "sons of lords", served both the king and the feudal lords. Supporting the whole system was the toil of the peasant-farmers, who produced an agricultural surplus (the first need of government), provided unpaid labour on public works (the fourth), and acted as seasonal conscripts for the royal forces (the eighth), so that the slave class in evidence under the Shang kings largely disappeared. Awareness of dependence on human resources, on "the multitudes of the people", as opposed to an all-benevolent supreme deity, finds expression in Early Zhou documents. The proclamation of Wu, just cited, is quite specific about the need for active co-operation between mankind and the powers above. While it is admitted that

> Heaven and Earth are the parents of all creatures, and of all creatures man is the most highly endowed, . . . Heaven (had to) help the inferior people, through the provision of rulers and the provision of teachers, that they might be able to aid Shang Di and secure the tranquillity of the four quarters of the kingdom . . . (Furthermore) the One Man (having) offered special sacrifice to Heaven and performed the due services to Earth, leads the multitudes to execute the will of Shang Di. Heaven has regard of the inferior people. What they desire, Heaven will effect. So the Son of Heaven needs their assistance in cleansing all within the four seas.

Fascinating as the humanist notion implicit here is, it was entangled with religious belief and would remain so in political theory at least till the end of the empire. Rebellions and natural portents did not trouble the upright ruler: neither the powers above nor "the multitudes" below would seek to harm an upright king, for "Heaven had no favourites except the virtuous".

The germ of the idea of the people's role in maintaining an ordered society may have arisen from Zhou sensitivity immediately after the conquest of the Shang. An edict against drunkenness points to worry about the softening effects of luxurious living; death was proscribed as the penalty for both princes and commoners addicted to wine. The extension of Zhou power into the lower Yellow river valley eventually caused the problems which the early Zhou kings seem to have feared. As time passed, local hostility to the Zhou overlords decreased and their kingship ties with their homeland in the Wei river valley became attenuated. Retainers were soon drawn from prominent families in the locality, with the result that a consciousness of place encouraged the formation of separate states. Population growth and economic development also put severe strains on the feudal structure. Curiously

enough, this was the time when the Chinese conception
of belonging to a unique civilisation was encapsulated in
the name given to their land, the Middle Kingdom
(*Zhongguo*).

In the *Book of Odes* the ideal of feudalism is expressed. The rural manor is represented as a picture of
peace and prosperity, where cordial relations exist between noble and peasant, no matter the heavy duties laid
upon those who tilled the soil. Yet even in this glori-
fication of a feudal world the fundamental importance
of the peasant-farmers for Chinese civilisation is fully
recognised, their welfare being secured in practice by the
construction of mud-walled villages that afforded winter
shelter as well as protection from marauders. Compassion for the sufferings of the people appears in historical
traditions too. In 984 BC a widespread insurrection
against the fifth Zhou monarch, Mu, collapsed when
"the chief rebel finding the royal army on its march
against him, out of pity for his people, fled without
meeting it". But the Early Zhou era was not entirely free
of strife. Recorded are military expeditions against the
troublesome barbarian tribes of the steppelands as well
as the more advanced peoples living in the Huai and
Yangzi river valleys. The bronze halberd (*ji*) and the
walled city remained the chief instruments of war, but
there is growing archaeological evidence to suggest that
both metal-working and city-building were becoming common amongst peoples beyond the territories under Zhou
control, which implies that the relative calm enjoyed
down to 771 BC depended on superior organization. The
area owing allegiance to the Zhou king covered the provinces of Shaanxi, Shanxi, Henan, Hebei and Shandong.

Internal difficulties first occurred during the reign of
Li, the tenth Zhou king. "Exceedingly cruel and re-
morseless in his treatment of those who dared to oppose
his will," Li is said to have allowed his suspicions of
senior members of the nobility to put his trust in a
magician, "who pretended to be able by his sorcery to
point out anyone, no matter how remote from the palace,
who had spoken ill of the throne." The resting reign

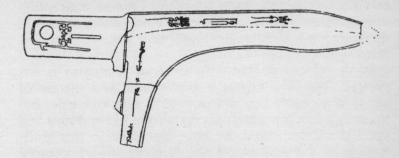

Fig. 13 The bronze halberd was a favourite Chinese weapon of war. It could be wielded from chariots at long range, at the end of a bamboo pole. This halberd was found in Anhui province and dates from the Spring and Autumn period

of terror lasted for three years. Then in 841 BC the people rose in rebellion, drove the king into permanent exile, and almost extinguished the dynasty. Only the steadiness and the self-sacrifice of a leading noble, the duke of Zhao, saved the heir apparent: to placate the multitude and save the royal house the nobleman magnanimously handed over—to their fury—his own son, who was about the same age as the prince. Although the dynasty recovered and in 788 BC was strong enough to withstand a severe defeat by barbarian tribesmen living in the provinces of Sichuan and Gansu, the reign of the twelfth Zhou king led to such a disaster that feudalism was put into irreversible decline. This king named You was, according to the Histories, "a thoroughly bad and unprincipled man". In 771 BC the capital of Hao, just west of modern Xi'an in Shaanxi province, was sacked through an alliance of barbarian tribesmen and relations of the queen, who had been set aside because of You's preference for a certain concubine. The king was slain but, once again with the aid of great vassals, the dynasty survived the catastophe, though a new capital had to be established in a safer position at Luoyang, some distance down the Yellow river. Royal prestige was shattered and real power, real energy shifted to the nobles who held the largest fiefs, and were independent in all except name. "Another unwise act", which tradition claims helped to diminish the authority of the crown, "was the ennoblement of the chief of the Qin people. Out of gratitude for sending soldiers to guard him on his way to his new capital, Ping (the rejected queen's son) not only raised the chief to noble rank but also gave him sufficient land to sustain his new position, the chief city of which was the old capital which he just abandoned." From this warden of the western march would eventually descend Zheng, the First Emperor of China.

With hindsight it was easy for ancient Chinese historians to conclude that the decision brought "great danger to the Middle Kingdom", for the reason that "the very duties ennobled Qin would be called upon to perform would inevitably develop his ambition, for the military skills of his people could not but be improved by their constant struggles with raiding tribesmen along the western frontier." But the inevitability of the decision was caused by the extreme weakness of the throne. In 707 BC the alteration of political reality became transparent to all in the humiliating defeat inflicted upon royal forces by a tiny territory previously under Zhou suzerainty. The age of feudal harmony had ended with the savage nomad attack on Hao, leaving as a permanent anxiety in the Chinese mind the threat of mounted raiders from the north.

2

THE CLASSICAL AGE

The Spring and Autumn and the Warring States Periods (770–221 BC)

FEUDAL DECLINE

The start of the decline of feudalism as well as the movement towards unity can be discerned in the Spring and Autumn period (770–481 BC), called after annals of the same name. It is here that the hereditary principle is found to be first weakened, the most conspicuous casualty of this change being the royal house of Zhou itself. The *Book of History* offers an insight into the straitened circumstances of the Son of Heaven after the nobles had rallied against the barbarian invaders in 771 BC. Whilst the great lords all declared their loyalty to the throne, the new king could not avoid acknowledging his dependence on their "compassion, without which the land enjoys no peace". Gifts of bows and arrows he made to leading members of the nobility indicate a patent lack of strength, for they represented the entitlement to punish any who were disobedient to royal commands. Gradually this devolution of authority left the Zhou kings with only a religious function and an impoverished domain surrounding Luoyang. The archaeological remains indeed show the growth of independent centres of power in the assemblages of bronzes found in walled-city sites and lavish

tombs, whose inscriptions no longer refer to the Zhou
monarch but proclaim the names of the lords for whom
they were made.

With the decay of feudal obligations and the undermining of central control, the leaders of the emergent states
fought each other for territory and competed to attract
technicians and peasant-farmers. In the west primitive
Qin encouraged immigration from rival states by offering
houses and exemption from military service. Incessant
warfare, either between the Chinese themselves or with
invading barbarians from the northern steppes, brought
about a substantial reduction in the number of states.
According to the *Record of Rites (Liji)*, a total of 1763
fiefs existed during the Early Zhou period (1027–771 BC).
At the start of the seventh century BC there were only
200 feudal territories; by 500 BC that number had dropped
to less than twenty. During the Warring States period
(481–221 BC) the internecine struggle became so bitter
and so intense that only seven feudal states were able to
concentrate enough resources for war. Powerless the Zhou
monarch, the One Man, watched as two great powers,
Qin and Chu, still incompletely sinicised, gained territory
through the quarrels of the older feudal states. By 221 BC
the strength of Qin was sufficient to destroy all its rivals
and unify the whole of ancient China in one empire. The
last Zhou king was rudely pushed from his throne by Qin
troops in 256 BC.

Prior to the rise of Qin an alternative method of government was tried, the hegemon system *(ba)* which maintained a semblance of order till the fifth century BC. The
first hegemon was Huan, duke of Qi (684–642 BC), a
prosperous north-eastern state in Shandong province.
Though its economic strength was securely based on salt,
iron and irrigation, the elevation to leadership of the
Middle Kingdom resulted from the energetic measures
Huan took in dealing with barbarian incursions and inter-
state rivalry. On the advice of his chief minister Guan
Zhong (died 645 BC), Huan called conferences to discuss
matters of mutual interest, such as sharing rivers, and
alliances were formed against truculent states such as

semi-barbarian Chu in the south. Signatories of the agreements drawn up at these meetings were charged with punishing the unfilial, defending the principle of inheritance, honouring the worthy, respecting the aged, protecting children and strangers, choosing talented officials instead of relying on hereditary offices, abstaining from putting officials to death, and avoiding acts of provocation, such as the construction of barriers, the unannounced placing of boundary markers, and the restriction of the sale of grain. But these good intentions had to be backed by force: in the forty-two years Huan was hegemon he went to war no less than twenty-eight times.

Huan always claimed to act on behalf of the Son of Heaven, but his protestations were really a cloak for his own policies. While he preferred to settle problems through diplomacy rather than on the battlefield, the events of his own life reflect the uncertainties of the times. Violence surrounded his accession to power and followed his own death in 642 BC: he had to kill his brother at the outset of his reign and the struggle between his sons delayed his funeral until the condition of the corpse became scandalous. Worms were seen crawling out of the room in which it lay, and so putrid was the flesh that preparations for burial could not be undertaken in daylight.

Yet as the first hegemon, Huan endeavoured to make political sense of what was a great turning point in the ancient history of China. And he was ably assisted by Guan Zhong, whom he spared as a supporter of his brother—an arrow fired by the minister had struck the clasp of Huan's belt during the bitter fighting over the succession. Even though the observations associated with his name were not written down till long after his ministry, Guan Zhong's ideas appear to have been seminal for Chinese political thought, since his elevation of the ruler's position not only anticipates Legalist ideas, in particular those of Shang Yang (c. 390–338 BC) and Han Fei Zi (c. 280–233 BC); they also look forward to the centralised order of the empire, which Qin inaugurated in 221 BC. Guan Zhong was equally concerned about the condition of the rural population, however. The growth of towns and cities, based on the fortresses of the nobility, absorbed the food and labour surplus of the land, so that the city-dweller was always better off. We are told that an artisan or a trader could earn in a single day enough money to live for five days, whereas a peasant-farmer might labour the year round and still be unable to feed himself. Caught between the tax-collector, the money-lender and the weather, the hard-pressed countryman could not survive without state relief. As Guan Zhong is said to have remarked:

> When the people are well off, they will be content with their villages and value their homes. Satisfied with their villages and valuing their homes, they will respect their superiors and be fearful of committing crimes. When they are respectful toward superiors and fearful of committing crimes, they are easy to govern. When people are poor, they cause trouble in the countryside and show scant respect for their homes. When the countryside is uneasy and people are not concerned for their homes, they will dare to show disrespect to superiors and break laws. When they show disrespect to superiors and break laws, they are difficult to govern. Thus it is that well-ordered states are always prosperous while disorderly states always are poor. Therefore those skilled in ruling will first enrich the people, and thereafter impose their governing on them.

Ensuring the people's livelihood constituted one of the essential actions of government, because they were the raft on which the state floated. Unlike Legalist thinkers, Guan Zhong neither despised ordinary men nor believed that terrible punishments were necessary to maintain control, but he did expect complete obedience to the wishes of the ruler.

Duke Huan himself, Guan Zhong admitted, was not without moral blemish. His avarice, drunkenness and lust were well known, "yet they were not crucial faults" in that his ability to rule was unaffected by them. Even stern Confucius told his disciples a century or so later that the hegemon's campaigns against the northern nomads had saved Chinese civilisation. "But for Guan Zhong," he said, "we should now button our clothes down the side and wear our hair down the back." He might have added that Huan was a patron of learning and his capital, Linzi, a welcome place of residence for scholars. But few states could compete with the magnificence of Qi. Many comprised little more than an enlarged feudal household, situated in the fortified city which housed the ancestral temple. In bigger territories the ruling house shared power with its chief supporters, who were granted lands and offices, and relied on the service of a knightly class, the *shi*, whose forefathers were officials or lords. The *shi* received the same training as their superiors, namely the Six Skills: manners, music, archery, chariot driving, writing and arithmetic. They were usually small landlords holding minor appointments. The growth of this class from 770 BC, a consequence of the blurring of feudal distinctions and the disappearance of many states, altered the balance of society and led under the empire to the *shi* becoming along with the peasant-farmers *(nong)* the mainstay of Chinese civilisation. In the teachings of Confucius, whose own family was undoubtedly *shi*, the pride and loyalty of the class were celebrated as the moral virtues which made up the essential character of the educated man.

The family feud for the succession in 642 BC ruined Qi and allowed the hegemony to pass first to neighbouring Song, and then in 636 BC to Jin, the biggest state of all until internal troubles in 403 BC split it into three separate units: Han, Wei and Zhao. Jin included large parts of Shaanxi, Hebei and Henan provinces, and its duke felt strong enough to summon and dismiss the Zhou king without any ceremony. A similar disregard for rank is evident in the intrigue and violence prevalent within the competing states themselves, a tendency towards disorder which become even more pronounced during the subsequent Warring States period.

One of the earliest accounts of battle is the defeat

inflicted on Chu by the hegemon Wen, duke of Jin, at Chengpu in 632 BC. During the winter of 633 BC the Chu army had besieged Shangqiu, the capital of Song, then an ally of Jin, and in the following spring Wen directed a force made up of soldiers from several northern states against the attackers. At the border town of Chengpu, Wen outmanoeuvred the Chu commander by luring him into a dangerous advance, and then caught his exposed troops in a pincer movement of infantry and chariots. The successful tactic was executed behind a screen of dust raised by chariots dragging trees. The historical record lays stress on ceremony and divination, the ritual before the start of the fighting, although good generalship obviously played a critical role in the sweeping victory. Afterwards Wen reported his good fortune to the Zhou king at Luoyang by presenting him with 1000 Chu captives and 100 chariots.

Warfare at this time contained the Chinese equivalent of chivalry. As well as following set procedures for joining battle, the nobles relied on divination in order to determine whether or not to fight at all. Everything was thought to happen within the sight of the ancestors, without whose aid victory could never be guaranteed. There are records of ancestral tablets being carried on campaign

Fig. 14 Divination was still very important in the Spring and Autumn period so that the ancestral spirits were consulted before any major decision was taken. Here offerings are being placed in front of a shrine before the start of worship

Fig 15. Chariot combat as portrayed on bronzes dating from the Spring and Autumn period. Such noble display was soon to be eclipsed by the crossbow

and it is known that it was customary before battle to ask "the spirits of former rulers" for protection against enemy weapons. Once the decision to engage was taken, nobles would mount daring raids and engage in archery duels from speeding chariots. Before the battle of Pi in 595 BC three Chu heroes taunted the Jin lines: one drove the chariot, the second loosed arrows, and the third protected the horses from foot-soldiers with a long spear. Pursued by a squadron of Jin charioteers, the Chu adventurers were making a daring escape, when a stag leaped up before them and they downed it with their last arrow. As a consequence of this, they halted and presented the beast to their pursuers, who accepted the gift and broke off the chase. In letting the Chu chariot get away the Jin nobles admitted the prowess and politeness of their foe.

But these mannered skirmishes were not to last. The abandonment of the chariot in the face of deadly shafts dispatched by the crossbow during the fourth century BC destroyed the link between aristocracy and war. Battles turned into largescale infantry engagements, massed armoured columns supported by crossbowmen, cavalry

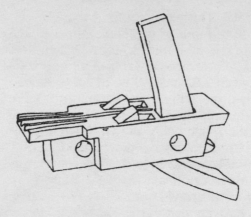

Fig. 16 The invention of the crossbow prevented the rise of an aristocracy in China. This Warring States period bronze firing mechanism allowed the crossbowman a deadly accuracy, while the later use of mounted bows made sieges equally lethal affairs

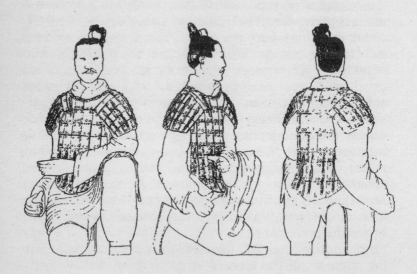

Fig. 17 Terracotta crossbowman unearthed near the tomb of the First Emperor at Mount Li, Shaanxi province. Note the scarf the soldier wore in order to protect his neck from the iron mail-coat.

and chariots. The excavations since 1974 at Mount Li, the site of the tomb of the First Emperor, have revealed how elaborate arms and armour became. Several thousand life-sized terracotta warriors and horses were placed there between 221 and 209 BC in subterranean chambers, apparently disposed in battle formation. Columns of foot-soldiers are modelled wearing iron mail-coats, even the heads of the rivets being shown. Such armour represents a major improvement on the padded jackets or treated sharkskin and animal hide used during hegemon Huan's lifetime. Most significant of all, though, is the vanguard of the terracotta army—three ranks of crossbowmen whose weapons had an estimated range of 200 metres. The heavy arrows they fired would have swiftly turned into colanders the shields of contemporary Macedonian or Roman soldiers.

During the two centuries prior to the unification of China in 221 BC war was not just professional and serious, it was also very expensive as larger states absorbed their smaller neighbours and diverted more resources to military purposes. The powerful states of Qin and Chu could each put into the field over 1 million soldiers. Because the core of Warring States' armies consisted of regulars, highly trained and well-equipped officers and men, rulers were anxious to protect what was a considerable investment. Sun Zi's *Art of War (Zhanshu)*, the oldest known military treatise in the world, relates how severe the contemporary code of discipline was in the fifth century BC. When a Chu officer succeeded in taking a pair of Qin heads prior to an attack, he was himself beheaded for acting without orders. As the Chu general remarked: "I am confident he is an officer of ability, but he is disobedient." Yet it was the state of Qin which first broke the power of the hereditary aristocracy in the army by promoting after 350 BC only the brave and the able to the highest ranks. Henceforth the army was simply a war-machine with no scope for noble display. Its ruthlessness could not be disguised any longer: "blood for the drums" ceased to be the ceremonial execution of a handful of prisoners after the fight when in 260 BC at Chang

Ping the Qin generals ordered the slaughter of 400,000 Zhao prisoners. Horrifying though this act of violence seemed at the time, the ultimate downgrading of the status of the military in Chinese society was to be a later achievement of Confucianism, especially under the Former Han emperors (206 BC–AD 9).

THE RISE OF QIN

Before its disintegration into three separate states in 403 BC, Jin was already threatened by two great rivals; Qin in the west and Chu in the south. Indeed, the intense struggle between these partly sinicised states comprised the driving force behind the movement towards imperial unification. Of the two contenders, Qin was the best placed after the collapse of Jin, since there was little unity of purpose amongst the other northern states (Qi, Yan, Zhao, Han, Wei, Song and Lu); while in the Yangzi estuary Chu had to deal with the belligerent powers of Yue and Wu. Not until 333 BC did Chu win a conclusive victory over these states and secure its eastern flank, by which time Qin had thoroughly reorganised itself under the guidance of Shang Yang (died 338 BC) and was ready to take the offensive. In 330 BC Qin extended its eastern border to the Yellow river, at the expense of Wei, and in 316 BC a south-western thrust brought about the annexation of Shu, a large portion of modern Sichuan province. Besides outflanking Chu, the Shu conquest added valuable resources to Qin once irrigation schemes were introduced on the Chengdu plain, thereafter called in the Histories "sea-on-land".

Credit for the massive Min river project which transformed the agricultural potential of the Chengdu plain is given to Li Ping, who was appointed governor in 250 BC. Although it is unlikely that Li Ping lived to see its completion, he no doubt witnessed in 246 BC the crowning of the thirteen-year-old Zheng, the future First Emperor, as the ruler of Qin. Under the superintendence of Li Ping's son the water-control scheme came into full operation well before imperial unification in 221 BC, and indeed the contribution its irrigation channels made to the state economy could have helped to tip the balance of power in Qin's favour. The irrigation system depends on the division of the Min river into two especially dug feeder canals by means of an obstacle of piled stones: one of these, following the old course of the river, also carries boat traffic and acts as a flood channel; the other, cut through the shoulder of a mountain, is concerned entirely with irrigation. The present tense is deliberately used because upon Li Ping's scheme the present-day prosperity of Sichuan province still rests.

Transparent to the Han historian Sima Qian were the benefits of irrigation engineering. Looking back on the triumph of Qin over the other feudal states, from the vantage point of the reign of the Han emperor Wu Di, Sima Qian understood the fundamental importance of the increase in agricultural productivity and the supply potential for maintaining a military supremacy, though his attention was caught by the intrigue surrounding the construction of a second water-conservancy scheme, the Chengkuo canal. Sima Qian relates

how the ruler of (the feudal state of) Han wished to prevent the eastern expansion of Qin by exhausting it with projects. He therefore sent the water engineer, Cheng Kuo, to the king of Qin to convince him that a canal should be dug between the Jing and Luo rivers. The proposed canal would be 300 *li* long and used for irrigation. The project was half finished when the plot was discovered. The Qin ruler was stopped from killing Cheng Kuo only by the engineer's own argument: "Although this scheme was intended to injure you, if the canal is cmpleted, it will be of great advantage to your state." The work was then ordered to be completed. When finished it irrigated 40,000 *ch'ing* of poor land with water laden with rich silt. The output of the fields rose dramatically and Qin grew rich and strong until it finally conquered the

whole of China. The canal was named after Cheng
Kuo, who built it.

The stratagem misfired badly; Han had bestowed on Qin
the means of eventual victory. The additional grain from
this vast area in the Wei river valley, about 227,000 hectares, supported extra soldiers and the strategic advantage
of the east/west canal was much improved communications. The Chengkuo canal, opened in 246 BC, turned the
Qin homeland into the first key economic area, a place
where agricultural productivity and facilities for transport
permitted a supply of tax-grain so superior to that of
other places, that the ruler who controlled it could control all China. It was a point noted by Ban Gu, who
wrote his *History of the Former Han (Qian Han Shu)*
towards the end of the first century AD. The Wei river
valley was

> in the abundance of flowering plants and fruits the
> most fertile of the nine provinces. In natural barri-
> ers for protection and defence it is the most impreg-
> nable refuge there is. That is why its influence has
> extended in six directions: that is why it has thrice
> been the seat of imperial power.

The three dynasties to which Ban Gu refers are the
Zhou, who launched from there the successful overthrow
of the Shang; the Qin, who created the unified empire;
and the Han, the first 200 years of whose rule was centred
on Chang'an, a city on the opposite bank of the Wei to
the old Qin capital of Xianyang. The last dynasty to have
its capital in the Wei river valley was the Tang (618–906).
    In the account of the construction of the Chengkuo
canal it is interesting that the Han king assumed the
willingness of Qin to adopt public works on a scale greater
than any other state. A reputation for innovation must
have been a legacy of Shang Yang's ministry, which shall
be considered next; yet it should not be overlooked that
the project was so extensive that even the Qin ruler
hesitated on hearing about the plot, though he was per-

suaded to continue by the engineer, who may have realised only during the course of the work what it would mean for Qin once it had been completed. Another version of the interview has Cheng Kuo saying: "I have, by this ruse, prolonged the life of the state of Han for a few years, but I am accomplishing a scheme which will sustain the state of Qin for ten thousand generations."

Since learning hardly existed in primitive Qin, its rulers were forced to look beyond their borders for talented people to employ. Cheng Kuo was but one of a long line of distinguished foreign advisers, which included Shang Yang, an eminent minister from 356 to 338 BC, as well as the architect of the First Emperor's ultimate victory, Li Si. Derived from a small fief on the upper reaches of the Wei river, to the west of the old royal domain of Zhou, Qin found itself responsible for the defence of the western frontier after the removal in 770 BC of the capital to Luoyang. According to one tradition, the house of Qin descended from a horsedealer, probably implying non-Chinese stock, and as late as 266 BC a noble of Wei could remark that "Qin has the customs of the Jong and Di tribes. It has the heart of a tiger or a wolf. It is greedy and untrustworthy. It is ignorant of polite manners, proper relationships, and upright behaviour. Whenever the opportunity for gain arises, it will treat relatives as if they were mere animals." But barbarian origins alone cannot explain the reluctance of the Qin court to embrace feudal etiquette. The Zhou dynasts themselves seem to have led a semi-barbarian, semi-civilised people against the Shang, but whereas the Zhou kingdom was characterised by ceremonial, albeit little more than a sham during the stay at Luoyang, the state of Qin eschewed aristocratic pretensions and concentrated on mundane tasks, such as the improvement of agriculture and metallurgy. Experience of the frontier may have engendered this more down-to-earth outlook, since the house of Qin inherited the lands of a disgraced ruler and the need to master barbarian intruders. Building up a power base was not just a pressing necessity, it was the very condition of survival that left no time for anything else. Qin was thrown back on its

own resources and therefore its ruler welcomed the reforms Shang Yang offered to introduce in order to deploy them for the fullest benefit of the state.

Yet it was the extreme rigour of Shang Yang's reforms
that excited contemporary admiration and terror, not
their basic intention. A new spirit of government, a quest
for efficiency without regard to traditional morality, already informed princely actions in the growing turmoil of
the fourth century BC. Its advent is usually connected
with Shen Buhai (c. 400–337 BC), a man of humble origin
who served as chief counsellor of Han for many years.
His fragmentary writings are concerned with efficient
administration and point towards a bureaucratic state.
The later philosopher Han Fei Zi summarised Shen Buhai's
theory of government as appointing officials according to
ability, demanding that they perform the duties of office,
examining the worth of all ministers, and keeping control
of justice. Although Shen Buhai stressed the role of the
ruler, he advocated the use of neither naked power nor
harsh punishments unlike the full-blooded Legalist Shang
Yang, but the strictness with which penalties were applied in Han remains chilling. When on one occasion the
king got drunk and fell asleep in a cold place, the crown-
keeper put a coat over him. Coming to, the ruler asked
who had covered him, and being informed, punished the
coat-keeper but put the crown-keeper to death, on the
principle that stepping outside the duties of an office was
worse than negligence.

Arriving in Qin from Wei, where Gongsun Yang or
Shang Yang descended from a royal concubine, the
would-be reformer in 356 BC found a ruler who was ready
for far-reaching change. King Xiao had invited able men
to his court on his accession five years earlier, but the
advice he was given seemed to offer nothing new. Sensing the impatience of the throne with conservative advice
which emphasised traditions, usages and customs, Shang
Yang recommended a complete break with the past. "A
wise man", he said, "creates laws, but a worthless man is
controlled by them; a man of talent reforms rites, but a
worthless man is enslaved by them. With a man who is

controlled by laws, it is useless to discuss change; with a man who is enslaved by rites, it is useless to discuss reform. Let your Highness not hesitate." Impressed by Shang Yang's intellect and resoluteness, the Qin ruler concluded: "One should in one's plans be directed by the needs of the moment—I have no doubt of it."

Given a free hand, Shang Yang introduced a new law code aimed at strengthening the military power of Qin. He sought to weaken the influence of the aristocracy, break up powerful clans, and free the peasants from bondage; in place of customary ties he substituted collective responsibility as the method of securing order. So Shang Yang

> ordered the people to be organised into groups of five and ten households, mutually to control one another's behaviour. Those who did not denounce the guilty would be cut in half; those who denounced the guilty would receive the same reward as if they had decapitated an enemy; those who concealed the guilty would receive the same punishment as if they had surrendered to an enemy. Families with two or more grown sons not living in separate households had to pay a double tax. Those who distinguished themselves in battle were given titles by the king, in strict order of merit. Those who engaged in private quarrels were punished according to the severity of their offence. Everyone had to assist in the fundamental occupations of tilling and weaving, and only those who produced a large quantity of grain or silk were exempted from labour on public works. Those who occupied themselves with trade were enslaved, along with the destitute and lazy. Those of noble lineage who had no military value lost their noble status. The social hierarchy was clearly defined and each rank allotted its appropriate fields, houses, servants, concubines, and clothes. Those who had value were distinguished by honours, while those without any value, even if they were wealthy, could have no renown whatever.

The implementation of these regulations was by no means easy, though dissension did not outlast the shaming of the heir to the throne. When the crown prince transgressed one of the new laws, Shang Yang demanded that at least he should receive a token punishment. King Xiao therefore agreed that the prince's guardian be degraded and the face of the prince's tutor tattoed, presumably on the grounds that these nobles shared responsibility for the prince's misbehaviour.

Such fanaticism cost Shang Yang dear. Unloved, and feared by the nobles and common people alike, he was safe as long as his patron remained on the throne, but after the death of Xiao in 338 BC, Shang Yang's enemies swiftly accused him of sedition and officers were sent to arrest him. There is marvellous irony in the story of his attempted flight. The ex-prime minister at first tried to hide in an obscure inn but the innkeeper, in ignorance of his identity, told him that under the new laws he dared not admit a man without a permit for fear of punishment. So it was that Shang Yang personally learned of the thoroughness of his own law code. Realising that escape from Qin was equally impossible because of his fame, he returned to the lands at Shang which he had been given for military service against his home state of Wei, and there prepared to resist. Defeat and dishonour were his fate, for as an example to the rebellious, the corpse of Shang Yang was torn limb from limb by chariots and all the members of his family were slain.

The Confucianist Sima Qian felt that "the bad end Shang Yang finally came to in Qin was no more than he deserved". In his *Book of Records (Shiji)* the historian lists the Legalist reformer's faults as dishonesty, guile, an inability to heed the views of others, and inhumanity. As an honest historian, though, Sima Qian records the achievement of Shang Yang's ministry:

By the end of ten years the Qin people were quiet. Nothing lost on the road was picked up and kept, the hills were free of robbers. every household prospered, men fought bravely on the battlefield but avoided disputes at home, and sound government existed in both towns and villages.

What this meant, nonetheless, was the subjection of the state to the needs of the ruler, a totalitarian ideal. "Of old," commented Shang Yang, "the one who could order the country was he who regarded as his first task the ordering of his own people; the one who could conquer the strongest enemy was he who regarded as his first task the conquering of his own people." Evident here is the Legalist assumption of an antagonism between the ruled and the ruler, between the people and the state. As Shang Yang believed, it had to be made worse for someone to fall into the hands of the police than to go to war.

By hastening the tendency of the age towards authoritarian government and despotism, Shang Yang turned comparatively backward Qin into the most powerful of the feudal states. And the fall of Shang Yang did not lead to the abolition of his reforms, for Qin kings were not unaware of the political and military advantages of centralised power, a disciplined bureaucracy, and a strong army. That they were able to behave in such an increasingly totalitarian fashion, right down to the unrestricted authority of the First Emperor himself, must mean in Qin that the lack of a developed feudal tradition ruled out effective opposition to the throne. On returning from a visit to Qin about 246 BC the heterodox Confucian philosopher Xun Zi wrote that the people feared the officials, while humanising rites and ceremonies were not observed, no music was performed, and scholarship did not exist at all. "The simple and unsophisticated inhabitants", Xun Zi tells us, "can only gain benefits from their superiors by achieving distinction in battle. And rewards increase to keep pace with achievement; thus a man who returns from battle with five enemy heads is made the master of five families in his neighbourhood." This singleminded dedication to Legalist aims achieved ultimate victory in 221 BC at a heavy price. As Aristotle wisely remarked of Sparta's miserable failure in Greek politics after the defeat of Athens in 404 BC, an exclusively military training

Fig. 18 Royal seals belonging to the state of Qi, period of the Warring States. Bronze artifacts stamped with these seals, excavated widely in Shandong province, indicate that regulation was not restricted to Qin despite the famous reforms of Shang Yang

was no preparation for peace and, in the last resort, was itself a cause of defeat. The Spartans "do not appreciate leisure and never engage in any kind of pursuit higher than war . . . Those like the Spartans who specialise in one and ignore the other in their education turn men into machines." In a similar manner the shortcomings of a military hierarchy troubled the Qin empire, once the strong hand of its founder was removed. The Second Emperor found himself beset in 209 BC by subjects driven to outright rebellion through the overbearing behaviour of Qin provincial governors.

The experience of Qin's rival in the south during the Warring States period was less satisfactory. In spite of being the last feudal state to provide a hegemon between 613 and 591 BC, Chu could not avoid becoming embroiled in a long and exhausting struggle with Wu and Yue. Wu, in particular, exercised the mind of the house of Chu, since exiled opponents were known to be instructing its forces in the most up-to-date techniques of war. There are indeed several tales in the Histories about fugitive nobles escaping to the mountains south of the Yangzi delta and helping the non-Chinese inhabitants to organise

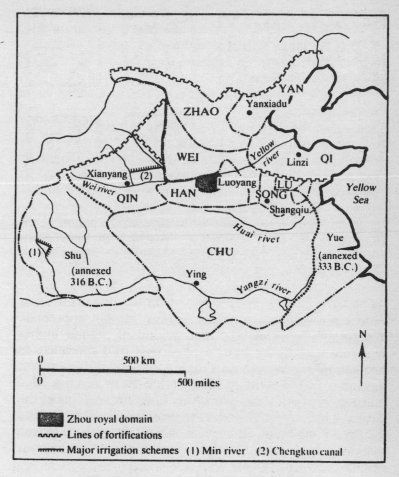

Fig. 19 The Warring States (482–221 BC)

themselves politically. Recent discoveries of Zhoustyle bronzes at sites along the southern border of Anhui province lend support to this idea of cultural development being stimulated by the arrival of an upper class from the north. One Chu exile stands out as the archetype of revenge: Wu Zixu. Having fled from the unjust wrath of the Chu king, who had killed his father and brother, Wu Zixu devoted all his energies to bringing about a war between Wu and Chu. In 506 BC he had the satisfaction of seeing Wu troops sack Ying, the capital of Chu, but his real delight came when he witnessed the humiliation of the Chu king, who was obliged to beg for assistance from an incredulous Qin before the invading force of Wu could be driven back.

Innovatory was the use made by Wu of a water-borne attack, following the winding course of the Yangzi river right up to the gates of Ying. Where the line of advance did not correspond with the direction of natural waterways, as in the northern attack of Wu on the small states of Song and Lu in 486 BC, a transport canal was dug for the ferrying of military supplies. This waterway, connecting the Huai and Yangzi river systems, eventually became the Han Kou section of the Grand Canal, which at the end of the sixth century AD was built as far north as the Yellow river. Perhaps overstretched by these adventures, Wu fell in 473 BC to a sudden invasion by Yue, the power in the lower Yangzi valley until Chu overcame it in 333 BC.

Military difficulties alone cannot explain the falling behind of Chu in the race for supremacy. Although Chu itself was endowed with a mild climate suited to intensive agriculture, there was no determined exploitation of this resource, unlike in its ruthless competitor Qin. It is quite possible that the loess soil of the northern state, with the consequent importance of irrigation, comprised the lever by which the ruler of Qin could move his people as a united force, whereas the ruler of Chu required less social cohesion in order to produce a reliable agricultural surplus. Another factor working against centralisation may have been an apparent scarcity of cities. While town and city sites in Chu compare favourably with those excavated in northern states, only a few have been located so far. From tomb finds, nevertheless, it is clear that the state possessed an advanced economy, which included bronze and iron manufacturing; the discovery of weapons amongst these funerary goods confirms the fear expressed in the Histories about the iron-tipped spears of Chu, "sharp as a bee's sting". Backward though Chu undoubtedly was, the absorption of so many feudal territories ensured that material progress had never been unduly slow. A feudal order as shallowly founded as in Qin naturally inclined Chu towards Legalist doctrines, but no Shang Yang appeared to give the sprawling state an organisation robust enough to withstand the political storms raging at the time. Though not until after the conquest of Chu in 223 BC could Qin be certain of final victory, the growing strength of its forces was signalled in the series of defeats inflicted on the Chu army during the earlier campaigns of 280 and 278 BC, which resulted in the annexation of large tracts of the middle Yangzi valley.

The most striking contrast between Chu and Qin was in the commissioning of public works; besides large-scale irrigation schemes, the latter is known to have engaged in extensive road and bridge building as well as the construction of defensive walls. Several of the states with borders adjacent to the steppe lands built walls as a method of dealing with the problem of mounted raiders. So serious was the threat to Zhao that in the fourth century BC its king, disregarding the derision of other rulers, bade his people adopt barbarian dress, for he took over not only Hu tactics of cavalry but even the trousers worn by these fast-moving Mongolian tribesmen. The solution adopted by Qin shortly after 300 BC was a long wall, a precursor of the Great Wall constructed on the orders of the First Emperor.

The ubiquity of walls in Chinese civilisation has often been remarked upon. Every Chinese city had its surrounding wall, while there is hardly a village of any size in northern China today which lacks at least a mud wall around its dwellings and stables. Within the historical city, walls divided the houses into lots and compounds, sections and districts, just as gates, sometimes set in large watchtowers, controlled the means of access from one part to another. Cities were planned and the arrangement of walls reinforced the power of the authorities—the lord and his officials. When the ancient Asian nomads also surrounded their camps with an earthen rampart, it is hardly surprising that the agrarian culture of China erected walls around its earliest settlements. The rural landscape was always dominated by the walled city, which contained the state granaries that held the grain-tribute or tax upon which organised government depended. This food stock maintained the army and fed the conscripted labour force employed in water-conservancy schemes. As canals and irrigation projects became more complex and more general, particularly from the Han empire onwards, the walled city in the countryside was the effective seat of local government and administration. Nightsoil being the chief fertiliser because the Chinese chose not to keep herds of grazing animals, it was inevitable that intensive agriculture developed in the fields just outside the walls of cities.

In the mind of the First Emperor, therefore, the Great Wall he ordered to be constructed in 214 BC would have no more than an enlarged version of a city wall, which was intended to separate the ordered world of China from the attentions of the uncivilised peoples roaming the steppe. Unequalled in human history is the length of 3000 kilometres that the Great Wall finally attained, making it the only work of man visible to orbiting space crews. As impressive to contemporaries was the road network Qin started to build in order to take advantage of newly acquired territories. There can be no doubt, too, concerning the superiority of these roads to Roman ones. Whereas a Roman road might be described as a heavy wall laid with difficulty on its side, the ancient Chinese road was essentially a thin, convex watertight shell, resting on ordinary subsoil. In this use of a light and elastic road surface Chinese engineers avoided the problems of temperature change and anticipated the technique of John McAdam by two millenniums. Another advantage in terms of traction appears to be the better fit of the Chinese animal harness which, unlike the throat-and-girth harness favoured in the West, did not choke the horse at all.

Although there is still insufficient information about bridge building, the growing interest of Qin in the lower Yellow river valley can be seen in the siting of two major bridges, one across the Wei and another across the Yel-

low river. The Wei bridge near Xianyang, in use by 290
BC, comprised sixty-eight spans of about 9 metres each,
giving an overall measurement of more than 600 metres.
While all its beams were wood, carrying a deck width of
12 metres, some of the piers close to the bank were
constructed of stone. The Yellow river bridge was composed entirely of boats, a method first pioneered by the
Zhou kings. This pontoon bridge, sited in 257 BC hard by
the junction of the Wei and Yellow rivers, is known to
have remained in use for several centuries.

The triumph of Qin was intimately bound up with
technology. Although the First Emperor had sponsored
large-scale projects before the conquest of the feudal states,
they were a matter of necessity after 221 BC. He was left
with an enormous army, besides countless prisoners, and
the *nong,* peasants freed from the old feudalism. In order
to occupy these idle hands and break up what remained
of the previous social structure, imperial policy greatly
expanded the programme of public works.

Sustaining the whole movement towards a centralised,
well-organised state, towards a civilisation in China entirely capable of surviving independently of other parts of
the Ancient World, was a revolution in metal working.
Late though bronze is in appearing in China, Shang craftsmen attained a far higher level of technique than other
bronze users. The advanced kilns of the older ceramics
industry must have played an important part in this development, as they facilitated the unprecedented leap
forward in iron metallurgy during the period of the Warring States (481–221 BC). Early references point to sophisticated iron-casting in Qi, but archaeology suggests
the sixth century BC as the beginning of iron metallurgy
as a major industry for toolmaking, although advanced
techniques were probably neither perfected nor widely
used until the following century.

Most surprising is the fact that iron-casting was practised almost as soon as iron was known, whereas in the
West iron metallurgy remained tied to the forge until about
1350. Steel could have been made at the end of the Warring
States period as well. Possible reasons for the swift prog-

ress in iron and steel technology include the high phosphorus content of Chinese iron ores, which have a low melting point; good refractory clays, permitting the construction of adequate blast furnaces and crucibles; the invention of double-action piston bellows, which gave a strong and continuous blast for furnaces, thus keeping temperatures high; the application of water-power to these bellows; and the use of coal for making very hot piles around the crucibles; and the expertise derived from the pottery and bronze industries.

Iron was thus a great gift for the Chinese peasantry. Cast into axes, adzes, chisels, spades, sickles, hoes and ploughs, the efficiency of the metal combined with irrigation to boost agricultural output to such an extent that the rural slavery of Greece and Rome was unnecessary. Exactly how many slaves existed at any particular time is impossible to calculate from the surviving evidence, but the smallness of this inferior class is generally agreed. However, in AD 44 there were 100,000 government slaves, the majority of whom were engaged in tending government-owned animals. Only convicts are mentioned as working in iron mining and manufacture; unlike slaves, they were sentenced to servitude for a definite period of time. Officials frequently complained about the uselessness of government slaves who "idle with folded hands" in contrast to hard-working peasant-farmers. Private slaves were kept too, but in striking contrast to Rome, the civil rights of the household slave were not inconsiderable. A master could not kill a slave of his own free will; even the usurper Wang Mang was in 3 BC obliged to order one of his sons to commit suicide for the murder of a slave. Government policy always aimed at the restriction of slavery, so that regularly edicts were issued freeing those who had become slaves because of poverty and famine. In Chinese history there is no equivalent of the slave-manned oared war-galley of the Mediterranean. When the water-mill first appeared in the first century AD it was welcomed as being more humane and cheaper than machinery driven either by men or animals.

In warfare the role of iron is at first unclear, except as

mail. At Mount Li, the terracotta warriors guarding the First Emperor's tomb are shown as wearing seven different styles of armour, their coats of mail consisting of numerous iron slates, joined so that the top pieces press on the ones below them. Only the remains of one actual coat of mail have been found, in Hebei province in 1965. Finds of iron weapons dating from the Warring States period are also rare, none at all coming to light in the excavations at Mount Li. The sharpest sword discovered there was manufactured by a unique process whereby bronze was coated with chromium. When taken from the ground after more than two millenniums, its edge was still keen enough to cut a hair.

With the coming of age of Zheng in 238 BC the state of Qin girded itself for the final struggle. Dismissing from office Lu Buwei, who had been instrumental in securing his father's accession to the throne, the young king turned to another outsider Li Si (280–208 BC), a former student of Xun Zi, whose sceptical tenor of thought must have helped to keep the new minister immune from the future First Emperor's superstitious enthusiasm for Daoist magic. The fall of "Uncle" Lu has been embroidered with unsavoury tales by later historians who have sought to besmirch Zheng's name. In a society that revered ancestors the temptation to represent the queen mother as a slut and her son as illegitimate could not be resisted. Apart from the powerful position he had established during the ruler's minority, Lu Buwei may have been seen as an obstacle to the will of the throne because of the 3000 scholars he maintained in the capital. This influx of opinion from the other feudal states was not to the young king's taste, and only the eloquence of Li Si prevented his own banishment with the other aliens in 237 BC. The career of Lu Buwei is unique in ancient China: he is the only example of a merchant holding high office. Traders *(shang)* were not usually allowed to enter officialdom, which meant that their wealth was impotent to raise them from a lowly stratum of society. Legalism was specially critical of the activities of businessmen, a law of 214 BC (in all probability the work of Li Si) compelling them to join military expeditions leaving for South China. This practice of sending active and former merchants as well as the sons and grandsons of merchants, together with convicts to be garrison troops and frontier guards, was revived later on by the Han emperor Wu Di. Echoes of this ancient attitude may be found in the banishment to the countryside of young people belonging to well-to-do families during the Great Proletarian Cultural Revolution in the late 1960s.

From the archaeological record, too, the degree of supervision exercised by the authorities can be discerned in the layout of cities. The best excavated Warring States city, Yanxiadu, capital of the north-eastern state of Yan, consisted of a rectangular enclosure measuring 4 by 8 kilometres, which was subdivided into three distinct sections by earthen walls. Quite separate were the industrial and commercial quarters from those containing residential accommodation. The presence of official buildings, as well as barracks close to the gates in the various walls, bear witness to the change in the function of the city from a fortified aristocratic stronghold to a regulated centre for administration and trade. A mint in Yanxiadu shows that money had become a significant factor in expanding the ancient Chinese economy, with cast bronze coins of various shapes circulating freely amongst the feudal states. Only after unification in 221 BC did the Qin coinage become standard; its coins were round with square holes in the middle, which facilitated their collection on strings.

Guided by the advice of Li Si, the future First Emperor deployed his troops resolutely against one state after another, in the words of Sima Qian "as a silkworm devours a mulberry leaf". The last Zhou king had already been forced from his tiny throne in 256 BC, an unmistakable sign of Qin intentions. Although the Qin army suffered reverses at the hands of Zhao and Chu, superior manpower and resources told in the end, Han going down in 230 BC, soon followed by Zhao (228 BC) and Wei (225 BC), but the decisive engagement did not occur till the year 223 BC when the rival state of Chu was vanquished. The over-running of Yan in 222 BC and the surrender of Qi without a fight a year later made the "Tiger of Qin", as Zheng was then called, the ruler of all China.

A HUNDRED SCHOOLS CONTEND

The turmoil of the final centuries down to the triumph of Qin called forth great intellectual ferment. The uncertainty of the age contrasted with an increasing prosperity as cities grew in size and number, technology made impressive advances, and commerce became important enough to suffer periodic repression. Rulers seemed indifferent to anything but personal gain, so that only the glibbest advisers could expect to make official careers for themselves and avoid miserable ends. Even a successful policy-maker such as Shang Yang could find that death and dishonour awaited him at the close of his ministry. The political troubles were lamented by scores of philosophers who felt keenly their own marginal influence on contemporary events. Their frustration produced an outpouring of ideas unmatched under the monolithic unity of the Chinese empire. They were obliged to write books because kings would rarely listen to their advice; not a few of these commentators sighed for the order of the Early Zhou period as conditions were not immediately suited to an alternative to feudalism. Not until 221 BC was the king of Qin able to win supremacy and impose a bureaucratic regime that left room for neither feudal sentiment nor local variation. Then everything was standardised, including thought. The reaction toppled the first imperial dynasty in Chinese history within a generation and inaugurated the compromise of the Han empire.

The Warring States period was the time of "the Hundred Schools", when roving philosophers offered advice to any lord who would listen or collected followers in order to establish a body of teachings. Apart from Han Fei Zi, who was a prince of the royal house of Han, the philosophers appear to have been *shi*, members of the

scholar-gentry and administrative class. Their social position entitled them to a freedom of thought and movement that was denied to the noblemen above, as it was to
peasant-farmers and artisans below them. In Lu Buwei's
sponsorship of philosophy during his premiership of Qin
(250–237 BC) may be detected something of the merchant's guilt about his own origins, at the bottom of
Chinese society. The fact that the self-made minister had
the arrogance to display publicly a book he commissioned along with a small fortune in gold, which was to
be a reward for anyone who could find in the text any
fault, only underlines the gulf which separated the untu-
tored moneymaker and the learned man. Amongst the
Chinese living overseas in South-East Asia today the
same feeling of inferiority forces its business community
to lavishly endow schools and colleges.

Four main philosophies evolved prior to 221 BC: Confucianism, Daoism, Moism and Legalism. Although the
first two were to have lasting importance in Chinese
history, and especially Confucianism, the most heatedly
debated philosophies before the Qin unification were the
last two. It has been said that traditionally the Chinese
were Daoist in private and Confucianist in public, but it
might be added that those who entered the imperial civil
service always felt the lingering influence of the administrative concepts of Legalism. Only the doctrines of Mo Zi
(*c.* 479–438 BC) vanished from the Chinese mind after the
First Emperor suppressed "the Hundred Schools" in 213
BC.

A moral philosopher, Confucius (551–479 BC) based his
social-mindedness on a feudal ethic which expected the
ruler to act with benevolence and sincerity, avoiding the
use of force at all costs. Like the Duke of Zhou and
other great princes of old, he had to manage the affairs
of state so that justice could be enjoyed by every subject.
Numerous soldiers were thus a sign of poor government.
While the biography of the philosopher in Sima Qian's
Book of Records reveals that Confucius "as a child often
set out the sacrificial vessels" and as an adult gained the
reputation of being "expert in matters of ritual", it also

shows how this delight in the elaborate ceremonies of
ancestor worship led him to formulate a code of conduct
which placed the individual in a tradition which was
linked firmly to the past. "I am a transmitter not a
creator," Confucius said. "I believe in things of old and
love them." For him tradition was embodied in the concept of *li,* which is translated usually as rites, etiquette,
ritual, but really means propriety. It is the courtesy that
is essential for a cultured person, and even today the
Chinese regard good manners as a sign of moral character. *Li* is not only the rules of politeness, but rather the
proper way of approaching every thought and deed. For
Confucius the ceremony of ancestor worship was the
meeting point of two worlds, the spiritual and the tempo-
ral, the past and the present, where good fortune was
bestowed upon the dutiful descendant, the preserver of
traditional values. He said that in accordance with the
rules of *li* affection and respect should be expressed during the lifetime of one's parents through obedience and
after their death by proper burial and the bringing of
offerings to their tombs. Filial piety *(xiao)* involved the
continuation of deference to parents into full adulthood;
it was never simply the natural attitude of children.

Confucianism so deeply instilled an appreciation of the
enormous role played by culture in civilised society that
subsequent Chinese thought can be said to have been an
interpretation of this underlying principle. Referring to
the Daoists, Confucius said: "They dislike me because I
want to reform society, but if we are not to live with our
fellow men with whom can we live? We cannot live with
animals. If society was as it ought to be, I should not be
seeking change." It is a point constantly made down the
ages by Confucian scholars whose outlook rested on a
profound sense of personal responsibility for the welfare
of mankind. Since they viewed the state as a large family,
or a collection of families under the care of one leading
family, the virtue of obedience also found a place amongst
the characteristics that defined the relationship between
the ruler and his subjects. When asked about government, Confucius replied: "Let the prince be a prince, the

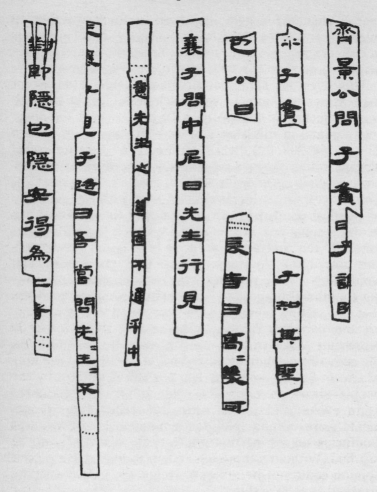

Fig. 20 Part of the teachings of Confucius, recorded on bamboo strips, from an archive found in a Former Han grave in Ding district, Hebei province. The text preserves the most original version extant, and is probably a copy made shortly after the fall of the Qin dynasty (207 BC)

minister a minister, the father a father, and the son a son." The cultivated man accepted the authority of his superiors because he cherished justice, unlike the selfish man who held nothing in respect but himself. When he sees a chance for gain, he stops to think whether to pursue it would be right; when he sees that his prince is in danger, he is ready to lay down his life; when he gives his word, no matter how long ago, he always keeps it.

This stress on submissiveness and loyalty was one of the features of Confucianism which in the first century BC was to secure it the position of the official ideology. Instrumental in this elevation were the teachings of Xun Zi (*c.* 298–238 BC), who recommended a strict social hierarchy and rigorous moral training because of his heterodox belief in the evil nature of man. In the thought of Confucius there is less emphasis placed on the necessity of political control for the reason that the decay of the feudal system was not as advanced as in Xun Zi's lifetime. On the contrary, Confucius held that it was important only that a state possess a compassionate ruler who would instruct the people by his own example in following traditional usage. He even warned progressive rulers that the setting down of laws was a dangerous practice for the nobility. Pointing out that a written law-code represents break with custom, he astutely predicted that the code of punishments inscribed on a tripod by the king of Qin in 513 BC would be learned and honoured by the people above all else. Those in authority could never again evoke tradition in order to declare their judgements were correct. Not for a moment, however, was Confucius suggesting that arbitrary decisions were to be justified. Without a thorough understanding of *li*, a proper opinion could not be reached. Hence the value which he attached to scholarship.

> Love of humanity without love of learning soon becomes silliness. Love of wisdom without love of learning soon becomes lack of principle. Love of rectitude without love of learning soon becomes harshness. Love of courage without love of learning soon becomes chaos.

Another influential idea of Confucius concerned the supernatural. His attitude to religion was purely practical. "I

stand in awe of the spirits," he told his followers, "but
keep them at a distance." This is neither the thorough-
going rationalism of Xun Zi nor even a sceptical point of
view, but an intimation that the celestial realm was far
above human comprehension; something not plumbed by
scrutinising the cracks made by heat on animal bones.
Nor could natural phenomena, like shooting stars, earthquakes and floods, be so readily interpreted as the will of
Heaven. The reluctance of Confucius to pronounce on
religion helped in introducing a sense of balance in the
supernatural world as well as on the earthly level, so that
in Chinese history "holy wars" have been conspicuous by
their absence. Though disappointment marked the final
years of his life because no ruler ever offered Confucius
an official appointment or heeded his teachings, the later
influence of his thought was so immense that he has been
rightly termed the "uncrowned emperor" of China.

Instrumental in advancing the fortunes of Confucianism were Mencius and Xun Zi, both of whom lived
during part of the final century of the Warring States
period. The elder Mencius dealt with opposing philoso-

Fig. 21 The grave of Confucius at Qufu, where his followers
remained in mourning for at least three years. From the Later
Han period (25–220) onwards, it became a custom for the emperor to offer sacrifices to the philosopher

phies, especially Moism, and propounded the doctrine of mankind's natural goodness. He was also the archetype of the filial son, the upholder of the family against the encroaching state. Whenever a ruler lost the goodwill of this subjects and resorted to oppression, the Mandate of Heaven *(tian ming)* was said to be withdrawn and rebellion justified. This democratic theory, a kind of safety valve in the Chinese constitution, derived from Mencius' belief that ultimate sovereignty lay with the people— Heaven granted a throne but succession depended on the people's voluntary acceptance of the new ruler. And the issue of approval did not apply solely in times of dynastic changeover when the people could indicate the choice of a successor by resisting or accepting him, but also in ordinary times the major policies of government had to reflect popular opinion. Continuity could thus be guaranteed only through the ruler's adherence to traditional values. He needed to nourish the people, thereby sustaining familial relations, the cement which held a civilised society together. Agriculture was of vital importance to Mencius because he felt that unless food and clothing were adequately supplied there could be no meaningful distinction between honour and disgrace. In times of famine he asks, "What opportunity does one have to cultivate propriety and righteousness?" A ruler should be concerned to enrich the people's livelihood, decrease taxation, end conflict and correct boundaries. "When a king rejoices in the joy of his people, they rejoice in his joy; when he grieves in the sorrow of his people, they also grieve at his sorrow. A common bond of joy will pervade the kingdom; a common bond of sorrow will do the same."

An ideal of Mencius was the "well-field system" *(jintian)*, which may have existed during the Early Zhou era. He argued that such a system of land tenure ought to be revived in order to alleviate the plight of the peasant-farmer, whose accumulating debts forced him to sell out and become either a tenant or share-cropper. The well-field is supposed to have contained nine squares of land; the central square belonged to the ruler, and the remaining eight were each cultivated by a family. Aware that a more flexible approach would be needed in areas of dense population, Mencius advised:

> In the remoter districts, let the nine-lot division be observed, and let the one lot be set out as a "helping lot"—a plot which the eight families help each other to cultivate on behalf of the lord. Near towns and cities, let the people pay a tax of a tenth part of their produce, and render military service.

The rate of tax recommended here was thought to have been one of the "ancient statutes" of the legendary Shun, which, according to Mencius, "no ruler ever fell into error by following". A fair distribution of land, salaries for feudal officials, and schools would best provide for the stability of a state. While Mencius evinced no confidence in the impotent Zhou king, his affection for the ancient rulers encouraged the hope that a new house would one day unite China and restore the old political institutions.

Protection from the authoritarian trend in contemporary philosophy came from Mencius' belief in natural goodness. Speaking of the inhumanity of rulers, he said: "A benevolent man extends his love from those he loves to those he does not love. A ruthless man extends his ruthlessness from those he does not love to those he loves." Kindness was the sign of a true man, unkindness and cruelty being explained in the very modern terms of social deprivation. Proper upbringing was essential. To a disciple Mencius once remarked: "A trail through the mountains, if used, becomes a path in a short time, but, if unused, becomes blocked by grass in an equally short time. Now your heart is blocked by grass." This accords with the traditional model for the Confucian scholar-official, who staffed the imperial civil service after the founding of the Han dynasty in 206 BC. He was a man firm in principle and benevolent in outlook: he served the throne and protected the lives of the ordinary people. Whereas the collapse of feudalism inclined Mencius towards ideal monarchy, with the virtuous ruler imitating the sage-kings of the past, Xun Zi had less patience with feudal niceties and declared that merit should be the sole basis for elevation. Dying in 235 BC, near the end of the Warring States period, Xun Zi was well placed to systematise the Confucian heritage and his thinking had great influence on the Han emperors, though in time the Chinese subordinated him to Mencius. His reputation has always suffered from the animosity directed at two of his students, Han Fei Zi and Li Si. At certain points, Xun Zi's theories came close to those of the Legalists, not least because his fundamental heterodoxy concerned human nature. In contrast with Mencius' strong emphasis on the potential for goodness in all men, Xun Zi decided that human nature was basically evil, a conclusion which led him to stress the need for education and moral training. For him the spiritual realm was a polite fiction and he poked fun at superstitious practices devised to obtain heavenly favours such as rain. "They are done", he said, "merely for ornaments. Hence the cultivated man regards them as ornamental, but the people regard them as supernatural." As rites and ceremonies were necessary for the maintenance of civilised society, "the ancient kings . . . established ritual practices in order to curb disorder, to train men's desires, and to provide for their satisfaction."

By appreciating the real purpose of rites and understanding how to appoint and control officials, Xun Zi believed it was possible for a king to rule effectively. He said,

> If agriculture is strengthened and its products are economically used, then Nature cannot bring impoverishment. If the people's livelihood is sufficient and their work in keeping with the seasons, then Nature cannot inflict sickness. If propriety is always cultivated, then Nature cannot cause misfortune. Therefore flood and drought cannot bring famine, extreme cold or heat cannot cause illness, and evil spirits cannot do harm.

Striking though the difference between Mencius and Xun Zi is on the question of human nature, the latter philosopher was never a supporter of the state of Qin. The disdain shown by Qin rulers for rites and their reliance on force he roundly condemned as shortsighted. "What proceeds by way of ritual will advance, what proceeds by any other way will fail," he noted prophetically.

Mencius and Xun Zi were equally agreed about the danger posed by Mo Zi's thought. Especially annoying to Xun Zi were the doctrines of frugality and simple burial rites. Little is known about the life of Mo Zi, and even his writings have survived only in a truncated form, but he seems to have lived sometime between the death of Confucius in 479 BC and the birth of Mencius in 372 BC. Apparently he held high office in the state of Song, where his expertise in defensive strategy would have been an asset. One Daoist tradition credits Mo Zi's rejection of Confucianism to a dislike of elaborate and costly ceremonies, but it is not unlikely that as an engineer he detested the ease with which so many Confucian scholars settled for comfortable careers as advisers on ritual.

Mo Zi appears to have travelled extensively, visiting one state after another and propagating a utopian doctrine of universal love. Harking back to the perfection of the Xia dynasty, when people were said to have treated each other as members of one family and looked upon all children as their own, he condemned the Confucian preoccupation with lineage as being socially divisive. In Lu, which may have been his native state, Mo Zi ran a school, and from there his followers intervened in political squabbles, offering both ethical exhortation and practical aid. The strength of Mo Zi's appeal to the contemporary mind was his interest in the technical rather than the moral side of state craft. Almost as if government were a machine, he sought methods of improving its performance and warned rulers of the dangerous strains introduced by wars; he said that states should seek ways of self-defence and self-preservation only as long as aggression troubled China. Deeply moved by the sufferings of ordinary people, Mo Zi said that "the man of Chu is my brother", lest those who heeded his word should imagine that compassion was restricted to relations, fellow citizens, or even the inhabitants of the purely Chinese states north of the Yangzi river.

The disappearance of Moist thought under the empire may have been the result of the affluence then enjoyed by educated men. Stable political conditions led to a growing sophistication and rationalism, which had little interest in the ghosts which Mo Zi believed were sent to punish evil-doers. The world of the spirits was instead appropriated by Daoism, the enduring opponent of Confucian ideology and until the arrival of Buddhism its most subtle challenger.

The first of the "irresponsible hermits", according to the Confucians, was a native of Song named Li Er, but it has become usual to refer to the founder of Daoism as Lao Zi, or the Old Philosopher. It is less easy to trace his life than Mo Zi's, though the tradition is unanimous that Lao Zi had no tomb, a significant omission in a civilisation moulded by ancestor worship. Like his greatest follower Zhuang Zi, he "lived without leaving any traces; engaged in activities that were not recorded for preservation". Both Lao Zi's birthdate of 604 BC and the book associated with his name are now the subjects of debate, but such is the power, however, of *The Way of Virtue (Daodejing)* that even if it is the work of a later follower, we cannot afford to overlook the originality of a message which has appealed to generations of Chinese readers.

Where it differs from the other schools of philosophy is in setting the senseless rivalry of princes in a cosmic perspective.

> Who would prefer the jingle of jade pendants,
> Once he has heard stone growing in a cliff.

Man's rootedness in Nature exercised Lao Zi's mind, an inner strength which made all men wiser than they knew. "Knowledge studies others; wisdom is self-known." The artificial demands of feudal society had so disturbed the innate abilities of men that instead of following the natural way *(dao)*, they were circumscribed by man-made codes of honour and love. Learning had become necessary, and charity was prized because kindness could no longer be expected from everyone. Most disliked of all by Lao Zi was the Confucian emphasis on the family as the cornerstone of the social order. For Daoists held that social evolution had taken a wrong turn with feudalism; their ideal was the primitive collectivist society that was supposed to have existed prior to the Xia dynasty. Reluctance to accept office or to try reform sprang from the belief that things were best left alone. It was summed up in the concept of yieldingness *(rang)*. "The wise man", Lao Zi maintained, "keeps to the deed that consists in taking no action and practises the teaching that uses no words." Daoist quietism was not something to be shouted from the rooftops. For those who knew remained silent in the presence of strangers: with regard to their disciples, they always took into account their readiness for wisdom. Anecdotes were thus favoured in teaching.

The sign of the sage was effective non-assertion. He gave up in order to get; he relinquished control in order to understand; he welcomed a relationship that was mutual; he was moved by a sense of profound non-possessiveness. *Rang* caused Zhuang Zi (350–275 BC) to turn down the premiership of the great state of Chu. The account of this rejection illustrates perfectly the Daoist fear of social entanglement:

One day the ruler of Chu sent two high officials to ask Zhuang Zi to assume control of the government. They found Zhuang Zi fishing. Intent on what he was doing, he listened without turning his head. At last he said: "I have been told there is in the capital a sacred tortoise which has been dead for three thousand years. And that the king keeps this tortoise carefully enclosed in a casket on the altar of the ancestral temple. Now would this tortoise rather be dead but honoured, or alive and wagging its tail in the mud?" The two officials answered that it would prefer to be alive and wagging its tail in the mud. "Clear off, then!" shouted Zhuang Zi. "I, too, will wag my tail in the mud here."

We can still catch something of the story's original impact. How bewildering it must have been for the two officials to make the difficult journey back to the Chu capital from the remote sage's hut, empty-handed. Zhuang Zi had rejected an office for which other thinkers strove: Confucianists, Moists and Legalists found his behaviour inexplicable. "A thief steals a purse and is hanged", commented Zhuang Zi, "while another man steals a state and becomes a prince." In the turmoil of the Warring States period, the only sensible policy for the sage was to live the life of a recluse.

Xun Zi was convinced that the Daoists were entirely misguided in their concentration on Nature, and he marvelled that they could waste time on the study of useless things. In fact this detached outlook proved to be important for the development of science in China, since it has been plausibly argued that Daoist observation and experiments in alchemy equal the dim beginnings of scientific method. Yet not everyone shared Xun Zi's scepticism when it came to the Daoist pursuit of the elixir of life. The First Emperor devoted a fortune to this end, dispatching embassies to the top of mountains in order to establish relations with the spirits and overseas to find "the three isles where the immortals dwell". The persistent belief in a chemical way to longevity is revealed in an incident recorded in the ninth century AD, when the chance excavation of a long-buried stone box filled with silk disturbed a grey-haired man of dignified mien who arose, adjusted his clothing, and then disappeared.

Not for nothing was the other root of Daoism the magic of the *wu*—female and male thaumaturges. Their sympathetic magic had long been at the service of the peasantry, but personal contact with these adepts and magicians after 221 BC fed the First Emperor's immense superstition. He found especially attractive the supernatural aspects of the Five Elements, a school of thought

strong in the eastern state of Qi. Although Sima Qian
admits a pressing need to sort out the muddle of inherited practices and customs once unification had taken
place, he also suggests that the First Emperor's anxiety
about orderliness and uniformity arose from his belief in
the Five Elements. He writes how

> Black became the chief colour for dress, banners
> and pendants, and six the chief number. Tallies and
> official headgear were six measures long, carriages
> six measures wide, one pace was six measures, and
> the imperial carriage had six horses . . . In order to
> inaugurate the Power of Water, Qin's element, it
> was believed that there must be firm repression
> with everything determined by law. Only ruthless,
> implacable severity could make the Five Elements
> accord. So the law was harsh and there were no
> amnesties.

Whatever the superstitious motives for Qin authori-
tarianism, it was the School of Law which provided the
means of enforcing correctness. The oldest meaning of
fa, the fundamental idea of Legalism, is "standard". Initially connected with standard measures of weight, length
and volume, the concept was extended as the general
regulation of an all-powerful ruler. The philosopher responsible for this shift in emphasis during the third century BC was Han Fei Zi, who argued that an elaborate
system of laws backed by inescapable punishments was
necessary for a strong state. "The ruler alone possesses
power," he insisted, "wielding it like lightning or like
thunder." Obedience to the letter of the law was demanded. As a result the morals of daily conduct were
termed the Six Lice by the Legalists: they proscribed
compassion, generosity, virtue, good faith, and learning.
It was not unexpected, therefore, that in 213–212 BC
books should be burned and scholars buried alive when
Confucianists dared to express reservations about the
harsh tendency of imperial policy. But it was this lack of
mercy in the community, an intolerable trait to the socia-

ble Chinese, that helped to engineer the downfall of the Qin dynasty. The success of Liu Bang, the usurping first Han emperor, was due in part to an overestimation of the bullying and oppression the people of the Middle Kingdom would stand.

PART II

IMPERIAL CHINA

3

THE EARLY EMPIRE

From Qin Unification till the Tartar Partition (221 BC–AD 317)

THE QIN DYNASTY (221–207 BC)

221 BC was the year in which the armies of Qin overran Qi, the last of the feudal states and once the leading power in the Middle Kingdom. Its surrender confirmed the Qin king as the unopposed ruler of the Chinese people, and to mark the great event of unification he adopted a new imperial title. Zheng chose to be called Qin Shi Huangdi, First Sovereign Qin Emperor, in order to show his supremacy over the kings whom he had dethroned. The character for emperor *(di)* in the title may have contained the notion of divinity, or at least divine favour. Already a very old and complex word by 221 BC, it had been used by Daoist thinkers as a means of elevating the semidivine figures they wished to claim as their own inspiration. They regarded the legendary Yellow Emperor, Huang Di, as the ancient sage from whom their teachings had descended. In Zheng's adoption of the new title, then, there was more than an element of political calculation, for the reason that the superstitious character of the unifier of China already inclined towards the supernatural aspects of Daoism. He could not have been unaware of the manner of the Yellow Emperor's

departure: after giving his kingdom an orderliness previously unknown on earth, Huang Di rose into the sky as
an immortal. The First Emperor first endeavoured to
communicate with the immortals in 219 BC so as to acquire the elixir of life. That he also commissioned at
Mount Li a mausoleum which modern archaeology has
disclosed to be one of the wonders of the world, shows
how as *Huangdi,* Sovereign Emperor, Zheng fully expected to join the select band of the immortals.

Possibly the three assassination attempts on Zheng's
life served to stimulate the pursuit of personal protection.
In 227 BC he narrowly escaped death in his own audience
chamber at the hands of Jing Ke, an agent sent from the
north-eastern state of Yan. Equipped with the head of a
fugitive Qin general, a map showing a gift of territory,
and a poisoned dagger, Jing Ke was charged with taking
Zheng prisoner or killing him. Sima Qian relates how

> King Zheng asked to see the map. Thereupon Jing
> Ke took out the map, unrolled it, and exposed the
> dagger. Seizing the sleeve of the Qin king with his
> left hand, Jing Ke grasped the dagger with the right
> and struck at him. In alarm King Zheng leapt back-
> wards so that his sleeve tore off. Though he tried
> hard, the king was unable to draw his sword, which
> was very long . . . Jing Ke pursued the Qin king,
> who ran round a pillar. The astounded courtiers
> were simply paralysed.
>
> In Qin law a courtier was forbidden to carry
> weapons. Moreover, the royal guard was not per-
> mitted to enter the audience chamber unless sum-
> moned. At this critical moment there was not time
> to call for the soldiers anyway. Thus Jing Ke chased
> King Zheng who tried to ward off the dagger blows
> with his two joined hands.
>
> At this juncture the court physician, one Xia
> Wuzu, struck Jing Ke with his medicine bag. King
> Zheng, however, continued to dash round and round
> the pillar, so distraught was he. Then a courtier
> cried out: "Put your sword behind you, king!" By

Fig. 22 A Later Han version of Jing Ke's attempt on the life of
the First Emperor, from a Shandong tomb. Most of the details
of Sima Qian's story are visible, including the box containing
the head of the fugitive Qin general

so doing, he found he could unsheath the weapon
and wound Jing Ke in the left thigh. Disabled, Jing
Ke raised his dagger and hurled it at the king, but it
missed and hit a bronze pillar. King Zheng then
wounded his assailant several more times . . .Then
it was that they killed Jing Ke.

The brush with death marked Zheng, who "was not at
ease for a long time". Except for Xia Wuzu, whom he
rewarded with gold, his courtiers had not rallied to the
defence. Anger and fear filled Zheng's thoughts and deepened his sense of being on his own. While the outraged
king threw himself into campaigns against the other feudal states down to 221 BC and the thorough reorganisation
of China after unification, the psychological impact of
Jing Ke's attack was reinforced by two other violent
assaults. In 219 BC a blind musician tried to strike the
First Emperor at court with a lead-filled harp, while a
year later a third would-be assassin ambushed the wrong
carriage on one of the imperial tours of the provinces.
Apart from increasing his dread of dying and spurring on
fruitless searches for a drug of immortality, these encoun-
ters led to his final aloofness from all but a small circle of

advisers and indirectly abetted those intrigues so disastrous to the dynasty on his sudden death in 210 BC.

Although the Qin dynasty was of short duration, such was the energy and determination of its founder that this period represents a turning point in Chinese history, for the bureaucratic form of government developed under the Qin monarchy became the model for future Chinese political organisation, lasting until the present century. The significance of the sweeping change that the First Emperor began and Liu Bang, the founder of the following Han dynasty, completed cannot be underestimated, as Chinese civilisation flowered within the framework of a unified empire. If the First Emperor did nothing else, he demonstrated to the Chinese the value of unity. Since 221 BC the country has been united for a longer period than it has been disunited, thus making China an exception to the rule that in the pre-modern era large states do not endure.

The vigour of the First Emperor can be seen in the stream of edicts he issued; they were intended to control his subjects, harness their strength, and exploit natural

Fig. 23 Standardisation was the hallmark of the Qin unification of China in 221 BC. Thereafter the Qin coinage was the only form permitted, its circular coins having a hole in their centres to allow collection on strings. Previously the Warring States had a diverse coinage—these examples come from Zhao, Lu, Yan, Qi, and Qin

resources in order to enrich and strengthen the state. In his drive for uniformity he became one of the great destroyers of history. Lacking any degree of economic integration, the Qin empire was insecure in two main directions—the east and the north. The deposed aristocracy of the old feudal states posed an internal threat, especially in the lower Yellow river valley, and on the northern frontier there was danger from the Xiongnu nomads, probably the Huns who invaded the Roman empire in the fifth century.

Military power seemed the best answer. Feudal holdings were abolished and noble families compelled to take up residence in Xianyang, now the capital of all China; peasant-farmers received greater rights over their land but became liable for taxes; the empire was divided into new administrative districts, garrisons were planted at strategic locations, and a body of inspectors was established to audit accounts as well as check on the administration of justice and government; there was standardisation of weights and measures, currency, written language and axle wheels; a national road network was built and canals improved for the supply of the army; and as a counter to the Xiongnu, the Ordos desert region was annexed and defended by the construction of the Great Wall, which ran from Gansu province in the west to the Liaodong peninsula in the east.

When, in 213 BC, the First Emperor discovered that these innovations drew criticism from the scholar-gentry, he listened to the advice of Li Si, his Grand Councillor *(chengxiang)*. In reply to the Confucianist contention that nothing would last which was not modelled on antiquity Li Si said:

> In the past the empire was divided. Because there was no emperor, the feudal lords were active and in order to confuse the people they harped on antiquity . . . Now Your Majesty rules a unified empire in which distinctions of right and wrong are as clear as your on unapproachable authority. Yet there are those who unofficially propagate teachings directed

against imperial decrees and orders. When they hear of new instructions, they criticise them in the light of their own teachings. At court they only dare to disagree in their minds, but in the streets they openly criticise your commands. To cast disrepute on their ruler they look upon as a duty; to adhere to contrary views they consider a virtue. The people are thus encouraged to be disrespectful. If this slander is not stopped, the imperial authority will decline and factionalism ensue . . . Your servant therefore requests that all persons possessing works of literature and discussions of the philosophers should destroy them. Those who have not destroyed them within thirty days after the issuing of the order are to be branded and work as convicts. Books to be spared from destruction will be those on medicine, agriculture, and divination. As for persons who wish to study, let them take the officials as their teachers.

The First Emperor approved the recommendation and the book burning took place in order to "make the people ignorant" and to prevent the "use of the past to discredit the present". Li Si's exemption of works on divination may have been calculated, given his master's interest in the spirit world, but he may have recognised that the deeply rooted and widespread belief in its efficacy would make suppression very difficult. Radical though Li Si's proposal was in its attempt to make knowledge an imperial monopoly, the proscription of books under Qin rulers was not new, Shang Yang having persuaded Xiao in the fourth century BC to order the burning of the *Book of Odes* and the *Book of History*. The ultimate result was decisive, nonetheless. When, in 206 BC, a rebel army burned Xianyang, the conflagration engulfed the imperial collection of books and in many cases destroyed the sole surviving copies. The loss caused a definite break in consciousness, for when, under the patronage of the Han emperors, ancient texts were painfully reconstructed from memory and the badly tattered copies hidden in 213 BC at

Fig. 24 Li Si, Grand Councillor of Qin, holding a seal of state. More than any other advisor of the First Emperor, he was responsible for the sweeping changes the first imperial government rapidly introduced

great personal risk were unearthed, the feudal age seemed historically remote.

Further frustration in 212 BC caused the First Emperor to conduct a purge of scholars, some 460 being condemned to death. Not even the protest of the crown prince, Fu Su, could stem the rising tide of his anger at "alchemists who had wasted millions without obtaining any elixir and scholars who said that the throne lacked virtue". Prince Fu Su had dared to suggest that the killing of so many Confucian scholars might unsettle the population. To counter dissidence, the First Emperor banished Fu Su, along with his supporters, and hastened the destruction of city walls.

Two years later the First Emperor died at the age of fifty, during one of his journeys through the eastern provinces, journeys which, though ostensibly tours of inspection, were really prolonged quests for immortality. Having had a dream of a sea-god interpreted as an evil spirit keeping him from contact with the immortals, he roamed the northern shore of Shandong province until he dispatched what was most likely a whale with a repeater crossbow. Shortly afterwards the First Emperor sickened and died, but fearing for their lives Li Si and the eunuch Zhao Gao suppressed the news and sent a forged edict ordering Fu Su to commit suicide. Then they turned the carriages towards Xianyang and placed a cartload of mouldering fish directly in front of the imperial litter. "It was summer," Sima Qian notes dryly, "and to disguise the stench of the corpse the escort was told to load a cart with salted fish." As a result of the terror inspired by the title of the First Emperor, there was neither an onlooker to question the arrangements made by the Grand Councillor and the eunuch for the homeward journey, nor on arrival in the capital an official to oppose the forged will which they used to place on the throne Hu Hai, the worthless second son.

This court intrigue gave the oppressed Chinese an opportunity to revolt. That the imperial armies were not then concentrated together but were dispersed in garrisons all over the empire played into the rebels' hands. Some of these troops, led by their commanders, also revolted. The Second Emperor, Ershi Huangdi, was the creature of Zhao Gao, who engineered Li Si's execution in 208 BC. Bidding for supreme power himself, Zhao Gao forced the Second Emperor to take his own life in the ensuing year, but the Histories state,

> no official would accept his usurpation, and when he entered the audience chamber, three persons there offered him harm. Realising that Heaven had refused to grant him the empire, and that the officials as a whole would not co-operate with his desire, he summoned a nephew of the First Emperor and reluctantly handed over the imperial seal.

While this was the only occasion on which a eunuch tried to usurp the throne, Zhao Gao was a prophetic figure in imperial history as eunuchs tended to assume great power whenever an emperor was weak. In the Later Han period (25–220) eunuchs were actually employed by rulers against powerful consort families, till they became a dangerous faction in their own right.

The hapless nephew of the First Emperor occupied the throne for only three months after the suicide of the Second Emperor. In early 206 BC rebel armies arrived in Qin, massacred the imperial house, and burned Xianyang

Fig. 25 One of the bronze chariots found near the tomb of the First Emperor in 1980. Its undisturbed state has led to speculation that the rebels in 206 BC may not have pillaged the emperor's grave itself

to the ground. The excessive burden of forced labour imposed by the Qin dynasty, in particular on the line of fortresses designed to contain Xiongnu; the enforced movements of population to newly conquered territories in the far north and extreme south; the cruelty of the legal code; and the onslaught on the feudal aristocracy had made the regime intolerable. A complicated struggle between several insurgent groups for the honour of replacing the Qin dynasty was eventually won by Liu Bang (247–195 BC), a man of the people. Tradition relates that in 209 BC, having lost several convicts en route to the First Emperor's tomb at Mount Li, Liu Bang released the others and put himself at the head of these "bandits". While the popular insurrection started as an attempt to restore feudalism the old aristocracy soon showed itself incapable of undertaking the task of government and, faced with the prospect of endless fighting, the Chinese put their trust in the ordinary men who had risen to prominence during the course of the revolt.

FORMER HAN (206 BC–AD 9)

The social origins of Liu Bang, who as the first Han emperor took the title of Gaozu, were extremely humble. Sima Qian and Ban Gu in their histories recall the remarkable physiognomy of Liu Bang, his prominent nose, dragon forehead, and the seventy-two black moles on his left thigh, just as they list the supernatural events attending his conception and early manhood, but they cannot disguise the historical fact of a peasant background. Han Gaozu was almost certainly illiterate and not a little intolerant of scholars. Prior to his final victory in 202 BC over all the other rebel leaders he displayed his dislike of the excessive ceremony attached to learning. When some scholars came to him in costume, wearing their elaborate hats, Gaozu snatched one of these pieces of headgear and urinated in it. But Gaozu was moderate in comparison with his chief rival for power, the Chu nobleman Xiang Yu. Capturing Xianyang in 206 BC before the main rebel forces arrived, Gaozu simply took charge of the Qin royal family and sealed up its treasures and palaces. He also forbade his troops to plunder or take captives. As Gaozu upbraided Xiang Yu later: "You fired the palaces of Qin. You desecrated the tomb of the First Emperor, you appropriated the wealth of Qin for your own use, and you executed prisoners who had already surrendered."

Gaozu's mildness was a genuine part of his character, a single virtue in what was a very violent age, and it made his accession something of a popular event. People felt that this commoner would govern in their interests, unlike the absolute rulers of Qin. On the throne he neither aped aristocratic manners nor slackened his compassion for his poorer subjects, and his habit of squatting down, coupled with an earthy vocabulary, unsettled polite courtiers and accentuated the kindly feeling of the people towards him. Yet Gaozu had the wit to appreciate the value of learned and cultivated advisers and assistants. During the civil war he had relied on the organisational skills of the clerk Xiao He in the difficult task of supplying his army. When the fighting was over, Gaozu awarded to Xiao He (died 193 BC) the top rank in his court, even though he had never borne arms, for the first Han emperor understood how much the country yearned for a sound administration. To the frugal policies of Xiao He and his assistants must be credited much of the dynasty's early success. It was Xiao He, too, who in 202 BC advised the removal of the capital to Chang'an, "Forever Safe", across the Wei river from Xianyang, as a means of breaking more readily with the traditions of the fallen house of Qin. To bring order to the daily life of the palace Gaozu himself commissioned the arrangement of a new court ceremonial for his boisterous followers. His only instruction was "Make it easy".

Following the brief period of unification imposed by Qin, China remained a confederation of states that only a generation before had been independent and still possessed regional cultures that were very much alive, but the combining of Confucian standards and rituals with inherited Qin practice gradually brought about cultural unity. By turning to scholars for advice, scholars untarnished with the excesses of Legalism, Gaozu started the process by which the Chinese empire came to be based on a Confucian model. The new cultural foundations of China were drawn from the old state of Lu, the birthplace of Confucius. The transformation was a slow one, Han Wen Di (179–157 BC) being the first emperor to openly adopt the teachings of the Sage of Lu. Wen Di was noted for "his generous, humane feelings, for his stern economy, and for the unceasing care that he took of his people's interests". His concern for welfare included famine relief at government expense, pensions for the aged, the freeing of slaves, and the abolition of the cruellest Qin methods of execution. He promoted additionally Confucian scholars to the highest offices of state, thereby assuring the triumph of this school of philosophy by the end of the first century BC.

Conscious of the fate of Qin, the early Han emperors ruled carefully and skilfully. Gaozu settled for a compromise on feudalism and granted fiefs to close relatives as well as members of certain feudal households, but these diminished holdings were intertwined with districts controlled by imperial officers. A rebellion among the eastern landholders in 154 BC was used by emperor Han Jing Di (156–141 BC) to alter the laws of inheritance. Thereafter all sons were co-heirs to their father and land was divided between them, an amendment which did much to quicken the breakdown of large units into little more

Fig. 26 The official seal of Li Cang, chief minister of the petty kingdom based on Changsha. The Han compromise involved ruling through a dual system: commanderies and kingdoms

than substantial estates. Emperor Han Wu Di (140–87 BC) completed the dispossession of the old aristocracy by means of harsh officials who moved against overpowerful families, whether of ancient lineage or recent origin.

Something of the wealth, and beliefs, of the nobility under the early Han emperors can be glimpsed in the impressive grave goods recovered from three intact tombs found at Mawangdui, a suburb of Changsha, Hunan province. Excavated in 1974, the tombs contain the bodies of Li Cang, marquis of Dai, who died in 186 BC, and his wife and one of their sons, both of whom died around 168 BC. Li Cang appears to have been the last prime minister appointed by the local ruler in Changsha; his successor was nominated by the central government. The deceased were each buried within several nested wooden coffins, at the bottom of a shaft some 16 metres in depth. This old method of burial was retained by the people of what had been once the state of Chu, long after the chambered tomb built of brick was adopted in north China. Apart from the almost perfect state of preservation of the marchioness' body, archaeologists were amazed at the decoration of the four inner coffins used in her burial. Dragons, leopards, and composite mythological animals appear amid swirling clouds, in the company of immortals, and on the ends of the third of the four inner coffins is represented a sacred mountain by which a soul might ascend to bliss. The ancient Chinese envisaged man as being made of a body joining two souls together. Whereas the *hun* soul came from the sky and returned to it, the *po* soul derived from the earth and fell back into it. Mention is made traditionally of two kinds of elixirs: one restrained the flight of the *po,* the other recalled the *hun.* Texts found in the Mawangdui tombs which relate to longevity are works on divination, including the *Book of Changes (Yijing),* and medical treatises illustrating Daoist breathing exercises.

Most fascinating of all at Mawangdui is the provision made for the nourishment of the deceased in the afterlife, or at least the prelude to it. Set out in the tomb of the marchioness were forty-eight bamboo baskets of pre-

Fig. 27 A cross-section of the nested wooden coffins in which the wife of Li Cang was buried at Mawangdui, Hunan province. No metal was used and their excellent preservation, and that of the marchioness' body, was due to the thick layer of charcoal and white clay encasing the coffin structure

pared meats and fruit as well as fifty-one pots containing cereals, vegetables and cakes. On small bamboo slips were recorded for each the details of preparation methods and ingredients. A favourite dish of the deceased was *geng,* a kind of stew that included cereals, pieces of meat or fish, and vegetables. Appreciation of cookery arose early in Chinese civilisation and, though the cuisine did not reach its peak until the Tang and Song dynasties, the art of blending fine flavours and of slicing ingredients into the thinnest slivers was already looked upon as the hallmark of excellence in Han times. A Han feast always began with wine, then came stew, followed by a series of dishes culminating in grain, and followed by fruit. The same pattern persists in the modern Chinese banquet, where fried rice or noodles are invariably the penultimate dish. Another aspect of diet that the Mawangdui finds indicate is the age-old closeness of food and health in China. Food was never simply a means to satisfy hunger; it has always been regarded as an aid to good health and a preventive medicine, so that today the Chinese housewife cooks according to the physical state of the family and the weather conditions.

We are fortunate to possess details of the dishes prepared for imperial ancestor worship during the Ming dynasty (1368–1644) because the first Ming emperor decided that the conventional sacrifices made to his forbears at a shrine maintained by officials outside the palace precincts were inadequate to show filial respect. As a result, the palace kitchens were reorganised to cater for the living members of his family as well as his deceased relatives at a specially built inner temple, which was titled the Shrine for Offerings to the Imperial Forbears *(feng xian tian)*. Quite probably the menus chosen for this private daily worship reflect the peasant background of the emperor's own family, for Liu Bang and Zhu Yuanzhang were the two commoners in Chinese history who overthrew tyrannical regimes and founded new dynasties. Having expelled the Mongols, Zhu Yuanzhang must have felt in 1371 a great debt of gratitude to his ancestors, an obligation he discharged through the offering of food they really prized. Thus the simple but wholesome fare the imperial kitchens prepared—rolled fried cakes, twice-cooked fish, honey rolls, steamed bread, noodles, pork, game, rice and fresh fruit and vegetables. Although there are no figures for the beginning of the Ming dynasty, an edict of 1435 mentions a staff of 5000 in the kitchens dedicated to the emperor's state banquets. Kitchen servants assigned to imperial sacrifices were fewer but, if anything, were selected even more carefully. Officials in charge of ritual observances investigated their family backgrounds and their own lives in order to avoid those with criminal records.

For the spiritual comfort of the deceased music was often performed. At Mawangdui the tomb of the marchioness contained both figurines of musicians and musical instruments: a twenty-five-string zither and a bamboo mouth-organ with twenty-two tubes. The musical tradition of Chu was much admired at the court of the Former Han emperors, although Confucian officials tried to direct imperial taste towards that of the older eastern states. For Confucius himself music had been very significant indeed. So affected was he once by the ceremonial music of the state of Qi that for three months "he did not know the taste of meat". Because Confucius sought an inner harmony of the mind and a balanced expression of emotion, the discipline involved in playing an instrument or singing greatly appealed to him. He was well aware, however, that there was music which encouraged frivolity, lewdness and violence, and he roundly condemned such barbarian pieces as being unworthy of the cultivated man. Sima Qian records an example of the courtly use of music in his story of Jing Ke's attempt on the life of First Emperor. After some hesitation, Jing Ke had accepted the commission from the king of Yan, who escorted him to the state border with his courtiers. Dressed in white, the colour of mourning, they all wept there as Jing Ke sang of his impending sacrifice. "Then he sang again", according to Sima Qian, "a stirring song. All the gentlemen assumed a stern gazé and their hair bristled up against their caps. At this point Jing Ke went into his carriage and departed without a backward glance."

The Bureau of Music (*yuefu*) was a favourite institution of the Han emperor Wu Di who ascended the throne in 140 BC at the age of fourteen. During his long reign the Bureau of Music was responsible for the collection of songs, the maintenance of orchestras and choirs, and for providing musical performances at certain occasions of state such as banquets, religious ceremonies and official audiences; its players also provided martial music in times of war. Having suffered when the pomp of court ceremonial was reduced after Wu Di's death in 87 BC, the Bureau of Music was finally abolished in 7 BC. Of the 829 virtuosi then in post only those staff who specialised in the "old music" were retained for official duties and assigned to other departments. This curtailment of extravagance was linked in the edict of emperor Han Ai Di (6–1 BC) with policies aimed at combating state bankruptcy and moral depravity, sentiments which would have certainly received the full approval of Confucius himself.

Although the general tenor of thought became primarily Confucian in Wu Di's own life time, the issue of intellectual supremacy was fiercely contested. There were

Fig. 28 Music has always been important in Chinese culture. Even today there is a lingering belief in the impropriety of certain kinds of music

strenuous arguments between officials who preferred a Qin-like method of government and those who looked back to the less centralised approach of the Zhou kings. Their debate was sharpened by the autocratic character of the emperor himself, by his determination to rule as well as reign; and it was given an extra religious dimension by Wu Di's desire to cultivate the immortals along similar lines to the First Emperor. The period was, nevertheless, one when fundamental changes took place and when precedents were set which influenced profoundly the remainder of imperial Chinese history. Through his persistence and severity, Wu Di not only ended the early Han compromise of shared power with the nobility but even more he subjugated the bureaucracy to his own wishes. Outstanding officials were regularly condemned for some crime or other, with the result that all important government business was referred to the throne and ministers were always obliged to accept a secondary role in the making of decisions. This gradual stifling of any criticism of policy, since the smallest protest was construed as disloyalty, helps to account for the serious economic and political errors of his reign. Many of these authoritarian measures reflected the worst methods of the Legalists, although Confucianism received imperial patronage and gradually came to form the nucleus of Chinese culture.

It was at the suggestion of Dong Zhongshu (*c*. 179–104 BC) that Wu Di proclaimed Confucianism as the recognised state cult in the year 136 BC. Other teachings were allowed to exist but did not have the benefit of official recognition and encouragement. An imperial university, which was set up in Chang'an twelve years later, founded its curriculum upon the Confucian canon and acted as a training ground for the highest officials of the administration. For each of the five classics—the *Book of Changes (Yijing)*, the *Book of History (Shuching)*, the *Book of Odes (Shijing)*, the *Record of Rites (Liji)* and the *Spring and Autumn Annals (Chunqui)*—several chairs were created in order that "scholars of great knowledge" could interpret their teachings.

It is an irony of history that this expansion of higher education relied on one of the reforms of Li Si; namely the standardisation of the Chinese script. We cannot be sure now as to the ancestry of the script adopted by the First Emperor's Grand Councillor as the standard, but it is not unlikely that Qin characters descended from the official script of the Early Zhou dynasts, whose capital of Hao stood in the Wei river valley until 771 BC. Early Zhou script would appear to have derived in turn from the pictographs found in the inscriptions on Shang oracle bones. It may well be that their eventual simplification in the official script of the Qin dynasty confirmed the non-alphabetical character of written Chinese. The specific cause of Li Si's reform was the growing confusion over

Fig. 29 A portrait of Dong Zhongshu from a Qing volume celebrating Confucian scholars who influenced imperial policy. Through this Former Han philosopher's work Confucianism became the state religion

etymology, however. The 3000 approved Qin forms probably represented a 50 per cent reduction of the characters previously used. Li Si did not put an end to the writing of corrupt characters—in the three-fold expansion of forms under the Han emperors further mistakes in etymology were inevitable—but his standardisation was sound enough to provide thereafter a workable basis for the written language. Though the Chinese empire subsequently suffered periods of disintegration and foreign conquest, such was the continuity and universality of the Chinese script that political breakdown did not automatically produce

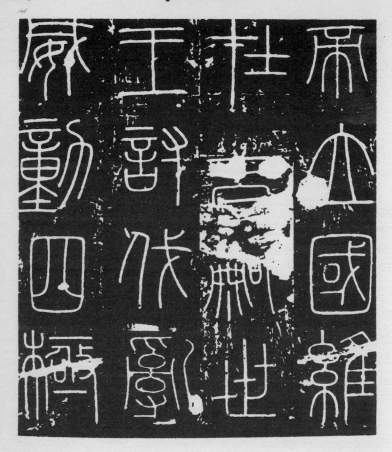

Fig. 30 Possibly an example of the hand of Li Si, who as the First Emperor's chief minister standardised the written script. It refers to the Qin unification of the Middle Kingdom

cultural disunity. Today its great advantage to the People's Republic can be seen in overcoming differences of dialect. Only the presence of a standard written language ensures that the same edition of the *People's Daily* can be read in both Beijing and Guangzhou.

An ideal graduate of the imperial university was said to be distinguished by abundant talents, respect for the family, loyalty to the emperor, moral rectitude, and deep learning. Either he took the central civil service examinations or he proceeded to an official college in the provinces and prepared candidates for local administrative posts there. The cleverest provincial students might be sent to the capital, where they attended the Grand School *(taixue)*, as the imperial university was called, and studied alongside the sons of top officials. The number of students enrolled was restricted to fifty under Wu Di, but increased steadily until it reached 10,000 during Wang Mang's usurpation (AD 9–23), and yet more still under the restored Later Han emperors.

Gaozu had summoned to the capital "men of wisdom" and "men of virtue", but Wu Di was the first emperor who set examination questions for the filially pious and incorrupt candidates seeking office. His interest extended to individual grades and he would revise the pass list whenever he spotted someone whose ideas he liked. Such a candidate was Hong Gongsun, to whom he entrusted in 125 BC the reorganisation of finance and education. Wu Di could not accept the low mark awarded to Hong Gongsun, who was so poor that he supported his family by breeding pigs. The emperor's close involvement is hardly surprising in the context of his personal style of government which depended upon a reliable and subservient civil service. The popular hatred of Qin ruled out any return to Legalism, however authoritarian his own character, while Daoism, to which he was attracted because of its expertise in supernatural matters, advocated too passive a role for the ruler: hence Wu Di's eventual support for an updated version of Confucianism, which achieved supremacy through the operation of the imperial university and the examination system. The consequences of the latter are still with us, though the Chinese themselves have shown less enthusiasm for selection by examination under the People's Republic. The ultimate origin of our school and civil service examinations lie in Wu Di's desire to recruit useful subordinates. As Robert Inglis, a British resident in China, correctly wrote in 1835: "The East India Company have adopted the principle . . . and the full development in India of this Chinese invention is destined one day, perhaps, like those of gunpowder and printing, to work another great change in the states-system even of Europe".

The revised form of Confucianism that Wu Di reluctantly endorsed drew upon both Legalist and Daoist ideas. Trying to find a mean between the teachings of Mencius and Xun Zi, Dong Zhongshu argued that since human nature possesses only the beginnings of goodness, society was only saved from barbarism through the institutions of kinship and education. He stressed three relationships—ruler and subject, father and son, husband and wife—and said that the ruler, the father and the husband correspond to the *yang* element and were therefore dominant, whereas the subject, the son and the wife tended towards the submissive *yin* element. Wu Di seems to have been astute enough to realise that this philosophy would be best anchored in the minds of the people by means of elaborate ceremonies. In addition to the costly cycle of sacrifices instituted in the capital, he therefore journeyed in a great state three times to the sacred mountain of Taishan in modern Shandong to engage in private worship of Heaven.

Two problems shaped the policies of Wu Di: the security of the northern frontier and the direction of the economy. The most severe was the threat posed by the Xiongnu, whose raids south of the Great Wall were a perpetual danger to the empire. Yet the fifty years Wu Di spent in fighting these fierce nomads exhausted the resources of China and almost brought the economy to ruin. His demands for manpower were insatiable and when regular conscription for military service failed, the prisons were thrown open and an amnesty granted to all who agreed to enlist in the army.

Manned by soldiers with crossbows, the Great Wall proved an effective barrier against nomad attack only when combined with the presentation of gifts to the Xiongnu equivalent of the Son of Heaven, because in return for substantial annual gifts the Xiongnu emperor undertook to police the steppe lands along the Chinese border. This arrangement had been first devised in 200 BC, following the decisive reverse at Pingcheng, near

Fig. 31 A ceremonial brooch derived from a nomad design. Such brooches were presented as gifts to Xiongnu chieftains by the Former Han emperors.

present-day Datong, where Gaozu was lucky to escape capture. By the reign of Wu Di it was accepted that conciliation would have to be abandoned, as nomad incursions continued and the growing strain on the imperial exchequer of what was a disguised tribute could no longer be borne. In 138 BC an envoy named Zhang Qian was dispatched westwards to stir up the enemies of the Xiongnu in Central Asia: to the amazement of the Chinese court he reported on his return that another civilisation existed in what is now Afghanistan. It was in fact the recently conquered Graeco-Buddhist kingdom of Bactria, a remnant of Alexander's dominions, but Zhang Qian does not seem to have appreciated that the former kingdom had been on the fringe of the Hellenistic world. No cultural exchange occurred between ancient China and the Graeco-Roman West: Chang'an became aware of other civilisations, but the only foreign influence at this early period came from India, in the form of Buddhism. Specific things brought back by Zhang Qian in 126 BC, after enduring ten years of nomad captivity, included the grape-vine, the walnut and the hemp plant.

What interested Wu Di in Zhang Qian's account of his travels were the large horses he noticed in the "Western Regions" *(xiyu)*, since they could be used to carry heavily armed men against the Xiongnu who rode the smaller Mongolian pony. The first campaigns had already begun the year prior to Zhang Qian's return, Chinese forces having driven the nomads beyond the line of the Great Wall. So in 115 BC he was sent out again on a diplomatic mission to the horse-breeding peoples of Central Asia. As a result one of the chieftains living near Lake Balkhash, in modern Kazakhstan, asked for the hand of a Chinese princess and sent a thousand horses as a betrothal present. The chieftain was given Liu Xijun, a princess of the royal blood, who in 110 BC set off with a large retinue for the distant land. Ever since the homesickness of the princess has proved a fascinating subject for both painters and poets: she who yearned "to be the yellow swan that returns to its home". But Wu Di was soon dissatisfied with indirect contacts and in 101 BC, after a three-

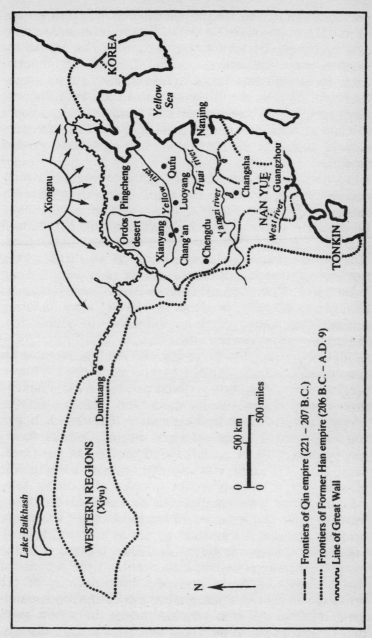

Fig. 32 Imperial unification: the Qin and Han empires

year campaign, a Chinese general succeeded in conquering the Ferghana basin, beyond the Pamir Mountains, and securing enough horses for stud purposes. The "Western Regions" were declared a Chinese protectorate, though it has to be said that the city-states based on its oases vacillated between the Xiongnu and China according to which side pressed them hardest. Nonetheless, the arrival of Chinese arms in Central Asia disturbed the old balance of nomad power and this in itself weakened the Xiongnu.

The military conquests in the "Western Regions" were matched by expansion to the south and the north-east. Notionally incorporated into the Qin empire, the southern kingdom of Nan Yue was finally reduced in 111 BC. This thrust to the far south took the authority of the Han emperor into modern Tonkin, then known as the commandery of Jiaozhi. Kingdoms in the border areas of Sichuan and Tibet also accepted Chinese supremacy, as did Yunnan, literally "south of the clouds", but its independent inhabitants were not securely annexed until the thirteenth century, when the Mongol invaders passed through the high plateau in an outflanking manoeuvre against the Southern Song dynasty. While the southern border was being secured, Chinese forces were simultaneously establishing colonies and administrative outposts in the north-east, where the military objective was the denial of supplies to the Xiongnu and the protection of the overland route to Korea, the northern part of which was divided into four commanderies between 109 and 106 BC.

Although the victories over the Xiongnu made Wu Di a famous ruler, the imperial borders were consolidated at great cost, even on the battlefield. The new cavalry helped to increase Chinese mobility, but the northern frontier remained a dangerous place to serve, in 102 BC some 20,000 soldiers falling in a single engagement. In 99 BC one of the best field commanders was obliged to surrender to the Xiongnu after an engagement that could have led to a revolution in tactics. Bereft of cavalry support, Li Ling managed with only 5000 infantrymen to keep at bay an overwhelming force of horse-archers. He positioned his crossbowmen behind a wall of shields and pikes so that their bolts could outrange the arrows shot from Xiongnu bows. The effect was devastating, and Li Ling almost showed that properly armed footmen could defeat horse-archers. But without support and with crossbow bolts running low, he ordered his men to find their own way back to the Great Wall as best they could. Only 400 soldiers reached the safety of its gateways, Li Ling himself being taken prisoner. When Wu Di heard of this, he was furious that the commander had not died in battle. Sima Qian wrote a memorial defending Li Ling, saying that the general had fought as long as possible, but the emperor was encouraged by the historian's enemies at court to regard this opinion unfavourably; the result was the charge of attempting to deceive the throne, a perfunctory trial, and castration. A year later, Wu Di

Fig. 33 Salt was made an imperial monopoly by the Han emperor Wu Di in 119 BC in order to finance his wars against the Xiongnu. Regulation of the economy was part and parcel of the dominant position of the throne in the early empire

recognised that he had been to blame for not sending a relief column to aid Li Ling, and he sent for the general, but the latter would not return to China. Eventually Li Ling's family were exterminated.

Because no emperor could afford a prolonged war lest the burden on the ordinary people caused a rebellion like the one that overthrew the Qin dynasty, Chinese foreign policy was always dictated by the need to contain nomad pressure, never by any ambition for foreign conquests. By 91 BC even Wu Di had to admit that there was no possibility of further campaigning. He was also aware that his foreign adventures spelt danger to the economic welfare of the empire. Mounting difficulties in the production and distribution of basic commodities, the worsening condition of the peasant-farmers, the growing wealth of merchants, and inflation caused by the private minting of coin, called for drastic action. To meet immediate financial commitments Wu Di sold titles and called in privately minted coins by issuing treasury notes made from the skin of a white stag. In 119 BC, the same year that merchants were forbidden to own land, a state monopoly had already been declared over the iron and salt industries, the control of which was given to leading officials until their incompetence compelled the recruitment of salt boilers and iron masters, merchants in the key industries. The *Yantielun (Discourses on Salt and Iron)* records the philosophical debate over this extension of public control in 81 BC, when emperor Han Zhao Di was attempting to review the new measures introduced by his illustrious predecessor. Despite the opposition of the Confucianists the arrangement became a fundamental part of imperial policy, though the monopoly on the production of alcohol declared in 98 BC was replaced by the payment of a tax. The iron and salt monopolies were simply too lucrative to be dropped. To counter speculation in foodstuffs Wu Di established public granaries and ordered provincial officials to buy when prices were low and to sell in times of shortage, a system known as the leveller *(pingzhun)*, which even the disgruntled Sima Qian noted was effective in stabilising prices.

Although on the death of Wu Di in 87 BC the empire was still impoverished by the long struggle against the Xiongnu, the late emperor had at least ensured the smooth succession of Zhao Di, his youngest son. Besides placing him in trusted hands during his minority, Wu Di took the precaution of seeing that the boy's mother died too. He seems to have been determined to avoid the court intrigues which beset other rulers. Political complications tended to arise in the imperial palace with plots centred on the consort family, the relations of the empress. Early imperial China had no civilised neighbours to provide royal brides for the emperor and so the ennoblement of the empress's family inevitably led to a power struggle with the old consort family, the relatives of the emperor's mother. The family of Wang Mang had been influential at court through marriage for two decades before his usurpation of the throne.

THE USURPATION OF WANG MANG (9–23)

Recurring difficulties with the economy and renewed activities by the Xiongnu were behind the brief Xin dynasty. The fall of Wang Mang, the sole Xin emperor, was similarly connected with the more radical reforms he proposed to solve these interrelated problems. A controversial figure, the elder statesman Wang Mang sought to limit the wealth of powerful families, whose holdings of land had increased considerably, and to alleviate the distress of the peasant-farmers, who were obliged to sell their farms and pledge their service to the rich during famine years. Emperor Han Ai Di (6–1 BC) had tried unsuccessfully to stem this quasi-feudal revival some years before Wang Mang usurped the throne and proscribed large estates. The difficulty for the imperial government was that so many peasants working on estates did not pay tax that there were too few taxable countrymen to fill the exchequer. So Wang Mang nationalised the land, forbade the buying or selling of slaves, and ordered small families in possession of large estates to surrender part of their holdings for distribution to those who had none. Reallocation was justified by reference to the "well-field system" of land tenure under the Early Zhou kings, when private property hardly existed. Government loans at low interest rates were offered to peasants for the purchase of tools and seed, the finance for this regeneration of the countryside coming from monopolies on salt, iron, alcohol and gold.

Wang Mang's methods of dealing with the economic crisis facing the empire were extreme, but his fundamental conception of farming as the basis of a sound state went back as far as the theories of Guan Zhong, who in the seventh century BC had said that the people's livelihood was essential for good order. The same idea appears in the *Discourses on Salt and Iron* as an argument in defence of monopolies. One of the officials taking part in the debate remarks:

> Agriculture is the great enterprise of the world, and iron implements are the great appliances of the people. When tools are easy to use, the necessary toil is less and the results better. The farmer enjoys his work and harvests are bountiful. When tools are inadequate, the fields are wasted and the results miserable.

Yet another participant makes the point that because of the high price of iron implements "poor people have to till with wood and weed with their hands". Still, a real improvement in farming methods and techniques was typical of Han agriculture. In 100 BC Chao Cuo had drawn the throne's attention to a system of ploughing in ridges and trenches that aided planting, irrigation and soil renewal. A further elaboration of this system was known as the pit-farming method, which consisted of an intensive concentration of labour and fertiliser within small pits evenly spaced across a field. The purpose of pit farming other than excellent yields was to counteract drought as well as to cultivate marginal land too small and inconvenient for regular ploughing. The use of night soil as a fertiliser was inevitable in an agriculture which neither kept grazing animals nor allowed land to lie fallow. Today the night soil of Chinese cities is still transported to nearby vegetable gardens and paddy-fields.

Large-scale water-control schemes also aided agricultural output. Between 134 and 131 BC a canal had been dug to join Chang'an with the Yellow river: it reduced the journey by half and irrigated 45,000 hectares. Other projects in the Yellow and Huai river valleys increased overall productivity, but these new key economic areas were soon found to be dominated by powerful families. The movement of whole populations to border areas was another policy employed by the Han emperors in dealing with uneven land holding. From 156 BC there was no longer any restriction on migration, although government support was only forthcoming to migrants moving into the newly conquered northern commanderies. Although an estimated two million settlers trekked northwards during Wu Di's reign alone, the most effective migration was in the opposite direction towards the Yangzi commanderies where the soil was fertile and the weather mild.

Notwithstanding all these measures, Wang Mang soon faced an economic crisis that was aggravated by the bursting of the dikes along the Yellow river at the same moment that military action was necessary against the Xiongnu. Since a mere 6 million of the 58 million population lived in cities it is hardly surprising that the seeds of rebellion were truly sown. Resistance to Wang Mang's reforms also was aided by the lukewarm attitudes of officials, who were often relatives of important landowners, but it became irresistible when famine and mismanaged relief drove the poorest people into open revolt. In Shandong province the desperate peasants banded together as the "Red Eyebrows", while their counterparts in the neighbouring province of Hubei, the "Green Woodsmen", even took control of the cities. When Wang Mang decided to send 400,000 troops to crush the rebels in 23, the arrival of large numbers of soldiers in famine areas turned the rebellion into a disaster, for the empty state granaries there obliged them to relieve the ordinary people of what little food was left. In the confused fighting which ensued the "Green Woodsmen" repulsed the imperial expedition and gave encouragement to anti-Wang movements elsewhere. Within the year the head of the usurper, exhibited in the market-place at Chang'an, was stoned by the crowd.

LATER HAN (25–220)

The enthronement in Luoyang of Guangwu Di, a member of the Han imperial clan, did not end the civil strife in 25. The "Red Eyebrows" had elevated an emperor of their own and, though Guangwu Di by 29 gained the upper hand, final resistance to the restored Han dynasty ceased only in 36 with the reconquest of Sichuan province.

Later Han emperors were much less independent because in the restoration of the dynasty Guangwu Di had to rely on support from the big landowners, who in 39 prevented him from conducting a survey of cultivated land for the purpose of reassessing the land tax. As a result of this central weakness there occurred a gradual resurgence of feudalism. The peasantry was once again tied to the land, either as sharecroppers or labourers, while artisans and scholars were compelled to associate themselves with local magnates strong enough to offer protection against bandits or rebellious soldiers. After the abolition of conscription in 46 the imperial government was entirely dependent on regular troops and the retainers of powerful families, an underlying military weakness that explains the less aggressive policy adopted on the northern frontier: for Later Han emperors could achieve victories over the Xiongnu only with the aid of friendly nomads. Eventually the Western Jin dynasty (265–316) found it impossible to cope at all with barbarian peoples who became allies of the various factions during civil disturbances. Nearly all the provinces north of the Yangzi watershed fell under Tartar dominion.

The decline of the imperial model of government during the Later Han was brought about by factors other than the growth of semi-autonomous estates, not least because the economic pattern of China as a whole was undergoing a significant change. When Guangwu Di moved the capital downstream from Chang'an in the Wei river valley, to Luoyang, in the lower Yellow river valley, he acknowledged the shift of the key economic area eastwards and southwards. The lower Yangzi river valley and the Huai river valley had overtaken the province of Shaanxi as the most developed region in the empire. This economic transformation is reflected in the census of 140: the northern provinces registered a fall in population, as marginal land was abandoned to herders, but figures for all the southern provinces showed steep increases. Population in Sichuan and Yunnan rose by over 50 per cent, in Jiangxi and Hunan it doubled, and for Guangdong in the far south the returns indicated that it trebled. The break-up of China in the Three Kingdoms period (221–265) can thus be seen as a continuation of the same process. The two southern kingdoms—Shu based on the Red river basin of Sichuan province and Wu on the lower Yangzi river valley—were sufficiently strong to challenge for many years the northern state of Wei, the rump of the Han empire. Perhaps the conflict can be attributed to something more than economic rivalry. The Qin empire had been regarded as an alien imposition throughout China, but the people of the old state of Chu, on which Wu was founded, had more reason to dislike its northwestern austerity, since they were heirs of a quite different cultural tradition that contained strong maritime and southern elements. Although the compromise of the Han settlement had worked for centuries, the possibility of economic independence in southern China may have been seized upon not so much by two ambitious families as by a people in delayed cultural reaction to the north.

The richness of the archaeological record for the Later Han is a direct result of the extravagant burials favoured by wealthy landowners. Everyone of any substance commissioned brick-built underground tombs and furnished them with precious objects. Decoration took the form of pressed bricks, engraved stone or just painting. The tomb

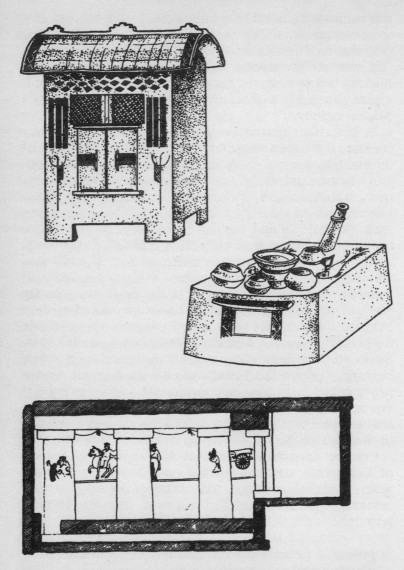

Fig. 34 Side elevation of a Later Han tomb, excavated in 1983 near the old city of Liaoyang, Liaoning province. Availability of stone explains its unusual construction, although the funerary goods are quite typical of the final century of the Han empire, including the terracotta models of a stove and a house as well as the tomb decoration

was itself surmounted by a tumulus and enclosed within a sacred precinct, a "spirit path" *(shendao)* ornamented with statuary leading from the entrance to the chamber; this was usually open-fronted and situated before the tumulus where it served for the worship of the deceased, whose genealogy and achievements were described on a column nearby.

In both their decoration and the funerary goods they contain, the tombs constitute one of our best sources of information for the early empire. For example, an engraved stone slab from a family tomb in Shandong province, dated around 150, shows Jing Ke's attempted assassination of the First Emperor: the distraught ruler is seen dodging around a pillar into which a dagger has been thrown. Apart from such records of historical events, tombs disclose the general outline of life in town and country. A certain falling away of quality is evident towards the close of the Later Han though, as growing demand for grave furnishings encouraged stereotyping, but pieces of exquisite workmanship were still being made for the after-life. One of these, excavated in 1969, was the famous bronze sculpture of a flying horse, cast at the beginning of the third century. From a tomb in Gansu province, this notable piece reveals one of Wu Di's western mounts at full gallop with one leg balanced on a swallow, the bird turning its head in surprise at the touch of the flashing hoof.

Conspicuous consumption accounts for full display cases of Later Han artifacts in museums today. Of the final years of the Han empire the Histories record that vast resources were concentrated in private hands. We read how

powerful persons possess several hundred houses, which are joined together, and extensive fertile land stretching all over the countryside. Their retainers are numbered in thousands and those who depend on them cannot be counted. They dispatch carts and ships to make trade in all directions, while their agents handle enough commodities to fill whole

Fig. 35 Elaborate decoration was typical of the Later Han tombs built for the landowning classes. Here something of its complexity can be seen in the bas-reliefs of a tomb excavated in 1973 in Zhejiang province

cities. Precious jade and valuable objects overflow their storerooms; horses, cattle, sheep and pigs are too many to be enclosed in a valley.

In contrast Luoyang appears modest, almost frugal. Elegant though the emperors Guangwu Di (25–57) and Min Di (58–75) endeavoured to make it, the new capital was smaller and in consequence more crowded than Chang'an had ever been. The splendours of Wu Di's reign were gone, a circumstance which gave some pleasure to those of Confucian persuasion, including the inventor Zhang Heng (78–139) and the historian Ban Gu (32–92). Equally sure of the value of decorous behaviour was Ban Zhao (48–117), the latter's sister, whose own rare access to an education allowed her to complete his record of the Former Han dynasty as well as compose the standard work on her own sex, the *Lessons for Women (Nujie)*. Because of her learning, she was even appointed as the governess of the empress and her ladies-in-waiting.

Lessons for Women assumed the subordination of women to men; they were expected to obey their fathers when they were children, their husbands when they married, and their sons when they were widowed. The ideal age for a girl to marry was fifteen, but wedlock could not be countenanced between persons of the same surname, lest the couple have a common ancestor. This taboo originated in late Zhou times, when social upheaval gave rise to family names, and its influence has not entirely disappeared among modern Chinese. There were seven grounds for divorce of a wife, namely disobedience to parents-in-law, barrenness, adultery, jealousy, incurable disease, loquacity and theft. It needs to be recalled, however, that in Han society a man could have only one wife. Concubines were not regarded as full members of the family and the status of a concubine was always inferior to that of a wife. Unfortunately for women in China Ban Zhao's recommendation that they should receive the same Confucian training that she had enjoyed was generally ignored.

During the Later Han the supremacy of Confucianism was unchallenged. By the end of Guangwu Di's reign it had become customary to offer sacrifices to the Sage of Lu, as one "who had given laws to the people". The following emperor, Ming Di, enjoyed expositions of Confucian doctrine, in which discussions he was sufficiently learned to take a leading part, and he even visited the shrine of Confucius at Qufu in 72, an event that really marked the state adoption of the philosopher's

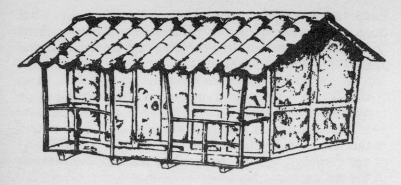

Fig. 36 Han grave model of a house from a tomb in Guangxi province

cult. His teachings had become a moral code, a yardstick for measuring correctness of behaviour, something ideally suited to the administration of "the Empire of all under Heaven". If the long struggle against the Xiongnu had any effect on China at all, it was to strengthen the confidence felt by cultivated Chinese in the scale of values on which their civilisation rested. As one memorial noted: "What distinguishes the people of the Middle Kingdom is that they are capable of honouring what deserves to be honoured." Unlike the Greeks and Romans, the Chinese lacked contact with peoples belonging to other ancient civilisations, as the expansion into Central Asia did not lead to any immediate influx of foreign ideas; by the time imported Buddhism became a powerful cultural force under the Tang emperors the Confucian framework of thought was firmly set in the minds of the official class.

Yet a leading thinker such as Wang Chong (27–97) could be sceptical of the subtle interpretations of the Confucian classics, then in vogue, and maintain that it was unnecessary to elaborate social distinctions into a universal theory. Established conventions and custom were sufficient. He also held similar views to the "Infinite Empty Space School" concerning the nature of the universe, insisting that Heaven was no more than a blind force and that there was no observable relationship between the movement of celestial bodies and human events. Strikingly modern were the theories of this school, which taught

> that the heavens were empty and void of substance. When we look up at it we can see it is immensely high and far away, having no bounds . . . The sun, the moon, and the company of stars float in the empty space, moving or standing still. All are condensed vapour . . .

But the appeal of Confucian theory as well as Wang Chong's scepticism was confined primarily to the scholar-gentry. Though the mass of the people agreed with Confucius about the importance of the family and respect for ancestors, they wanted something less austere and clung to Daoism, which was then absorbing the magical practices of the countryside. The local deities of ancient tradition escaped the chill waters of Confucian ridicule under the spreading umbrella of Daoism. What completed the transformation of Daoist philosophy into a popular religion was competition with the new faith of Buddhism, during the centuries of confusion that succeeded the dissolution of the Han empire. The first heavenly teacher *(tianshih)* of the Daoist church was Chang Daoling, who established a small, semi-independent state on the borders of Sichuan and Shaanxi provinces. His organisation of the peasants living there in a quasi-religious, quasi-military movement was the first of many such rural ventures. In 184 the great rebellion of the "Yellow Turbans", centred on Hubei province, also drew on Daoist revolutionary doctrines. It is reputed that Chang Daoling dramatically acquired immortality when in 156 he suddenly disappeared except for his clothes.

While alchemical theory preoccupied Daoist adepts in their search for an elixir capable of turning men into immortals, the Later Han witnessed a number of significant technical advances that anticipated discoveries traditionally attributed to the West. The talented Zhang Heng

shone as a poet, a calligrapher and a scientist. About 130
he invented the first practical seismograph, his "earth-
quake weathercock", which though not furnishing a scientific explanation for seismic disturbance, at least gave
to the One Man immediate notice of a disaster and its
direction from the capital. The theory of the Mandate of
Heaven and the corresponding benevolence of Shang Di
made the throne sensitive to the interpretation of natural
phenomena or marvels *(zaiyi);* hence the importance of
the imperial observatory which Zhang Heng ran. Other
inventions to his credit were an improved armillary sphere
to trace the paths of planets and the first known application of motive power to the rotation of astronomical
instruments. Recognition of magnetism came from Daoist
geomancy, the art of adapting the abodes of the living
and the dead so as to be in harmony with cosmic forces:
it was achieved by means of a lodestone spoon. A passage written in 83 states, "But when the south-controlling
spoon is thrown upon the ground, it comes to rest pointing south." This is the earliest record of magnetism, yet
by Tang times a compass was in use, the original self-
registering instrument.

A provincial official is said to have introduced a water-
powered metallurgical blowing-machine in 31. The continuous blast thereby afforded was of inestimable value
to the state-owned iron industry and may have led directly to the production of steel. There is no doubt that
steel was being produced during the sixth century by a
technique that foreshadowed the Siemens-Martin process
of combining cast and wrought iron. Another invention
of the imperial workshops was paper-making, announced
in 105 by the eunuch Cai Lun, formerly emperor He Di's
confidential secretary. A fragment of paper discovered in
1957 reveals that a coarse version made of hemp fibres
was available from the reign of Wu Di, but after the
advance overseen by Cai Lun rolls of paper became
commonplace. When later combined with block printing,
paper caused a fundamental revolution in communications that is still in progress throughout the modern world.
The earliest known printed book, a Buddhist text, dates

from 868 and was found in the immense complex of cave-temples at Dunhuang near the western terminus of the Great Wall. But Chinese prisoners of war had already introduced by that date paper-making to the Arabs, who eventually passed the technique to Europe about the eleventh century. Paper-making assisted the spreading of hygienic habits throughout society too: in lavatories toilet paper became available.

The state-controlled salt industry was able to exploit wells in Sichuan province because of the improvement in the manufacture of iron and steel bits. Bamboo tubes fitted with valves were lowered to a depth of nearly one thousand metres in order to extract brine, which was evaporated in large iron pans with the aid of natural gas collected from other bore-holes. The ability to tap this source of salt so far from the sea has been invaluable in times of national crisis, the last such occasion being the Japanese invasion of China during the Second World War. An advantage for early Chinese technology was the abundance of natural piping in the form of bamboo. Besides its usefulness in salt mining, split bamboos could be arranged as irrigation flumes, thus providing a means of overcoming unsatisfactory surfaces for water.

Vital as hydraulic engineering undoubtedly was to agriculture, the imperial programme of canal construction aimed at improving water transport, whose advantage in the shipment of heavy goods was not fully appreciated in the West until the industrial revolution of the eighteenth century. The Chinese emperors were naturally interested in the movement of tax-grain to the capital, not in the development of trade. Navigation itself had been aided by the invention of the sternpost rudder, whose prototype was discovered in a pottery model of a vessel excavated in Guangdong province. Taken from a Former Han tomb in the early 1950s, the model has a large rudder positioned below a steersman's cabin in the stern. The steering oar, general in the West till the Middle Ages, put a severe limitation on the size of ship that could be safely constructed, besides giving the steersman a hazardous task of control in rough weather. The stern-post

Fig. 37 Water-powered blowing-engine for blast furnaces and forges as depicted in a Yuan book. The early perfection of their iron- and steel-making process gave China excellent tools

rudder first appears in Europe about 1180, a time almost exactly identical with the appearance and adoption of the magnetic compass there. In China the evolution of the stern-post rudder and the watertight compartment allowed junks to become large deep-ocean craft. Some of the vessels in the Ming fleet that visited Africa before Vasco de Gama rounded the Cape of Good Hope in 1497 displaced more than 1500 tonnes. The recovery in 1962 of one of their actual rudder-posts at the site of the Ming shipyards in Nanjing has permitted the calculation of 180 metres for overall length. In 1602 the largest ship in the English navy was still under 1000 tonnes.

On land several technical advances also contributed to better transportation. First, the "wooden ox" or wheelbarrow eased the lot of porters. A second improvement was the perfection of the equine collar harness, first invented during the Warring States period. Last but not least, the advent of the stirrup represented a decisive development in the use of the horse. Possibly stimulated by the Indian toe-stirrup, news of which could have been transmitted via Buddhism, the Chinese foot-stirrup made riding easier and in the process gave rise to the armoured cavalryman. The feudal knight that Chinese stirrups helped to elevate in the West ironically was later unseated by another Chinese invention, gunpowder.

Another field of advance under the Han emperors was medicine. Analysis of the foodstuffs in the Mawangdui tombs has revealed herbal preparations intended for the health of the deceased, and their supposed value can be judged from a hitherto unknown medical guide left with them. That great care was also taken to delay physical corruption is evident from the state of the marchioness's body on excavation, which was much better preserved than those belonging to Liu Sheng and Dou Wan, a local ruler of Zhongshan in Hebei province, and his wife. The son of the Han Emperor Jing Di, Liu Sheng chose to be clad on his death in 113 BC in a jade shroud, as did his wife shortly afterwards. Dou Wan's own shroud, the centrepiece of the Chinese Exhibition in London in 1973, comprised 2160 pieces of jade, wired together with gold

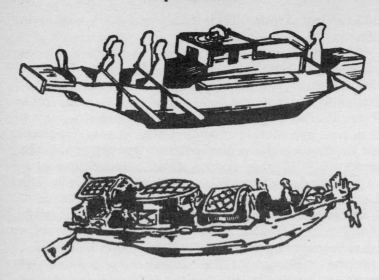

Fig. 38 Two model boats from Han dynasty tombs excavated in Guangdong province. The top one is a reconstruction of a wooden vessel, while the bottom terracotta boat provides crucial evidence for the invention of the rudder

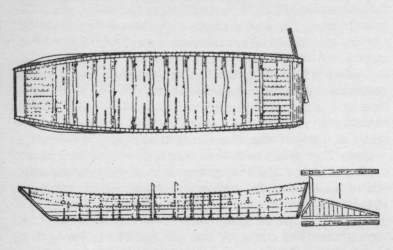

Fig. 39 The earliest boat with an intact rudder dates from the Song empire (960–1279). It was found in 1978 at Tianjin, Hebei province

and silk-wound iron. Their tombs were discovered in 1968.

Although the earliest pharmacopoeia was written prior to imperial unification, interest in longevity, even immortality, from the First Emperor onwards stimulated research into the treatment of disease as well as the activities of the Daoist magicians whom Liu Sheng must have employed. Whilst Han medical theory was still permeated by the idea of universal balance, as expressed in the balance of Yin/Yang, doctors never rejected cures because of the fear of upsetting established principles. The first official dissection was carried out in 16 by order of Wang Mang. This operation on the body of a criminal, according to the historian Ban Gu, was conducted by a skilled butcher under the direction of the court physician; it involved "measuring and weighing the five entrails and tracing the course of the cavities with the aid of fine bamboos to see where they begin and end, so that it would be possible to know how to cure illness". The basic elements of Han therapy were medicines derived from plants and rocks, acupuncture and moxibustion, diet, massage and small-scale incisions. While pills of deathlessness could be purchased, a practical approach to health was already in existence, and one founded on careful observation and diagnosis. The examination of the pulse was systematised, and in about 200 a work appeared that described various infectious diseases including typhoid. It would seem that Hua Tuo (190–265), an expert in physiotherapy, even devised a general anaesthesia by the use of a wine containing Indian hemp.

Despite all this material progress, the final century of the Later Han witnessed numerous risings, the most serious of which was the "Yellow Turban" insurrection in 184. Its leader was a certain Zhang Jiao, a Daoist healer who travelled the north-western provinces declaring how the moment had come for the renewal of the world in a Great Peace *(taiping)*. Wearing yellow turbans as their rallying sign, the rebel peasantry seized control of vast areas in the lower Yellow river valley, executing officials and landowners as they advanced. Repression was swift and violent, nearly 500,000 rebels dying in the nine-month campaign, but the extent of rebellion shook the Later Han dynasty to its foundations.

Also a contributory factor in weakening the imperial regime was the political conflict between the rival factions in the palace itself. Against powerful families the Later Han emperors were tempted to employ eunuchs, but these conflicts only tended to make them in turn more powerful, until at last their machinations drew the army into politics. The assassination of a renowned general at court brought in 189 an immediate response from his troops, who stormed the palace and slaughtered every eunuch in sight. The beneficiary of this coup was another general, the soldier-poet Cao Cao (155–220), who assumed authority in all but name: the Later Han dynasty was continued as long as he considered it was politically useful. In the ensuing anarchy the empire disintegrated as owners of estates fortified their dwellings and recruited soldiers to defend them. When in 220 Cao Cao's son, Cao Pi, deposed the puppet emperor and founded the Wei dynasty, his chief rivals set up their own houses in Chengdu and Nanjing. With the foundation of these Three Kingdoms (*sanguo*), the edifice of the early empire began to crumble.

THE CRISIS OF THE EARLY EMPIRE

Having become the dominant figure in northern China, Cao Cao obliged the shaken throne to let him eliminate other military leaders. In 208 he felt strong enough to tackle the Sun family, a serious rival established on the Yangzi river at Nanjing, but the superior nautical skills of the southerners discomforted Cao Cao at the battle of Chibi and he had to accept a division of China. Following the accession of Cao Pi as the first Wei emperor, the Sun declared itself in 229 the imperial Wu, and not long afterwards at Chengdu in Sichuan province Liu Bei, who claimed to be connected with the Han royal house, added his own claim as the imperial Shu. The latter was fortunate in obtaining the services of Zhu Geliang, an ingenious minister who was more than a match for Cao Pi. Zhu Geliang (181–234) is credited with the first large-scale use of the wheelbarrow for transporting military supplies.

The rivalry of the Three Kingdoms is celebrated in the famous novel *The Romance of the Three Kingdoms (Sanguo Yanyi)*, written in the fourteenth century by Luo Guanzhong. To the Chinese the period has always appeared romantic and legendary, so much so that from one of its generals they have derived Guan Di, the Confucian god of war. However, he was neither bloodthirsty and cowardly like Ares nor an implacable foe like Mars; on the contrary, he was the deity who sought to prevent war. Guan Di is still regarded as the antithesis of Cao Cao, whose famous epigram was "I would rather betray the whole world than allow the world to betray me."

Fig. 40 Liu Bei's chief minister, Zhu Geliang, whose efficiency in war and diplomacy ensured the survival of the Shu state. He was also a distinguished mathematician and inventor

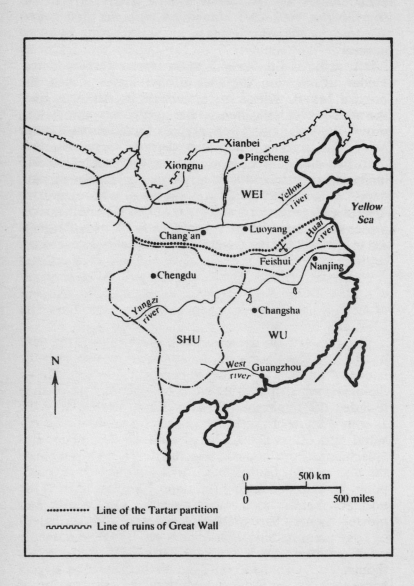

Fig. 41 The Three Kingdoms (221–265)

The long struggle between the Three Kingdoms was ended in 280 by the Western Jin dynasty, which had toppled the Wei house fifteen years earlier. The first Western Jin emperor, Sima Yan, was another northern general in the mould of Cao Cao, but he outdid him by briefly achieving the reunification of the whole country. Under his direction, the ancient heartland of China, the original Middle Kingdom, reasserted its authority over the newly developing areas in the south and southwestern provinces. What stood behind this triumph was a greater concentration on agricultural productivity and water transport as a means of strengthening military power. Local magnates were stripped of their retainers—though the tendency of the age soon transformed the officials planted in their place into new magnates themselves—and extra manpower came from barbarian migrants who were permitted to settle within the Great Wall. This policy of barbarian settlement was to have the dire military and political consequence it had in the Roman empire. But, by avoiding pitched battles and merely waging an economic war of attrition the Western Jin was able to reduce both Shu (264) and Wu (280).

The Western Jin dynasty lasted only till 316, the year in which most of the northern provinces passed into the hands of peoples from the steppes and the remnant of Sima Yan's line fled southwards to Nanjing, where they founded the diminished Eastern Jin dynasty (317–420). A combination of pressures caused this collapse and ensured that China should be divided for 273 years. Encroachment from nomads had worried the empire since the time of Han Gaozu, but it was the more conciliatory policy inaugurated during the Later Han that opened the northern frontier to invaders, because the price of employing friendly barbarians as allies was their settlement of large areas within the empire itself. That these people posed an internal threat was not readily understood, although Cao Cao had contrived to disperse the largest tribes into smaller groups, each under the supervision of a Chinese official. Periods of civil strife were the most dangerous as opposing sides were tempted to call upon friendly tribes for aid. This occurred in 304, when the Hunnish Xiongnu backed one prince and the Tartar Xianbei were enlisted by another. In 311 Luoyang was sacked and the emperor captured; then in 316 the last Western Jin emperor was taken prisoner on the fall of Chang'an.

Sima Yan himself must bear some responsibility for the disaster, since he made the fatal error of allowing his twenty-five sons to govern separate territories, a policy which weakened the central government, encouraged fragmentation into quasi-feudal holdings, led to family conflict after his death, and gave the nomads their chance. But it would be wrong to suppose that ferocious invaders vanquished an enfeebled China. They did not. In 383 the better discipline and equipment of the small Eastern Jin army secured a decisive victory at Feishui over an infantry force of 600,000 accompanied by 270,000 nomad cavalry. This engagement confirmed the independence of the Chinese settled south of the Huai river valley.

4

THE MIDDLE EMPIRE

From Disunity to the Tang and Song Renaissance (317–1279)

THE TARTAR PARTITION (317–589)

With the downfall of the Western Jin dynasty in 316, the hold that Chinese rulers had fought to maintain over north China following the end of the Han empire was lost. The sacking of the great cities of Luoyang and Chang'an led to an exodus of scholars and officials from north to south, where they settled around the Eastern Jin capital of Nanjing. There they assisted in the establishment of a diminished state, which nonetheless was felt to be the true heir and preserver of Chinese culture; and in conjunction with local Buddhist monks they also helped in the development of a faith that appealed to educated people. The loss of the ancient heartland of China raised doubts as to whether Confucian ideology was a sufficiently strong shield in troubled times and, in this mood of despair, scholars were prepared to open their minds to both Daoist and Buddhist ideas. Since the imperial house was inevitably weak, Buddhist monks were able to assert their independence of secular authority on similar lines to the monastic community in India. This was in contrast to the situation in the barbarian north, where Tartar rulers expected unqualified obedience to their orders.

Fig. 42 A Daoist recluse with a follower, after a fifth-century painting. During the uncertainties of the Tartar partition scholars turned from Confucianism to the mystical comforts of Daoist and Buddhist teachings

North China had become little more than a battleground for competing barbarian kings. Once the southern thrusts of these warring chieftains were halted at the battle of Feishui in 383, and a line of partition drawn virtually along the northern boundary of the wet-rice growing area (countryside unsuited to the military tactics of nomad cavalry), then the focus of conflict switched to the control of the northern provinces themselves. The unexpected reverse at Feishui seems to have disturbed the balance of power, for there occurred a fresh barbarian invasion by the Tuoba Tartars, a branch of the Xianbei that was already urbanised. These people founded a new dynasty, the Tuoba Wei (386–550), which through a succession of able rulers gradually defeated all rival princes. But tribal difficulties, clashes between the different eth-

nic groups, prevented the Tuoba emperors from doing
more than securing their position in north China. The
dynasty indeed went through a series of title changes—
Northern (386–532), Eastern (534–43) and Western
(535–50)—that reflected the incessant power struggles
around the throne. By the reign of Xiao Wen Di (471–99),
however, the Chinese at court formed the leading element, and they persuaded the emperor to move his capital from Pingcheng, modern Datong, to Luoyang as a
token of his claim to rule "all under Heaven". In the
490s Xiao Wen Di introduced further measures which
were dictated by the administrative needs of what was
then a large state, stretching from Dunhuang in the west
of Korea in the east. He prohibited Tartar speech, dress

Fig. 43 By the Sui reunification of China in 589 the Buddhist
religion was a serious threat to both Confucianism and Daoism.
Communities of monks were busy translating the scriptures and
propagating the faith. This portrait of a Buddhist monk comes
from Dunhuang

Fig. 44 A Tartar aristocrat and his lady obeying the edict of Xiao Wen Di in the 490s and adopting Chinese manners. This move began the process through which the country was reunited by the Sui dynasty

and customs; henceforth Chinese culture was to be the standard for the Tuoba empire.

This astonishing instance of the integrative and absorptive power of Chinese culture in part explains the survival of the empire, even its continuation down to modern times. The impact of barbarian settlement on the western provinces of the Roman empire was entirely different, since a definite cultural break occurred with the retreat of Latin learning behind monastery walls. In north China, on the contrary, there already existed in embryo alternative social arrangements to a centralised authority. On the large estates could be found an effective organisation for production and defence, with a corresponding quasi-feudal order that was capable of filling the power vacuum caused by the decline of central government, particularly in the fourth century. The powerful family, which controlled the locality with fortified encampments, offered security to the peasants and employment to the scholars, albeit on a smaller scale. Although these local magnates could be troublesome, they were accepted by the Tartar invaders as a permanent feature in the political scene, a decision which ultimately produced the Sino-barbarian synthesis in north China under the Tuoba Wei dynasty. Their advice to Xiao Wen Di in dealing with an increasingly restive peasantry was wholesale sinicisation.

As the Tartar habit of plunder was unsuited to a state based on agriculture, salaries were introduced to dissuade officials from the practice and land was redistributed to the peasants in order to provide adequate tax-grain. Incessant uprisings in the countryside therefore drove the Tuoba Wei into an accommodation with the people they ruled. There were simply too many peasants to be ignored, a vast cultural reservoir not easily drained of Chinese traditions, and though many scholars had migrated southwards, enough stayed behind to influence decisively thinking at court.

The transfer of the capital from Pingcheng to Luoyang also favoured the spread of Buddhism. While Xiao Wen Di wanted to place emphasis on Confucian institutions and practices, he found that popular pressure would not allow him to restrict the number of temples and nunneries to be built within the city walls. Once the imperial palaces were completed, he had to bow to demands for rock sculpture at nearby Longmen, as the inhabitants of the capital missed the gigantic cave sculptures they had left behind at Yungang, a few kilometres west of Pingcheng. It was under his successor, the ardent Buddhist emperor Xuan Wu, that most of the carving took place at Longmen as well as the construction of notable monasteries in Luoyang itself. One of these monasteries, with over one thousand cells, was built like a palace among hills and ponds, amidst groves of bamboo and pine.

In the last years of the Tuoba Wei rule, there were 30,000 recorded temples occupied by 2 million monks and nuns: in Luoyang alone the scholar Yang Xuanzhi remembered 1367 religious buildings. "No place was without a monastery," he wrote in his *Memories of Luoyang's*

Temples. "They spread almost into the meat and wine markets, so that their statues and stupas were wrapped with unsavoury smells." Written after 547, the year Yang Xuanzhi is known to have visited the ruins of Luoyang, the *Memories* give a detailed picture of Buddhist influence in the capital before its enforced abandonment. In 534 a military adventurer named Gao Yang, a Chinese who had adopted Xianbei customs, captured the emperor and forced him to order the removal of the capital eastwards to his own stronghold in Hebei province. But this transfer of population was as unsuccessful as the dynasty Gao Yang's son sought to establish in 550 as the Northern Qi. The latter was toppled after thirty-one years by the Xianbei general Yang Jian, the future Sui emperor Wen Di and reunifier of China.

The earliest reference to Buddhism, whose phenomenal rise in popularity was the salient historical event of the period of disunity, was made in 65 by the Later Han emperor Ming Di, when he addressed his nephew as one who "recites the subtle words of Huang-lao, and respectfully performs the gentle sacrifices of the Buddha".

This early Buddhism was looked upon as a sect of Daoism. Indeed, Daoist communities may have served to spread certain Buddhist symbols and cults, thus playing a role analogous to that of the Jewish communities which helped to spread early Christianity in the eastern provinces of the Roman empire. But eclecticism was born as much from the circumstances of the Indian religion's arrival as the ability of the Chinese mind to hold simultaneously without apparent distress a number of different propositions. The earliest Buddhist converts had few texts, depended on the testimony of foreigners, and had scant idea of the society in which the Buddha had preached. *Mahayana* (the Great Vehicle) was the form of Buddhism carried to China and this more evolved version of the faith had already many opposing schools. At a congress called by the Kushan ruler Kanishka (78–123), a gathering held in the Punjab and known as the Fourth Buddhist Council, the representatives of no less than eighteen Buddhist sects were in attendance. To overcome uncertainties a Chinese pilgrim such as Fa Xian travelled to India in order to receive instruction and collect manuscripts. The account of his travels, *A Record of the Buddhist Countries*, illuminates developments in Mahayana doctrine as well as China's sea and land communications with the outside world. In 399 he took the overland route from Chang'an down the Silk Road, descending onto the north Indian plain from modern Afghanistan. His homeward journey by ship from the Ganges delta took him to Sri Lanka and Sumatra before landing in 414 on the coast of Shandong province.

Translation of the manuscripts brought back by pilgrims, or introduced into China through the agency of foreign monks, quickly drew criticisms from Confucian scholars, who accused the new teachings of being unfilial, but they were not immune themselves from Buddhist speculation, once translations of high literary quality came into general circulation. Instrumental in making such texts available, as well as emancipating Buddhist ideas from Daoism, was the Central Asian missionary Kumarajiva. He arrived at Chang'an in 401 after learning Chinese during a long captivity in Gansu province, where the local military commander had detained him on his journey eastwards. At Chang'an, which only passed into Tuoba Wei hands two decades after Kumarajiva's death in 413, every facility was made available to help in the mammoth task of translation. Over a thousand monks worked with Kumarajiva on the revision of old and imperfect translations as well as the production of entirely new ones. Even the Later Qin ruler Yao Chang occasionally lent his personal support by holding the old translations which were used as the basis for comparison. Possibly of Tibetan ancestry, Yao Chang had seized power in 385 but his kingdom foundered after an attack in 417 delivered by an expedition from southern China. The would-be liberators were unable to maintain their conquest, as Chang'an was first captured by Xiongnu forces, then the Tuoba Tartars.

Thanks to the efforts of Kumarajiva the ideas of Mahayana Buddhism were presented in Chinese with greater clarity and precision than ever before. In particular he rescued from Daoist influence the fundamental concept of *sunyata,* "emptiness", the unreality of all the elements of existence. Tradition has it that Yao Chang was so impressed that he assigned ten girls to live with Kumarajiva in order that his qualities of mind should be transmitted to offspring. Although the great translator submitted to the ruler's wishes and children were born, he was modest enough to tell his followers that they need only pluck the holy lotus that grew out of the mud: the mud should be left well alone.

To counter the charge of filial impiety, an inevitable accusation against a faith which aimed at individual salvation through the realisation of *sunyata,* scriptures were translated that showed concern for the family. One text relates how a *bodhisattva,* or "being who is possessed of the essence of the Buddhahood", chose to be reborn as the son of a childless, blind couple who wanted to retire to the forest in order to lead a life of contemplation. Under the Tang emperors the Buddha was to be transformed into the epitome of the dutiful son as the Buddhist church accepted a place within the structure of the Confucian state. Much of the conflict between the imperial civil service and the Buddhist monasteries that brought about this singularly Chinese compromise stemmed from the different experiences of the northern and the southern provinces during the Tartar partition. Coming from the north, where the Tuoba Wei had kept strict control over ordination and temple-building, both the Sui and Tang dynasties were ever watchful for signs of religious disobedience.

Of all the southern rulers, the Histories depict emperor Liang Wudi (502–550) as the greatest patron of Buddhism. Though satisfactory relations with the Tuoba Wei eluded him, the energy he expended in propagating the new religion bore plenty of fruit—to which he seems to have been converted from Confucianism in about 511. Shortly afterwards he invited 3000 monks to Nanjing from India, a request the reigning Gupta king was pleased to allow, though his most famous import was Paramartha, who arrived only in 548. Rebellions in the final years of Liang Wudi's reign prevented the setting up of a translation school in the capital, but it did not stop Paramartha from embarking on important translations of his own. "Each day", the Histories noted, "the emperor and the empress became more and more absorbed in their devotion to Buddhism. The empress built a magnificent temple close by the palace, where she could worship at all hours of the day, and as a work of merit she erected a pagoda thirty metres in height, which could be seen for a long distance in every direction, and which reminded the people of the grip that Buddhism was taking upon those

Fig. 45 The most ardent supporter of Confucianism amongst the southern rulers was Wen Di (424–54), who in his final years tried to stem the rising tide of Buddhism. He was the antithesis of Liang Wudi, the would-be imperial monk

in high positions in the land." Only with difficulty was Liang Wudi himself dissuaded in 528 from permanently becoming a monk.

There was consternation over this attempted course of action, as well as over the prohibition of meat in the rites of ancestor worship, but the emperor was not easily deflected by the criticism of anyone. For him the highlight of his whole life happened in 538 with the receipt of sacred nails, hair and bones; these relics of the Buddha were ceremoniously incorporated in a splendid temple and an amnesty was proclaimed throughout his territories. Yet one Buddhist is supposed to have confused Liang Wudi. This was Bodhidharma, the founder of the Chan sect, which in Japan eventually became Zen. When asked by the emperor what merit he had acquired by good works, Bodhidharma replied, "No merit at all!" Amazed, he then asked his visitor about the first principle of Buddhism. "There isn't one," was the reply, "since where all is emptiness, nothing can be called Holy." Despite this rather splendid interview, evidence now points to the arrival of this enigmatic monk in Luoyang sometime before 526, rather than south China. Certainly it was in a monastery there that he spent his days "gazing at a wall".

SUI REUNIFICATION (589–618)

The sinicisation of the Tartars living in north China left the way open for imperial reunification. Like the Qin dynasty which first united the country in 221 BC, the Sui began its reconquest in the northern provinces, only to fall itself within a few decades. And, once again, a subsequent imperial house built on the new foundations it laid. For the empire succeeded in weathering the crisis of partition, as well as a ruthless reunification, and under the Tang emperors saw the beginnings of a brilliant cultural renaissance. Even today Chinese people still call themselves *Tangren*, men of Tang, in recognition of the way their civilisation was moulded by the dynasty's achieve-

ments. The distinction between the Han and the Tang
periods is indeed expressed in a common form of address. *Hanren,* men of Han, embodies a sense of exclu-
siveness, Chinese as opposed to Xiongnu or barbarian,
whilst *Tangren* incorporates the diversity and tolerance of
a China stretching from the steppes to the tropics on one
hand and from land-locked mountains to the sea on the
other.

The reunification movement started in 581 when Yang
Jian overthrew the Northern Qi dynasty. Something of
the Xianbei ancestry of this hardbitten soldier may be
apparent in his thrift and his sternness. He demanded
from his officials the same sense of duty as from his
soldiers; and he set his face resolutely against luxury,
forbidding the ostentation of powerful families, until he
could be sure of the revenues due to the imperial exchequer. A census in 585 discovered an extra 600,000 adult
males, confirming Yang Jian's worst suspicions about the
self-interest of the landowners. Thus after capturing Nanjing
in 589, and reuniting the north and south, he cracked
down on their retainers and gave notice that an effective
imperial government could not allow any lingering feudalism.

Sui Wen Di, as Yang Jian was titled, was not without
compassion for the sufferings of the common people. In
595 such a dreadful famine struck the province of Shaanxi
that even the wealthy had to undergo privation. Discov-
ering the plight of the poor, the Histories say, the Sui
emperor "ordered his troops to assist in a general evacuation of Chang'an. On the long and painful trek eastwards he showed the greatest humanity to his suffering
people. The soldiers helped the very old and young
along the road and over the difficult passes amongst
the mountains they had to cross. As Wen Di felt that
this terrible visitation upon the land was a sign of
divine disapproval, he went as a pilgrim at the beginning
of 596 to Taishan and prayed on the mountain for
forgiveness."

Abundant harvests ensued, although Yang Jian was
less fortunate in the affairs of his own court. The plotting

Fig. 46 The reunifier of China, Wen Di, the first Sui emperor, after a Tang painting. The Xianbei-Chinese ruler is shown in the company of his chief ministers

of his wife brought about the downfall of the heir-apparent and the elevation of his second son Yang Guang, who in 604 assassinated him. Of Yang Guang, the second and final Sui ruler, the Histories state:

He shortened the life of his dynasty by a number of
years through his extravagance in public works, but
benefited posterity unto ten thousand generations.
He ruled without benevolence, but his rule is credited with enduring accomplishments.

This ambivalence sums up the Chinese attitude to the Sui
house as a whole, not least because its repressive rule
was looked upon as the price which the people had to
pay for the reunification of the country.

Yang Jian transplanted two of the distinctive institutions that were developed in north China under the Tartars; namely the *jintian* system, a revival of the land
reform programme unsuccessfully tried by Wang Mang in
9, and the *fuping*, the militia: together they formed the
power base of the restored empire. The militia comprised
locally recruited units, either drawn from families with a
tradition of military service or from ordinary families
who chose to furnish soldiers rather than perform labour
duties on public works. The length and frequency of the
service required of militiamen is unclear in Sui times, but
we know that even in the mobilisation of 1 million soldiers against the kingdom of Koguryo in 612 Yang Guang
could call upon sufficient of their numbers to strengthen
the crack troops of the regular army without recourse to
raw recruits. Earlier in 590 Yang Jian had tried to spread
the burden of war more evenly; he ordered the territorial
military bureaux to ensure that all soldiers should be
subject to the local officials and cultivate land like the
peasant-farmers. The militia was not wound up until 749,
a significant date in Chinese history because it left the
Tang emperor dangerously exposed to the whims of military leaders at the head of professional soldiers. The
disastrous rebellion of the barbarian general An Lushan
in 755 was a direct consequence of the throne's reliance
on full-time troops. Although the militia suffered during
the fighting that accompanied the fall of the Sui dynasty
in 618, the system was continued by the early Tang rulers
who had risen to power as commanders of local contin-
gents. In fact the first emperor, Tang Gao Zu, lost no

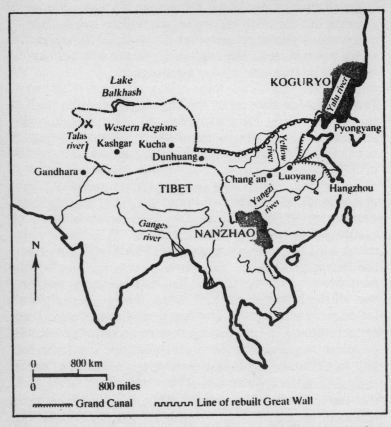

Fig. 47 The Tang Empire prior to the rebellion of An Lushan (755)

time in establishing local militia units to provide a reliable and widespread source of manpower for the military needs of the dynasty. At his abdication in 826 the total number of units had passed the 600 mark.

As soon as Yang Guang came to power as the Sui emperor Yang Di though, he brushed aside the financial restraint of his father and commissioned a new capital in Luoyang. It was built by hundreds of thousands of workmen in 605. His next project, which lasted from 606 till 610, was the digging of the Grand Canal in order to link the northern and southern provinces permanently together.

Construction involved the reopening of older sections of existing but derelict waterways as well as the cutting of extensive sections of new canal. Over 2500 kilometres were brought into use, stretching from Beijing in the north to Hangzhou in the south, with Luoyang in the middle. At the same time labourers were ordered to continue with the repairs Yang Jian had initiated on the Great Wall. Millions toiled on these gigantic projects; for those who shirked there awaited decapitation, flogging, neck weights and the confiscation of property.

Yet for all this, it was the foreign policy of Yang Di that ruined the Sui. Peasant rebellions began in 611 with a rising in Shandong province, but their number and intensity increased in the north-east as pressure bore down on the population with each successive failure of the campaigns against Koguryo, a kingdom which occupied what is now southern Manchuria plus the northern part of the Korea peninsula; its capital was on the site on modern Pyongyang. Following border difficulties, Yang Di determined to invade Koguryo and secure the Chinese position by reasserting authority over the Liao river valley. In 612 an expeditionary force tried to take the enemy capital through a quick thrust, but the walled cities along the eastern bank of the Liao river held up the pace of the advance. In the following year a second, and larger Chinese army, moved forward and engaged Koguryo forces on the Yalu river, the present-day border between the People's Republic and North Korea. The battle ended in a resounding defeat, according to the Histories, "with Yang Di fleeing for his life, while all the baggage and war materials of the great host fell into the victor's hands, together with a very large number of prisoners". Ignoring widespread insurrection in the provinces, and opposition from the officials at court, the emperor led another ineffectual expedition against Koguryo in 614. Only the exhaustion of the enemy ended this expensive conflict, when the king of Koguryo agreed to accept the status of an imperial vassal.

Fig. 48 An official seal of "the lord of Yiyang", in the Sui empire a large district in Jianxi province. Of Sui or early Tang provenance

Fig. 49 Sui tombstone in the form of a building. It reveals the classical form of the Chinese roof

While Yang Di convinced himself all was well, "the empire was honeycombed with rebellion and everywhere", say the Histories, "those in revolt gathered extra supporters because of the unpopularity of the government".

As disturbances grew and spread, Yang Di withdrew into a private world of his own that was only shattered by the knife of an assassin in 618. A half-hearted effort to place Yang Di's nephew on the throne followed, but it was too late, China had already slipped into civil war.

THE TANG RENAISSANCE (618–906)

The man who did most to preserve the reunified empire was Li Shimin, the second son of the first Tang emperor Gao Zu. It was his straightforward and economical government which confirmed the belief of the Chinese people in the value of unity. He kept the military establishment to a minimum through improving the quality of the militia, whose members were self-sufficient farmers performing only an annual tour of duty. Properly trained and equipped, this body of part-time soldiers formed the dependable core of the early Tang armies; even after his accession to the throne in 626 as Tang Tai Zong, Li Shimin insisted on personally instructing the militiamen in the finer points of shooting the crossbow. The military background of the imperial family made Tai Zong very sensitive to dangers from this quarter and led him to shift the balance of power from the military to the civil. Therefore he increased the number and frequency of official examinations for entry to the civil service and instituted a scholarship system to encourage learning. Examinations had been held under the Sui emperors, as well as Tang Gao Zu, but the aristocracy really began to decline in power during Tai Zong's reign (626–49), when its place in government was gradually taken by professional bureaucrats recruited on the basis of personal talent and education. The rise of men committed to the service of a dynasty changed the position of the emperor: he was no longer the chief aristocrat whose pedigree, as in the case of the Li family, might even be suspect; on the contrary, with no aristocracy to challenge his authority, and with a loyal and hard-working bureaucracy, the imperial clan became set apart from ordinary people in

Fig. 50 Emperor Tang Tai Zong with his senior officials, after a contemporary painting. During his reign (626–49) the government was gradually taken over by professional bureaucrats recruited through examinations

a quite new way, and the emperor started to accrue powers that culminated in virtual despotism under the Ming (1368–1644).

Already in the reign of Tai Zong there appeared a gulf between the emperor and the officials through whom he ruled. Though less forceful and superstitious than Han Wu Di, Tai Zong shared that ruler's flamboyance and impatience at delay and, readily provoked, his face would turn purple with rage and intimidate those in his presence. Early experience of war—the normal upbringing of contemporary noblemen of mixed Chinese and Turkish blood—had taught Tai Zong to rely on human effort alone, a belief in direct action that was further strengthened by the bloody struggle he waged against his brothers, which in 626 left them dead and forced his father to abdicate. Yet the family feud did not close his eyes to the merit of men who had advised his brothers. One of these was Wei Zheng (580–643), whom he promoted to the highest offices. The emperor is said to have appreciated his frankness, though the advice he received from this Confucian scholar was often very unpalatable.

The ruler-minister relationship of Tai Zong and Wei Zheng, which lasted for seventeen of the twenty-three years of the reign, has always been regarded as an ideal one. Whilst openness of discussion reflected a bureaucratic self-confidence quite impossible in later Ming times, Confucian commentators have not been able to avoid embroidery in their account of Wei Zheng's period of office. It has to be admitted, nevertheless, that the tone was set by his literal acceptance of the Confucian dictum that a minister was duty-bound to rectify his ruler, never hesitating to denounce any aspect of conduct that worried him or to resist any policy he believed detrimental to the interests of the state. A valuable counterweight to imperial pretentions though he was, the influence of Wei Zheng on Chinese consciousness is not unconnected with the return of Confucian officials to the halls of government after an absence of more than three centuries. His eminence at court represented for Confucianism a welcome recovery of status.

A weapon that Wei Zheng was adept at deploying against Tai Zong was the judgement of posterity, as the emperor was a very self-conscious ruler and deeply concerned about the record of his reign. On more than one occasion Tai Zong endeavoured to influence the officials in charge of supervising the compilation of dynastic history. In China it was customary from the Former Han onwards for specially appointed scholars to write the history of their times, and no one but themselves was ever allowed to read what they had written. As each document was composed, it was deposited in an iron-bound chest, which remained locked until such time as the dynasty had ceased to rule. Then at the order of a later ruler the chest would be opened and the documents it contained edited into a history of the previous dynasty. This method of storage had been devised to protect scholars who might have to record facts unpleasant to the throne.

When in 641 Tai Zong asked one of these officials

about the possibility of examining documents before they were deposited, he was respectfully told that "in recording the ruler's words and deeds, good and evil must be written down so that the ruler will not act improperly. For that reason they are never made available." On being pressed by Tai Zong about adverse comments on his reign, the official said: "My duty in office is to uphold the brush, so how could I not record bad points?" The emperor was still not satisfied however. In 643 he wanted to know how the deaths of his brothers were treated. Even Wei Zheng appears to have shared some of his concern over this distressing episode and indeed there is evidence that sections of the dynastic history came under Tai Zong's strong editorial influence.

Despite his unprepossessing appearance, Wei Zheng was never awed by the emperor's powerful personality and was completely unafraid of him, even when he heard that Tai Zong in rage at his opposition had cried out, "I'm going to have to kill that old country bumpkin!" His daring independence rested on the unshakeable conviction that the fall of the Sui dynasty was attributable to Yang Di's reluctance to heed the advice of loyal officials. He believed that its inability to deal with internal problems resulted from a preoccupation with foreign conquest, a belief which led him in 640 to oppose an expansionist policy in Central Asia, much to Tai Zong's annoyance. Yet there were times when the emperor was melted by the minister's rectitude. So cold was the attitude of Tai Zong towards his father, even after he had died, that orders were given for the construction of a very modest tomb on the outskirts of Chang'an. In contrast for himself, and his courtiers, a tomb city was laid out on a mountain site some distance from the capital. Its first occupant was the empress, for whom a veritable mausoleum was built in 636. Since on a clear day from the palace one could see the mountain on which the tomb was situated, the sorrowful emperor had a tower especially built in order to gaze at it. Not long after the empress's burial, Tai Zong invited Wei Zheng to accompany him in ascending the tower. To the emperor's consternation the minister said that his poor eyesight prevented him from seeing anything. When he was at last pointed in the right direction, Wei Zheng commented: "Oh, that's it then . . . I thought Your Majesty was looking at another tomb." Realising that the minister referred to the poor resting place of his father, Tai Zong wept and ordered the observation tower to be destroyed at once—the Confucian scholar had touched that potent Chinese nerve, filial piety.

With the aid of officials of Wei Zheng's calibre, Tai Zong finally established the notion of China as the territory of the unified empire. Division was simply not to be seen as an option even after the devastation caused by the rebellion of An Lushan: military commanders were obliged to restore the imperial house in 763, although the fact that their troops comprised regulars rather than militiamen meant that the civil service had to forfeit some of its pre-eminence. From then onwards, it was customary for officers and men of the frontier commanderies to chose their own commanding officers, whose positions tended to become hereditary. It was a practice that the Tang court disliked but dared not alter. Yet the empire owed to its armies not only security along the frontiers but beyond them, the creation of an outer zone of independent states, increasingly dominated by Chinese culture and using Chinese script. This outward extension contrasts with policies followed during the Han empire, for there was a two-way flow of influence that now seems positively modern. The attitude of the Tang emperors indeed reflected a genuine readiness to accept foreign peoples and their ideas. In the capital, Chang'an, there were priests from India, Indochina, and South-East Asia, merchants from Central Asia and Arabia, and travellers from West Asia, Persia, Turkestan, Korea and Japan. These people made their influence felt in the fashions, amusements and cuisine of the court; at the simple level of cookery a bewildering variety of vegetables, nuts, fruits and spices became known for the first time. Particularly popular among all classes was Persian confectionary and vendors offering foreign cakes *(hubing)* thronged the streets of Chang'an, then the largest city in the world with a population of over 1 million.

Side by side with the arrival of new culinary ideas went an influx of Buddhist scriptures from India and Central Asia. Tai Zong gave a personal interview to the famous Buddhist monk Xuan Zhang, or Tripitaka, on his return from India with manuscripts in 645. Although the emperor was inclined to Daoism, he supported the Confucians for the sake of the civil service, besides welcoming Buddhism and other foreign faiths. A decade earlier, according to an inscription set up in Chang'an, a Nestorian monk had been welcomed at court by Tai Zong, who commented on his Christian message:

> The Way has more than one name. There is more than one Sage. O Lopen, a man of great virtue, has brought his images and books from afar to present them in the capital. After examining his teachings,

Fig. 51 A palace entertainment for the court ladies. Good food and drink were enjoyed in Chang'an, since the Tang capital was able to draw upon culinary ideas from the "Western Regions" as well as from the traditional provinces of the empire

Fig. 52 Tripitaka, or Xuan Zhang, the Buddhist pilgrim to India, shown carrying back the scriptures to Chang'an. From a stone carving

we find that they are profound and pacific, stressing what is good and important. This religion benefits all men. Let it be preached freely in Our Empire.

The inclusive habit of mind in evidence here, coupled with Confucian scepticism, has tended to keep religion and the priesthood as minor elements in Chinese civilisation, with the result that persecution barely figures in the historical record. The severe, though short, repression of foreign faiths in 845 can therefore be seen as an attempt to prevent a Buddhist church from securing a stranglehold over the economic affairs of the empire. Its method was confiscation of property and compulsory laicisation of 260,500 monks and nuns. Unlike resilient Buddhism, however, Nestorian Christianity did not survive this purge and disappeared almost without trace.

The expansionist policies of Tai Zong were followed by his immediate successors. So secure was the Chinese position in Central Asia, which had been annexed in 640, that another unsuccessful campaign against Koguryo failed to diminish Tang authority along the northern frontier. A renewed offensive in the north-east, ordered in 645, had turned into a disaster when a great blizzard caught the imperial forces on their march home. Remembering the prudent counsel he had previously received, Tai Zong sadly noted, "If Wei Zheng were alive, he would not have allowed us to do this." Vigorous action in the 660s, however, brought the greater part of the Korean peninsula to heel. Pyongyang, the Koguryo capital, fell in 668 and was garrisoned by 20,000 Chinese troops. A similar irritant to the empire was Tibet, which under Srong-btsan-sgan-po (605–649) became for the first time a single kingdom. Tibetan pressure on Gansu province threatened China's trade routes to the West and Tang emperors were forced to maintain large garrisons there. When, in 775, the An Lushan rebellion forced the central government to withdraw these troops for the defence of the capital, the Tibetans occupied most of Gansu, and later reduced the Chinese outposts further west as well. Only the disintegration of the Tibetan kingdom after 842 saved China from the need to mount a major counterattack. A dispute between the king and the great Buddhist monasteries left the latter dominant in Tibetan society, and also effectively sealed off the rugged country from Chinese influence, which had begun through dynastic marriage and the nobility sending their sons to study in China. As a result Tibet adopted a script derived from India, and

Fig. 53 Tai Zong greeting in 641 an ambassador from Tibet, which under Srong-btsan-sgan-po had emerged as a powerful kingdom. Chinese influence over the Tibetan court was maintained by marriage with princesses of the imperial house: this scene from a contemporary painting records the negotiations leading to a betrothal

remained culturally separate from China until very recent times, in spite of the Manchu conquest in the eighteenth century.

Intrigue at court, including banishment and executions, resulted in Tai Zong's ninth son becoming the heir-apparent and succeeding him in 649 as emperor Gao Zong. The doubts that Tai Zong had about the ability of his successor to lead the country effectively proved to be well-founded. Weak in character and prone to physical illness, Gao Zong was overshadowed by his empress Wu Ze Tian, a beautiful and intelligent woman with a natural genius for politics. Once the experienced ministers who had advised Tai Zong died or retired through old age, the empress was able to concentrate power in her own hands. After the death of Gao Zong in 683, she continued to control the court and pushed aside two of her sons before, in 690, the time was judged right for her to ascend the throne. For fifteen years empress Wu Ze Tian styled herself as emperor Sheng Shen, the only woman ruler in Chinese history. Allowing for the hatred of Confucian commentators towards her usurpation, it is quite apparent that she was exceptionally gifted and the author of constructive policies, even though her use of secret agents and sudden killings did much to undermine the authority of officials. A streak of cruelty ran through empress Wu Ze Tian's character: it caused a reign of terror, but she was always careful to balance those who served her violent ends with a group of talented administrators. These gifted individuals had risen to the highest court offices via the examination system, by means of which, the Histories report, the usurping empress "wished to cage the bold and enterprising spirits of all regions".

Her deliberate choice of examination graduates for key posts may represent an effort to weaken the opposition from powerful families living near the capital, among whom the supporters of the imperial house were likely to be found. Not until the rise of the minister Li Linfu in 733 did they recover their position at court. This policy of favouring less privileged families naturally introduced to high office men of real ability as well as giving opportunities to scholars residing in other provinces of the empire. Perhaps empress Wu Ze Tian's greatest claim to fame is her patronage of poetry, since it was through her influence that poetry became a requisite in examinations for higher qualifications and promotion. So in 800, because of his talent in writing verse, Bai Juyi obtained a first class grade in the palace examinations and was appointed a collator of texts in the imperial library, a sinecure for bright young men whose future careers had yet to be decided. Bai Juyi went on to be a distinguished official and a famous poet. Although he tells us that his "bluntness did not suit the times" when he chose to criticise courtly extravagance, there can be no doubt that his lighter poems enjoyed an immense popularity. "One found them everywhere", a friend of his observed, "on the walls of palace buildings, Daoist and Buddhist monasteries and posting stations. Everyone recited them, princes and nobles, wives and concubines, ox-herds and grooms. They were copied out, printed and sold in the market and brought to give in exchange for wine and tea. This happened in many different places".

The invention of block printing sometime in the eighth century met the demand for books and encouraged the spread of literacy. It also helped to enhance the Tang renaissance which reached its highest expression in poetry. The poetic impulse responded to the loosening of cultural restraints, not least under the long reign of Xuan Zong (712–56), a ruler who consciously sought to make Chang'an the capital of refinement as well as that of an empire. The *Complete Tang Poems* comprises over 48,000 poems by no less than 2200 authors. This prodigious output becomes even more impressive when we appreciate it contains the great names of Chinese poetry: Wang Wei (699–761), Li Bai (701–762), Du Fu (712–70) and Bai Juyi (772–846). Of these poets only Wang Wei was a painter, revealing that those apparently indissoluble Chinese arts of calligraphy, poetry and painting date as a unity from the period of the Song emperors (960–1279). At this time painting, which later became one of the chief distractions of educated men, was a craft practised almost exclusively by specialists. But the surge of creativity in writing affected prose composition too, although stylists such as Han Yu sought to recapture the earlier clarity of the Han historians. His motive for purging ornament was the creation of an instrument capable of exposing the stupidities of the age, and especially Buddhism.

The first thirty years of Xuan Zong's reign were marked by good government, cultural achievement, prosperity and population growth. Census figures for 754 indicate that there were 9,069,154 families, giving for the empire a taxable population of 53,000,000. Migrant families, groups of people who had moved from one area to another in order to avoid taxation or to find better land for cultivation, probably account for another two or three millions, the majority of whom would have moved to the southern and south-western provinces. This final shift of the key economic area out of the north-west partly explains the siting of the two Song capitals at Kaifeng on the lower Yellow river valley and at Hangzhou, Zhejiang province.

Disaster struck the Tang empire in 755. An Lushan, a

Turkish general in command of the imperial forces in the north-east, rebelled and overran Hebei and Henan, then the richest and most productive provinces in the empire. Threats from powerful and mobile enemies had caused permanent armies of long-serving troops to be stationed along the northern frontier, replacing the militiamen whose ranks had been thinned by the wars of Gao Zong and the empress Wu Ze Tian. That Chinese arms were already overstretched was patently clear from two serious defeats in the year 751. One occurred in Yunnan at the battle of Dali, when an army of 60,000 men was annihilated by the forces of Nanzhao, an independent kingdom; the second reverse took place on the banks of the Talas river in distant Turkestan, where Arab soldiers wrested Central Asia from the Chinese sphere of influence and incorporated large areas of it into the Muslim world. No Chinese Charles Martel was on hand to turn back the flood of militant Islam as at the battle of Tours nineteen years earlier.

An Lushan's rise to such a dangerous position of power must ultimately be blamed on the emperor himself. Xuan Zong was too willing to listen to praise of the commander from Li Linfu, a scheming minister, and Yang Yuhuan, his favourite concubine. Since Li Linfu died in 752 before the rebellion broke out, opprobrium was attached to Yang Yuhuan, whom mutinous troops compelled the emperor to hang during the flight of the court to Sichuan province. Although fighting spread into the lower Yangzi valley, the rebellion reached its peak in the north-eastern provinces, where resentment at the resurgence of Chang'an families at court may have added fuel to the fire. By the time the rebels had been beaten in 763, the empire had abandoned outlying territories and was struggling to fend off enemy thrusts, the Tibetans even managing to sack Chang'an in a surprise attack.

The Tang dynasty survived the devastating civil war and the empire, though reduced, enjoyed another century of peace before popular insurrections arose, those tell-tale signs of impending dynastic change. But central government was weakened by the growth of local government in the provinces, a compromise necessitated by demands for greater freedom of action from the military commanders who had restored the imperial house. As taxes from the provinces became less reliable, the imperial exchequer turned to monopolies for regular income and tea was added to the state preserves of iron, salt and liquor. The problems of the court were made still worse in 835 by the emergence of the eunuchs, who soon came to occupy the highest ranks of the bureaucracy and manipulated several emperors. Although their influence was checked under emperor Wu Zong (840–6), the chaos resulting from the great peasant rebellion of 874–84, when Luoyang and Chang'an were captured, gave them ample opportunity for manoeuvre, just as it did provincial governors. When the last Tang emperor was deposed in 906, the country fragmented into nearly a dozen states, an unprecedented disunity possibly connected with new methods of warfare, as reference is first made to the use of gunpowder in the tenth century.

One event stands out in the late Tang era, Wu Zong's suppression of Buddhism in 845. Calls for a check on the growing influence of the Buddhist church originated with Fu Yi (555–639), a sceptic who in 624 asked the first Tang emperor Gao Zu to abolish the religion altogether. Another outspoken critic of its excesses was Han Yu (768–824). In his lucid memorial to the throne, *On the Bone of Buddha,* the rational outlook of Confucian philosophy was pitted against the superstition so transparent in imperial patronage of the new faith. What particularly worried Han Yu was the hysteria which greeted the arrival of the relic at Chang'an. The Histories record how "a soldier cut off his left arm in front of the Buddha's bone, and while holding it with his right hand, he reverenced the relic each time he took a step, his blood sprinkling the ground all the while. As for those who walked on their elbows and knees, biting off their fingers or cutting their hair, their numbers could not be counted." The answer was quite simple, Han Yu contended: just allow the authorities to destroy the "decayed and rotten bone, outlaw Buddhist superstition, and end the uncertainties of the people". He pointedly reminded the emperor that China had known little peace since the time of Han Ming Di, when Buddhism first appeared.

Although Han Yu's daring onslaught of 819 only drew imperial disfavour upon himself, it helped to set a climate of opinion among officials that encouraged the decrees of 845. Successively emperor Wu Zong issued orders to shut down country retreats, shrines and monasteries, then the enormous temples situated in the towns and cities. The persecution lasted nine months and, despite an easing of regulation under the next emperor, left the Buddhist church forever in a subservient role within the Chinese state. In 956 an edict of the Later Zhou, one of the Five Dynasties, nationalised some of the larger statues of the Buddha, the bronze of which was melted down and turned into coins.

THE FIVE DYNASTIES (907–960)

The fifty-three years of disunity that separate the Tang and Song empires are known as the age of the Five Dynasties *(wu tai)* because of the habit of Chinese historians in tracing a "legitimate" succession for ruling houses, irrespective of the territory each might control. This traditional practice does not imply any political blindness on the part of commentators but rather a preference for dynastic chronology. There were indeed ten royal houses in south China, besides the five dynasties which in rapid succession ruled the northern provinces.

Neglect of hydraulic engineering after the An Lushan rebellion doubtless assisted the development of local separatist movements, whenever a military leadership arose to direct them, but the establishment of so many small states in south China can be explained only in terms of its geographical character—a land of mountains and valleys. Economic development had still to transform the region into a homogeneous unit, something that was to be accomplished under the Song emperors. The pace of development, though, was accelerated by a steady influx of

Fig. 54 Scholar-officials playing a board game *(weiqi)* similar to draughts. From a painting dated to the mid-tenth century

people fleeing the troubles in the north from the mid-eighth century onwards. The consequent increase in agricultural production caused the late Tang administration to look to the Yangzi valley and the south for the bulk of its grain shipments. The Wei river valley, the site of Chang'an, even found itself in great economic difficulties during the ninth century, owing to the disrepair of the irrigation system upon which it had depended for more than a millennium; and much land had been abandoned in north China because of devastation too. Lip-service was still paid to the *jintian* system of landholding so favoured by Mencius, but no dynasty succeeded ever again in imposing a system of land allocation as a means of ensuring a reliable agricultural surplus. Effective land reform had to await the foundation of the People's Republic in 1949.

In north China the brief military dictatorships that compromised the Five Dynasties were unable to hold their own against nomadic incursion. The first dynasty— the Later Liang—survived the longest, seventeen years (907–23). Taking advantage of such chronic instability, a Qidan tribe based in southern Manchuria penetrated the north-eastern frontier and obliged the first ruler of the

Later Jin (936–47) to cede a large tract of Hebei province, including the gates in the Great Wall and what is now Beijing. In 947 the Qidans called their state the Liao, a sinicised name, and adopted Chinese culture. As admiration was not the same as absorption, the Hebei cession remained outside the empire for centuries until, at last, through it came the Mongols to conquer all of China in 1279. Reluctance on the part of scholars to serve the military adventurers in north China who so swiftly deposed each other brought about another exodus from north to south; this repeat of the experience on the fall of the Western Jin dynasty in 316 did a great deal to advance civilisation in the southern provinces. The spread of literary culture also received stimulus from contemporary advances in the art of printing. The Confucian classics were block-printed between 932 and 953, but after 1040 the invention of movable type allowed the Song emperors to sponsor a revolution in consciousness through the government publication of standard works.

In 960 another northern general, Zhao Kuangyin, seized power and declared himself the first Song emperor Tai Zu, naming his dynasty after a district he had governed in the province of Henan. While he advanced upon the throne in the same manner as the emperors who had immediately preceded him, the new imperial house did not disappear as quickly as the Five Dynasties. A reason for its preservation, apart from the character of Zhao Kuangyin himself, was the priority given to the reunification of China. When one of the southern kings begged for independence, the first Song emperor asked, "What wrong have your people done to be excluded from the Empire?"

THE SONG ACHIEVEMENT (960–1279)

A mutiny by troops he was leading against the Qidans forced Zhao Kuangyin to ascend the throne. He had been appointed commander-in-chief of the army because of his rectitude and respect for learning; these qualities,

Fig. 55 A ruler of one of the Five Dynasties (907–60) giving audience. Despite attempts to claim imperial descent from the Tang, these short-lived houses were a pale imitation of previous authority

it was hoped by the ruling house, the Later Zhou (951–60), would make him the trusted protector of the seven-year-old emperor, but the plan took no account of the temper of the soldiers. "While Zhao Kuangyin was still recovering from the effects of a drinking session," the Histories relate, "a party of his officers burst into his tent and hastily wrapped a yellow robe around him. Once the ordinary soldiers heard that he had been saluted as the One Man, they also acclaimed him and thereby ensured the end of the Later Zhou dynasty. But the next morning Zhao Kuangyin would only agree to their wishes on certain conditions. These were that the lives of the existing imperial family should be spared, as well as those of the officials in the palace, and that there should be no robbing of the treasury, but the question of rewards to those that had been loyal to him should be left to him." These conditions were readily agreed, much to the relief of Kaifeng, then the capital of the northern provinces.

Once on the throne, Tai Zu ended the vicious circle of suspicion and military revolution that had raised and

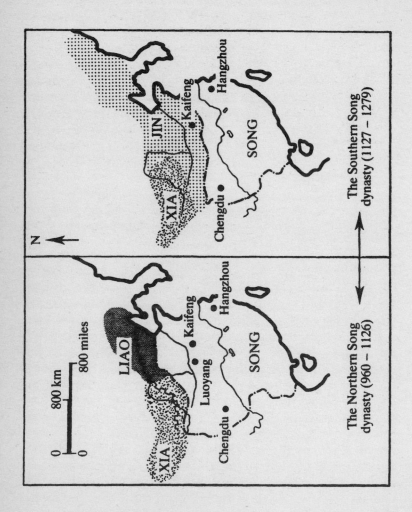

Fig 56 Song China (960–1279)

1 Detail of a partly
reconstructed hut at
Banpo, the famous
neolithic village near
Xi'an, Shaanxi
province

2 An entrance to a
compound in Shaanxi
province: the wall and
gateway are con-
structed of rammed
loess earth, a building
method going back to
neolithic times

3 Officers from Pit No 1 of the terracotta army, buried close to the tomb of the First Emperor at Mount Li, Shaanxi province

4 General view of the front ranks of Pit No 1: the vanguard comprised unarmoured crossbowmen

5 The Small Wild Goose Pagoda (*Xiao-yan Ta*) at Xi'an, Shaanxi province; built about 710, it once stood in the centre of the Tang capital of Chang'an on a street that led south from the entrance to the imperial palace

6 A Buddhist saint: one of the painted terracotta figures at the Great Wild Goose Pagoda at Xi'an, Shaanxi province

7 Country transport: so docile are Chinese donkeys and horses that it is not unusual to pass a moving cart on which the driver is fast asleep

8 Stones feature in every Chinese garden; here is a group positioned against a wall at the Summer Palace, near Beijing

9 A worshipper resting in the Huajue Mosque, Xi'an, Shaanxi province. Today there are 13 million Muslims in the People's Republic, drawn largely from minority peoples

10 The Phoenix Pavilion at the Huajue Mosque, a Ming dynasty construction; the pavilion, with its ornamental garden, stands in front of the building which contains sacred niches

11 Ceremonial sculpture of a military official on the route to the imperial necropolis laid out by Yong Le in the early 15th century for the Ming dynasty

12 Another ceremonial sculpture on the road to the site of the imperial Ming tombs, about 30 km north of Beijing

13 A bastion of the Meridian Gate (*Wumen*), the entrance to the Purple Forbidden City, undergoing restoration in 1980

14 An incense burner on a lower terrace of the Hall of Supreme Harmony in the Purple Forbidden City, Beijing

15 A fabulous bronze tortoise. This symbol of longevity stands guard in one of the terraces in the Purple Forbidden City

16 An inner courtyard of the Purple Forbidden City. Whereas the model building symbolised the divine authority of the throne, the bronze containers in the background were simply functional and held an emergency supply of water in the event of fire

17 The innermost court of the Purple Forbidden City open in imperial times to non-residents of the palace. The small door below the stairway admitted only eunuchs to the domestic quarters of the emperor

18 Dr Sun Yatsen in 1924, a year before his death. Both Beijing and Taibei look upon him as the 'Father of Modern China'

19 Yuan Shikai, President of the Chinese Republic and would-be dynast

20 Public execution of a Boxer rebel, watched by European soldiers, 1900

21 The overthrow of the Chinese empire, 1911–12. High officials making their escape from Beijing

22 Three powerful warlords of the late 1920s: Jiang Jieshi (Chiang Kai-shek) flanked on the left by Feng Yuxiang and on the right by Yan Xishan

23 Destruction caused by Japanese bombing of Shanghai, 1932

24 Guomindang troops on the march along the Great Wall in 1937. Japanese forces were soon to drive them southwards

25 Communist infantry taking Lanzhou in early 1949, prior to the Guomindang collapse

26 Zhou Enlai at the Geneva Conference, 1954. His attendance marked the start of world recognition of China's return to great power status

27 Chairman Mao and Lin Biao being acclaimed by members of the People's Liberation Army at the height of the Great Proletarian Cultural Revolution – a ritual that was satirised after Mao Zedong's death in Gu Hwa's novel *A Small Town called Hibiscus*

28 The Nixons, with Zhou Enlai, during their historic visit in 1972 to the People's Republic. That a former supporter of the 'China Lobby' should radically switch US policy towards 'the Reds' is one of the ironies of contemporary politics

29 Deng Xiaoping shortly after the deaths of Zhou Enlai and Mao Zedong in 1976. Military support seems to have ensured his emergence as China's subsequent leader

30 Foreign exchange for reconstruction has been earned partly through agriculture. Here, in 1959, silkworms were being bred specially to increase output

31 Young men and women at work in the Sanyo Electrical Machinery Company, a Japanese-owned enterprise and the first foreign-owned business to open in the Shenzhen Special Economic Zone, facing Hong Kong

32 The 'dragon pavement' of the Purple Forbidden City, Beijing. Besides
the dragon, a symbol of imperial authority from the time of unification in
221 BC, other auspicious animals decorate the centre of the path reserved
only for the Son of Heaven

degraded the Five Dynasties. He told his senior commanders at a celebration dinner just how uneasy he was. When everyone assured the emperor that his position was safe, Tai Zu reminded the diners of his own unexpected elevation. So the officers asked him to take whatever steps he felt necessary. At which Tai Zu said:

> The life of man is short. Happiness consists of the means to enjoy life, and then bequeath the same to one's descendants. Now what I propose is that you should all resign your military appointments, retire

Fig. 57 The first Song emperor, Tai Zu, playing football with members of his court. In China the game consisted of skilful passing and ball control rather than tackling and scoring: women also took part in games that could have up to eight players, when it was known as "Eight Immortals Crossing the Sea" From a contemporary painting

to the provinces, and there select for yourselves the best estates; on these you will be able to live at ease, drinking day and night, in the knowledge that you have provided for your descendants. Any man that is willing to accept my proposal I shall treat as my friend and ally our families through marriage.

Next day all the commanders tendered their resignations on grounds of ill-health, and Tai Zu kept his part of the bargain, ennobling them and generously distributing lands and wealth.

Then the first Song emperor fundamentally reorganised the administration of his territory. The army was no longer permitted to administer any lands, as the entire supervision was placed under civil officials. Not surprisingly the southern principalities viewed these developments with interest and sympathy. Two of them submitted to the Song dynasty by diplomatic arrangement; others surrendered after brief campaigns, whilst the last independent state held out against his successor, Tai Zong, only till 979. But in the same year Tai Zong (976–97) met a disastrous defeat at Gaolinghe, near present-day Beijing, when he tried to retake the part of Hebei occupied by the Qidans. Further reverses were suffered in 986, when four separate armies took the field in order to co-operate with a Korean force striking from the east. From then onwards, the Northern Song dynasty (960–1126) was on the defensive in its relation with the Liao kingdom. It is known as the Northern Song because in 1126 the warlike Jin, having disposed of this northern neighbour, fell upon Kaifeng and drove the dynasty south to Hangzhou, where, as the Southern Song, the imperial house lasted till 1279.

Apart from the Qidans, the northern frontier was threatened by another powerful group, the Tibetan Dangziang, a partially sinicised tribe which had secured in Gansu province a base from which to expand southwards at the expense of the Chinese. Between 1032 and 1044 Song generals fought a complicated, defensive war against Xia, the name the Dangziang gave to their state. The compromise eventually reached was an annual gift of silver and silk in exchange for peace; this unofficial tribute to Xia, and a parallel one to Liao, recalls the arrangements initially forced on the Former Han by the Xiongnu. For in striking contrast to the Han and Tang empires, the foreign policy of the Song was never expansionist in design: it aimed solely at the strictest containment of the northern peoples. Even though foreign invasion remained a perpetual threat and was the cause of the final overthrow of the Song dynasty, the subjection of military officials to civilian control reflects the pacific tenor of the times. The century of calm that followed the wars with Liao and Xia was a splendid epoch for China: many today would regard its achievements as the climax of Chinese civilisation.

Learning, as enshrined in the civil service examinations, formed the basis of the Song achievement. The administration was modelled on the Tang and the recruitment of officials aided by government-sponsored universities and colleges. Not only were more students allowed to pass their final examinations and take up an official appointment, but also there was a significant widening of the curriculum. During the ascendancy of the reformer Wang Anshi (1021–86), technical and scientific subjects could be offered. Previously the questions set, though concerned with administrative, governmental and economic problems, were expected to be answered within the context of orthodox Confucian literature and philosophy. Although subjects such as engineering and medicine did not long survive the fall of Wang Anshi in 1076, this extension of official knowledge is an indication of the contemporary rise in scientific consciousness among the educated classes. Wang Anshi's humble background may account for his interest in labour-saving devices, but no country could then compare with China in the application of natural knowledge to practical human needs.

During the Song dynasty the empire reached the edge of modern science and underwent a minor industrial revolution. The world's first mechanised industry was born at the same time that the printing of books facilitated the exchange of scientific knowledge derived from observation and experiment. But it remains an intriguing histori-

Fig. 58 Elaborate architectural decoration in a temple dated to 1001, Ding district, Hebei province

cal fact that China, far ahead of other cultural areas in scientific and technical understanding between the first century BC and the fourteenth century, did not generate modern scientific method. Nor was the commercial development under the Song emperors followed by anything which faintly resembled the rise of capitalism in Europe, for China was to continue on its own distinct course, a society dominated by the scholar-bureaucrat. Only in the late nineteenth century were the educated classes convinced that the country needed to import modern technology, the early stages of which had been acquired by the West, albeit indirectly, from China.

Western debts to Chinese science are now admitted. The major information flow occurred after the end of the Southern Song, when Mongol conquest of all between the Don and the Mekong rivers encouraged overland trade and travel. Yet the fundamental ideas of Chinese science were largely neglected in favour of specific inventions or processes. An instance of this short-sightedness is Marco

Polo. His *Travels* hardly touch upon scientific topics though in the 1280s he had been governor of Yangzhou, a centre specialising in the production of armaments and military supplies in Jiangsu province. By the thirteenth century Europeans were using the magnetic compass, the stern-post rudder and the windmill, and in the fourteen century mechanical clocks, water-powered textile machinery, blast furnaces, gunpowder, segmental-arch bridges, and block printing are recorded. Whilst the exact origin of these inventions was unknown to the inhabitants of Europe at this time, their significance as agents of social and economic change was not unnoticed. In the early 1600s Francis Bacon was fully aware that the metamorphosis of the continent stemmed from the applications of these inventions. He wrote:

> It is well to observe the force and virtue and consequences of discoveries. These are to be seen nowhere more conspicuously than in those three which were unknown to the ancients, and of which the origin, though recent, is obscure; namely, printing, gunpowder, and the magnet. For these three have changed the whole face and state of things throughout the world, the first in literature, the second in warfare, the third in navigation: whence have followed innumerable changes: insomuch that no empire, no sect, no state seems to have exerted greater power and influence in human affairs than these mechanical devices.

The clue to this acute observation was Bacon's own scientific activities. What he was pointing out was a crucial watershed in European history, the divide between medieval and modern times. Knowledge became readily available in printed form, whereas previously only the very rich layman could afford the long, tedious and expensive process of hand-copied manuscripts. The Renaissance and the Reformation followed. Gunpowder eclipsed both knight and castle, besides in the Thirty Years' War inaugurating conflict on a continental scale, while the magnetic compass had sent Columbus to America in 1492 and helped Magellan circumnavigate the globe in 1520.

Nothing like this transformation occurred in China. Despite the commercial activities of the great cities—Marco Polo was stunned by the sheer size of the economy—the merchants were never permitted to acquire any lasting influence in state affairs. Neither were cities free as in the mercantile centres of Europe, where a charter granted privileges to the burghers not enjoyed by those in the surrounding countryside; nor had the merchant guilds any social standing. The merchants, victims of sumptuary laws and state regulation, sought admission for their sons to the official class, which by tradition disdained commerce. Because of his unchallenged authority and the intimate relation of mankind with Nature in Chinese thought, the scholar-official was interested in the benefits of technology, so that the imperial government acted as an important stimulus to advance. Its own direct revenues were therefore enhanced by the introduction of advanced metallurgical bellows, which worked through the conversion of longitudinal motion by crank, connecting-rod and piston-rod.

Another remarkable water-powered machine was capable of spinning thirty-two threads simultaneously; in different versions it was used for silk-reeling and hemp-spinning. The leather driving belt of this piece of textile machinery had an interesting parallel in the chain-drive belonging to Su Song's astronomical clock. Su Song (1020–1101) and other engineers applied the principle of regular and controlled water flow to an armillary sphere, a model of the heavens used in astronomy. It allowed the sphere to move in accordance with the apparent movements of the planets and the stars. Though the hours were struck on a gong, it was not seen as the perfection of the water clock, which essentially it was.

Imperial patronage also extended to medicine, in 1111 the twelve most eminent practitioners at the throne's behest compiling an encyclopedia of current knowledge. This work was part of a general movement towards the codification of medical disorders—symptoms, diagnosis

Fig. 59 Su Song's astronomical clock at Kaifeng, built between 1088–92. This reconstruction shows clearly a celestial globe and an armillary sphere. There was a striking mechanism but no outside dial

and treatment. Its novel concern to standardise medical practice and reassess early theory in the light of new evidence reached its culmination in the comprehensive study of diet and health undertaken by the Ming doctor Li Shizhen (1518–93), whose work is still used by Chinese doctors today.

Just as active as the engineers and doctors under the Song dynasty were the philosophers, the result of whose wide-ranging speculation is usually termed Neo-Confucianism. This recasting of Confucian thought, like the earlier revision that Dong Zhongshu made in the Former Han period, occurred when political and social change had brought new problems which traditional reasoning was ill equipped to deal with. The late Tang saw a steady weakening of governmental institutions, an erosion of central authority that the chaos under the Five Dynasties served only to accelerate. Although the early Song rulers tried to reassert control through a revived civil service, society was far different from what it had been prior to the rebellion of An Lushan. Central weakness had permitted the growth of commercial centres, unwalled cities largely beyond state regulation, while in the countryside competition for land was sharpened by the use of paper currency. Shortage of copper coinage had been the spur for the 956 edict of the Later Zhou, which brought back into circulation the metal locked up in Buddhist statuary. Though another 6 million strings of new coins were issued in 1073, the supply of money always lagged behind demand. Bills of exchange, the antecedents of paper money, were commonplace from the late Tang, but overprinting of currency notes ended with such chronic inflation that in 1265 the imperial government was obliged to issue new notes backed by gold and silver.

Thus Song society presented problems of control for the throne that were not easily susceptible to direct action. An appeal to the mind, therefore, was the solution offered by Zhu Xi (1130–1200). He breathed new life into Confucianism by incorporating in his system many of the rival doctrines belonging to Buddhism, which though less potent a force than in the ninth century, still exposed the paucity of cosmological explanations in traditional Confucian thought. Following the idealism of Zhou Dunyi (1016–73), who argued that the empire was in harmony with a pre-ordained pattern in Nature, Zhu Xi placed emphasis both on the understanding of this relationship and the pursuit of moral perfection. But reliance on the ideal that the universe and men are one did not lead Zhu Xi into pantheism, as he denied the immortality of the soul and the existence of a deity. "There is", he remarked succinctly, "no man in heaven judging sin."

Zhu Xi's scepticism was never indifference. His strong social conscience was a reflection of contemporary concern for works of charity and relief. In contrast to the Tang, during which charitable works were generally a preserve of the Buddhist church, Song measures were initiated and administered by the government, and particularly directed at the needs of the ill, the infirm, and the orphaned. Even public cemeteries were established to allow the poorest families the opportunity for paying proper respect to their forbears. It might perhaps be said that the compassion of the Buddhist saint had been appropriated by the Confucian state.

In his voluminous writings Zhu Xi remoulded the Chinese mind, since Neo-Confucianism became under the Southern Song the official orthodoxy and the curriculum for the examination system, through which in the late empire all who sought honour, status and official wealth had to pass. Study for these examinations was prolonged

Fig. 60 Respect for learning reached its zenith during the Song empire, when the civil service examinations formed the basis for advancement. Here retired scholar-officials are finding amusement in the comparison of texts

and, at the lowest level, indefinite, for there was an obligation to pass a regular repeat examination for holders of a first degree *(shengyuan)*. Hence scholastic competition absorbed the energies and aspirations of the ablest men almost until our century. A cynic might well have concluded that an extended examination system favoured a despot, but nonetheless its graduates gave China an unmatched administration for more than half a millennium. Only in the late eighteenth century did the serious shortcomings of a conservative outlook reveal themselves, and even then the weakness of antiquarian attitudes was made manifest by events beyond the borders of the empire. The modern world was taking shape in Europe, a circumstance which left China dangerously unprepared for the impact of its technology in the final century of the empire.

While the Song was the most active period culturally in Chinese history, with the possible exception of the Warring States, its greatest achievement lay in the visual arts. Painting became respectable under emperor Hui Zong (1101–25), a keen artist himself, and would-be officials were allowed to offer painting as one of their subjects in the palace examinations. The examination question, closely modelled upon that in the literary paper, consisted of a line or phrase from the classics or a well-known poem, which had to be illustrated in an original way. Hui Zong liked to set painting competitions as well, in special cases adding a poem of his own to the winning work. By so doing the emperor combined "the three perfections" *(san jue)* of painting, poetry and calligraphy: though his inimitable style, known as slender gold, can be seen on several surviving paintings, there is uncertainty as to whether he was responsible for more than the calligraphy. Hui Zong is said to have specialised in bird-and-flower paintings and led something akin to a movement. But it was in another form that Chinese art found its perfect mode of expression. That is the painting of the landscape, which began to replace figure and animal painting as the cherished form towards the end of the Five Dynasties; it was fostered as much by Buddhism as the mystical elements in Daoism. Although China abounds with splendid scenery, the Tang poets first articulated the pleasures of hermit in his remote hut, with the result that a romantic appreciation of the landscape became common amongst the educated. The poet and painter Wang Wei had shown a practical way of finding rural contentment by designing a garden. Typically his retreat, about forty kilometres from Chang'an, cannot be separated from a growing personal commitment to Buddhism. After his wife had died in 734, Wang Wei refused to marry again and chose to remain celibate like a monk. Around 750 permission was given for his house and garden to be turned into a monastery. In the later imperial confiscation of 845 the property, with thousands of others, was returned to secular use.

Interest in gardening as an art ran parallel to that of landscape painting. Both were looked upon as possessing

Fig. 61 "A single stone may evoke many feelings", a Ming garden treatise states. This Qing print of a garden near Suzhou illustrates the Chinese use of gnarled stones, unusual trees, water, and buildings.

a symbolic as well as an artistic value. They were aids to meditation. More spontaneous than either the geometrical arrangements favoured in Europe or the stereotyped landscapes in Japan, the Chinese garden always sought irregular and unexpected features which appealed more to the imagination than the reasoning faculty of the observer. The basic elements were the same as landscape painting, mountains and water *(shan shui)*, which could be interpreted simply as gnarled rocks and a pond. In an extensive essay, the Northern Song painter Guo Xi wrote that, as filial duty and social obligations prevented most people from seeking peace in retirement, the task of the landscape painter was to bring the sights and sounds of Nature into the living room of every household. "When you are planning to paint," Guo Xi maintained, "you must always create a harmonious relationship between Heaven and earth." The popularity of paintings in the houses of Hangzhou is mentioned in *The Travels,* but Marco Polo's aesthetic sense does not seem to have been awakened by what he saw. Yet the roll-call of Song artists includes nearly all of the famous names in landscape painting: Fan Kuan (990–1030), Guo Xi (1020–90), Mei Fei (1051–1107) and Xia Gui (1180–1230).

The literary skills of Guo Xi should come as no surprise during this period, since even the Song reformer Wang Anshi composed 1400 poems. As a consequence of advances in printing, scholars were able to communicate as never before, and there was an impressive outpouring of poetry and prose. Ouyang Xiu (1007–72) continued the austere tradition of Han Yu's prose style, arguing no less forcibly that the empire's ills derived from Buddhism. The other outstanding prose-writer was Sima Guang (1019–86), who shared Ouyang Xiu's dislike for the new measures introduced by Wang Anshi. His monumental work, *History as a Mirror (Zi Zhi Tong Jian),* is a commentary on events in China from the Warring States till the Later Zhou, a span of 1362 years. An arch-conservative, Sima Guang believed that disobedience was the worst crime in society. Another scholar who disagreed with Wang Anshi was the poet Su Shi (1036–1101); harassed

Fig. 62 The Song poet Su Shi, who is remembered today for his culinary skills as well as his poetry. In 1097 he was banished to the island of Hainan following disagreement over the policies of Wang Anshi. A poem written in 1100 relates his pleasure on recall—"calling back my soul"

during the reformer's ministry, he did not enjoy senior posts until after the death of emperor Shen Zong in 1085. In the southern provinces Su Shi was celebrated for the installation of bamboo water-mains as well as the invention of succulent dishes, besides his poetry.

Su Shi's poems contain many references to eating, which under the Song emperors was considered to be the essence of civilised living. This was an age of great cities, even after the removal of the imperial palace in 1127 to Hangzhou. Their growing populations were largely sustained by a shift to rice cultivation, which was helped by double cropping, using a drought-resistant strain introduced from Champa, modern Cambodia. At the same time the commercialisation of agriculture made produce more easily available, and to the surprise of contemporaries, supply kept pace with the increase in population, so that the Song Chinese were undoubtedly the best-fed people then alive. By 1270 the number of residents in Hangzhou had passed the million mark, and to feed them 200 tonnes of rice was brought in daily. The overall population of the empire, according to a census taken earlier in 1083, already exceeded 100 millions or nearly twice that of the Tang. Hangzhou, a city "greater than any in the world", in Marco Polo's estimation, had humble beginnings and was little more than a sprawling town in late Tang times. With reluctance the Southern Song dynasty (1127–1279) agreed that its irregular and unplanned features would be graced by the construction of an imperial palace. Kin-sai, the name given in *The Travels,* is a corruption of "temporary residence", the only title the emperors could bring themselves to confer on Hangzhou, despite the charm and attractiveness of its environs. On West Lake, an expanse of water immediately beyond the city walls, the pinnacle of urban luxury was found in the floating restaurants that catered for private parties, even to the extent of advice on matters of etiquette. Amid this prosperity chefs had ample scope for experimentation; they were able to cook for a sophisticated official class as well as wealthy merchants, and they took full advantage of an acceptance of innovation in order to shape the cuisine we associate with China today.

In Hangzhou, an official reported, "new settlers arrive every month". Although refugees from north China after the fall of Kaifeng in 1126 may account for part of this novel expansion, the evidence for an overall increase in the size and number of towns and cities throughout the Song era points to a rural exodus of peasant-farmers, one of the problems Wang Anshi's reforms attempted to redress. There is no accurate way of gauging the extent of serfdom, since poverty could be overcome by various degrees of subordination, but the impact of a cash economy on the smallholder was severe enough for Wang Anshi to introduce between 1069 and 1074 state credit at a low rate of interest. Loans were intended to help farmers across the difficult period before harvest, when financial weakness might compel them to pledge their crops to rich brokers. The "New Laws" for which Wang Anshi gained the approval of emperor Shen Zong (1068–85) were fundamentally practical in conception. In effect they were aimed at improving the performance of the civil service so as to allow it to assume an active role in national economic planning. Of prime concern were the boosting of agricultural output and the increasing of tax revenue.

Wang Anshi's effort to make sense of the monetary revolution failed, not least because the "New Laws" struck at the privileged position of the propertied classes. Practical measures, like the technical subjects introduced into the civil service examinations, were attacked as dangerous lapses from tradition, but Confucian rhetoric could not disguise entirely the self-interest of the large landowners whose surplus wealth was increasingly available for buying out struggling peasant-farmers. Wang Anshi suffered the additional handicap of corruption amongst the civil servants he was obliged to employ in running the empire's economy. The austerity of his own life was not enough to persuade senior officials that a change was necessary. In vain, therefore, Wang Anshi stood against the growing affluence of the cities, before the loss of

Fig. 63 Although the Chinese never went to the extreme of the Japanese tea ceremony, they came to look upon the drinking of tea together as an essential part of social life. Tea parties were held indoors and outdoors, usually at places thought to be excellent for brewing. Here tea-sellers gather at a tasting competition. From a Yuan painting

Shen Zong's confidence drove him in 1076 from office. The only one of his innovations that endured was the *baojia* system, intended for internal and external security. This required groups of families to provide soldiers in an emergency and to guarantee the peace of their neighbourhood. Families living in north China were also obliged to keep a government horse in fodder during the winter months.

Unfortunately for the Song empire the obligation to sustain cavalry mounts lapsed some years before Jin horsemen fell upon Kaifeng. These nomads were originally vassals of the Qidans, but ten years of war with the Liao kingdom had given them mastery of the northern frontier and direct contact with the Chinese. Emperor Hui Zong, the patron of art, had been willing to cooperate with the Jin at first, on the understanding that the occupied part of Hebei would be returned to the empire, but he soon realised his mistake because, once the Liao kingdom was overrun, Jin detachments pressed on to attack Kaifeng. In 1126 the city surrendered and into captivity went Hui Zong and his son, in whose favour the disgraced emperor had abdicated. For several years the Jin army dominated China until the populous south rallied under the generalship of Yue Fei (1103–41) and at the battle of Yancheng, in Henan province, destroyed its best units. A year later in 1141 emperor Gao Zong decided to end military operations and accept a partition almost identical to that won by the Tartars in 317. To the dismay of many Chinese, Yue Fei was executed in compliance with the Jin's demand.

Fig. 64 The execution of Yue Fei in 1141 at Jin insistence ended Southern Song military operations against the invaders. In this portrait, after a contemporary painting, the general is wearing clothes similar to that favoured by the Qidans and the Jin

Fig. 65 Jin or Qidans preparing to parley, from a Southern Song painting. In order to maintain peaceful relations with the northern peoples, the Song Chinese were obliged to pay a large tribute, usually in the form of silver

A greater threat, however, appeared in the rear of the Jin. Having destroyed in 1210 Xia, amid scenes of untold ferocity, the Mongol horde under Genghiz Khan turned its attention to the reduction of China. Only forays against other enemies gave a respite to the Song empire, for once the Mongols conquered the Jin in 1234, the full force of their strength was directed southwards. That nearly half a century of war was necessary before in 1279 the last member of the Southern Song dynasty perished in a sea battle off what is now Hong Kong is testimony of the stubborn resistance put up by Chinese armies, exploiting terrain unfavourable to cavalry tactics. But another factor in lengthening the struggle was military technology, since gunpowder had been adopted by the imperial armies. Explosive grenades and bombs were launched from catapults; rocket-aided arrows with poisonous smokes, shrapnel and flamethrowers were deployed alongside a primitive armoured car as well as armoured gunboats; and in close combat the "flying-fire spear" *(fei huo qiang)* discharged both flame and projectiles. From the latter—in all probability a Jin invention—derived the bombard and the gun sometime during the late thirteenth century. The hand-held "flying-fire spear" was noted for the discharge of its contents with a very loud report. The Mongols, like the Tartars, became irresistible only when they adopted Chinese equipment. Yet they outdid these previous invaders in becoming the first nomadic people to conquer the whole of China. In 1263 the grandson of Genghiz Khan and the first Yuan, or Mongol emperor, Kubilai Khan, founded Beijing as his capital.

5

THE LATE EMPIRE

From the Mongol Conquest till the Foundation of the Republic (1279–1912)

THE MONGOL CONQUEST (1279–1368)

During more than half the period of the late empire which began with the Mongol conquest, China was under foreign rule. For 356 years Mongol and Manchu emperors directed the destiny of the most populous country in the world; but the approach of these foreign rulers was very different, in spite of a common need to preserve their positions. Whereas the Manchus as the Qing dynasty (1644–1911) became patrons of Chinese culture and in so doing forfeited their own language and traditions, under the Yuan dynasty (1279–1365) Mongol emperors preferred to exclude scholars from office and rely upon a civil service chiefly staffed with officials of non-Chinese origin. As a Yuan civil servant, Marco Polo could express admiration of Kubilai Khan's great empire, its cities, commerce and canals, for the good reason that he was unaware of the level to which Chinese civilisation had attained prior to the fall of the Southern Song. Although the narrative of *The Travels* opened the eyes of medieval Europe to the magnificence of East Asia, Marco Polo never penetrated deeply into conditions in China, which, during his stay from 1260 to 1269, had scarcely begun to recover from the destructiveness and disruption of the Mongol conquest. For the impoverishment of whole provinces had lowered the number of people liable to taxation to 58,837,711, less than half the total recorded in the last years of the Northern Song.

The Mongol onslaught was a definite set-back for China. Although sinicised barbarians such as Yelu Chucai (1190–1244) were able to mitigate the harshness of the Great Khan—dissuading Genghiz Khan on one occasion from genocide—the Mongol imperium remained an alien usurpation even after the accession of Kubilai Khan, who in 1263 transferred the capital from Karakorum to Beijing. What the Yuan dynasty represented was the greatest clash in world history between the nomadic culture of the steppe and the civilisation of intensive agriculture. There is a revealing incident reported in *The Secret History of the Mongols,* commissioned by Genghiz's successor Ogodei (Khan, 1229–41). During one of his bloody campaigns in Central Asia, Genghiz Khan questioned two learned men from Turkestan about the puzzling phenomenon of the city. To the Mongol leader, the city was something unnatural, a threat to the world of the nomads, whose arms during the thirteenth century for the first and last time came very close to conquering the Old World. But understanding was not the same as acceptance and in the attack on the Jin Genghiz had encouraged Mongol ferocity. "The greatest joy", he told his men, "is to conquer one's enemies, to pursue them, to seize their belongings, to see their families in tears, to ride their horses, and to possess their wives and daughters."

As every tribesman was a soldier, the continuous military activity started by Genghiz Khan forced the Mongols to rely more and more on servile labour, even in the crucial task of cattle-breeding. When necessary both women and children entered the fray and acted as military auxiliaries. At most there were 300,000 Mongol males of fighting age, but this horde had several inestimable advantages over rival armies. The Mongol warriors were unswervingly loyal and obedient: the *yasa,* or military code, prescribed death for nearly all breaches of discipline. In these brave horsemen, too, Genghiz possessed a

Fig. 66 Mongol horsemen hunting. The cavalry skills of the Mongol horde, coupled with a severe military code, gave to Genghiz Khan an unbeatable army, despite advanced Chinese weaponry

highly trained and mobile cavalry. "Their horses", *The Travels* records, "are so well-broken-in to quick-change movements, that upon the signal given, they instantly turn in every direction; and by these rapid manoeuvres many victories have been obtained." Not least the Mongol horde proved capable of adopting military technology from other nations and using non-Mongol troops to deploy the new weapons. Polish chroniclers relate how at the battle of Wahlstadt in 1241 the Mongols used a smoke-producing device to cause disarray among the combined forces of the Poles and the Teutonic Knights.

The critical moment in Mongol attitudes to conquered peoples occurred shortly after 1218, the year Yelu Chucai was summoned by Genghiz to Karakorum. The Khan expected that this Qidan nobleman, descended from the royal house of Liao, would welcome service in the Mongol court because of the enmity between Qidan and Jin. But Yelu Chucai spoke respectfully of the Jin, to whom his father and grandfather had rendered loyal service. Pleased by such rectitude and honesty, Genghiz found a place for him in his retinue as a secretary-astrologer. When Mongol advisers later recommended the extermination of the Chinese, in order to turn their cultivated fields back into pasture, Yelu Chucai played upon the cupidity of Genghiz and convinced him that it was better to extract from them taxes and military supplies. Calls for the wholesale slaughter of the Chinese were repeated throughout the dynasty, and notably amid the peasant rebellions that troubled the reign of the last emperor Togan Temur (1333–68): the moment for action, however, had passed and Yuan policy was based upon an uneasy truce between the very different interests of the steppe and the sown.

Although Yelu Chucai's influence increased after the election of Ogodei Khan, when he rose to become head of the secretariat, the proposals he put forward drew the animosity of the anti-Chinese faction at court. From his diary it is known that Yelu Chucai hoped the regime would base itself on the teachings of the Three Sages: Lao Zi, Confucius and the Buddha. His temporary restarting of examinations in 1237 at least freed a thousand scholars from Mongol slavery, but it could not arrest the drift of the dynasty towards becoming an entirely alien imposition. The decision in 1239 to permit tax-farming by Muslim businessmen was the last straw for Yelu Chucai, who died of a broken heart four years later.

The reign of Kubilai Khan (1260–94) comprised the best years for the Yuan dynasty, although abortive expeditions of conquest to Japan, Indo-China and Java overstretched its military resources. In the early fourteenth century the strain was clearly evident in the differences between the Mongol clans, which in twenty-five years raised nine candidates to the throne. This conflict opened the way to a partial recovery of influence by Chinese officials in the civil service, but the restarting of the examination system in 1315 came too late to rally lasting support to the Yuan, against whom popular rebellions steadily increased in number and extent. Unrest was widespread in the 1340s, culminating in the uprising of the "White Lotus", a secret society whose doctrines were an amalgam of Daoist and Buddhist cosmology. Centred

Fig. 67 Mongol aristocrats in the period after Kubilai Khan had established his capital on the site of modern Beijing. The Mongols, however, remained a foreign dynasty for all the efforts of Yelu Chucai

on the Huai river valley, the rebels halted grain supplies to the capital via the Grand Canal and defeated imperial troops sent against them. Though the area was pacified in 1362, through the combined efforts of the Mongols and local Chinese landowners, the movement encouraged insurrection and mutiny elsewhere so that the authority of Togan Temur was soon restricted to Kanbula, as the Mongol capital at Beijing was called, and isolated areas such as Yunnan. All the conditions were ready for a successful national rising, save for a leader. That person was found in the former monk, beggar and bandit, Zhu Yuanzhang.

MING: THE CHINESE RECOVERY (1368–1644)

The Chinese rebel leaders could not agree together, and therefore the Yuan dynasty enjoyed a brief breathing space before it faced the combined wrath of the insurgents. Once Zhu Yuanzhang had overcome the last of his rivals at the battle of Boyang lake in 1367, and organised the superior resources of the lower Yangzi valley, the fate of the Mongol emperor was sealed. Togan Temur did not even wait for the arrival of the rebel forces in the capital: he fled to Mongolia in 1368, leaving the impoverished empire in the care of the first Ming emperor, Hong Wu (1368–96).

At Nanjing Zhu Yuanzhang acceded to the throne and titled his dynasty the Ming. Although there was more than a millennium between them, Ming Hong Wu and Han Gaozu are often compared as the two commoner-emperors who overthrew tyrannical regimes and founded new dynasties. Both were of very humble origin and gained the throne because of a combination of outstanding leadership and peasant cunning. Both were prepared to use the administrative skills of the scholars in order to consolidate their authority, but in the perceived relationship between emperor and official there were marked differences between them.

In 202 BC Han Gaozu had been anxious to dissociate his house from the worst excesses of Qin rule, identified in the minds of the people with officials who subscribed to the doctrines of the School of Law. There was indeed a popular expectation that the change of dynasty meant a change in the style of administration, which Gaozu tried to accomplish by adopting the role of the Confucian prince, the benevolence of whose actions would elicit virtue from all his subjects.

The situation in 1368 was different in several ways, Ming Hong Wu had led a successful national rising against foreign invaders. Without rivals and without the political uncertainties which had faced the founder of the Former Han, Hong Wu was in a very strong position, his personal authority more absolute than any previous Chinese ruler other than the Qin Shi Huangdi himself. The scholar-gentry welcomed the overthrow of Togan Temur, because they had been indifferently treated under the Yuan dynasty, and they were quick to take up appointments in the Ming administration. Yet from the beginning of the Ming it was transparent that the old independence of senior ministers was a past tradition. Hong Wu, in 1380, reacted violently to the alleged sedition of Hu Weiyong, a high official, striking down the minister's family and friends; the total number of people directly or indirectly implicated was over 30,000, all of whom were executed. In 1393 a leading general, Lan Yu, was killed, along with 15,000 of his supporters. Few of those who had helped Hong Wu in founding the Ming dynasty died naturally, in contrast to the peaceful accommodation the first Song emperor reached in 961 with the field commanders responsible for his coup.

To strengthen the power of the throne, Hong Wu used the fall of Hu Weiyong as an excuse to abolish many senior official appointments, thus bringing the heads of bureaux and the armed forces into direct relation with the emperor. This move towards despotism, which was to be the major trend in Chinese politics until the end of the imperial era this century, had considerable dangers for the stability of the empire, particularly at times when children or weak individuals were seated on the throne. It was not until many years later, in 1449, that the disadvantages and dangers of this change were apparent. Then, emperor Ying Zong was so much under the influence of his personal attendants, the eunuchs, that he was persuaded into an unnecessary military expedition on the steppes which ended in his own capture by Mongol tribesmen. Finally, the new position in which the scholar-bureaucrats were placed can be glimpsed in the introduction of corporal punishment for maladministration or impropriety. Flogging in court was undoubtedly a barbaric legacy of the Mongols, but there can be no question that Hong Wu had an intolerance of opposition that tended to manifest itself in cruelty. No longer was it the practice for unworthy officials to be banished to a distant province, or for those condemned to commit suicide.

To perpetuate the imperial house, Hong Wu successively appointed his sons, nephews and grandsons to fiefs scattered throughout the empire. These holdings were kept small and separate from the civil administration, but the military unit each was allowed to maintain could be

summoned to the capital in an emergency. In 1399, a
year after Hong Wu's death, a fierce struggle between
the fief-holders erupted when his grandson, the emperor
Hui Di, took steps to curtail the system. The civil war
ended in 1402 with the capture of Nanjing by Hui Di's
uncle, who declared himself to be the third Ming emperor
Yong Le. At the time it was believed that Hui Di had
been burned alive in the destruction of the palace, but it
later became known that the young emperor, disguised as
a Buddhist monk, had escaped into the countryside, where
he lived a wandering life for forty years. Apprehended in
1441, after the death of the usurping uncle, he was allowed to spend his final year in quiet seclusion.

The most dynamic period of the Ming empire were the
reigns of its founder and the third emperor, Yong Le. In
breaking the time-honoured custom of taking for the
dynastic title an ancient name of a locality associated
with the imperial house and choosing instead the epithet
brilliant or bright, Hong Wu was perhaps making the
point that the empire needed to be restored to its former
brightness. As the provinces had been racked by warfare
for thirty years, reconstruction and economy were essential. "We should not pluck the feathers of an infant
bird," Hong Wu said, "nor should We shake a newly
planted tree." The extravagance of the court was reduced—
its running costs had soared under the harem-loving
Mongol emperors—and surplus monies immediately diverted to reclamation schemes. Aware that hydraulic conservancy projects were a unifying force in imperial history,
Hong Wu stimulated the responsible officials into fre-
netic activity, so that a progress report of 1395 covering all the provinces mentions the completion of 40,987
water-control works. The Grand Canal, last dug in the
Yuan empire to connect Kanbula with the agricultural
wealth of south China, was brought to perfection in
1411 by Song Li, who solved the problem of water-flow
along the summit section with a mile-long dam and
sluice-gates. This reservoir formed from the in-flowing
rivers was divided into "water boxes" by fourteen locks,

Fig. 68 Emperor Yong Le, the usurping uncle. A determined autocrat who oversaw the revival of Chinese fortunes after the Mongol conquest. He subdued the Mongols, strengthened the Great Wall, built the city of Beijing, and dispatched Zheng He into the "southern oceans"

which controlled the water through opening and shutting their gates.

Song Li's renewal of the waterway was necessitated by the decision of Yong Le to move the capital from Nanjing to Beijing, where the Mongol one had stood. From this time onwards the sea route for transporting grain-tax declined, a circumstance which may have served to inhibit maritime shipbuilding and sea power in general towards the close of the Ming period.

Hong Wu had preferred as his capital Nanjing because it was well sited to govern the prosperous southern provinces, now culturally advanced by emigration from the north of China which had borne the brunt of nomadic invasions ever since the twelfth century. On Hong Wu's orders, displaced peasant-farmers were set to reclaim abandoned fields, with government-loaned oxen and seed. Others received aid to open up new lands, especially along the frontiers, where soldiers also spent the greater part of their time engaged in cultivation. By the establishment of military agricultural colonies the problem of the army's food supply was partially solved. When in 1409 Yong Le sent a force against the resurgent Mongols there was no difficulty in supplying it with 30,000 grain-wagons.

The Histories note, too, the measures Hong Wu introduced for "the encouragement of education. Schools that had been allowed to fall into decay were reopened throughout the provinces, and a system was set in operation by which a supply of competent teachers could be obtained. The Imperial University received special attention, its graduates receiving honours and privileges which inspired scholars everywhere to aim at becoming members of it. To encourage study he founded libraries in all the provincial capitals and in a good many of the other large cities of the empire." Two avenues were fixed as the routes to officialdom: the examinations conducted by the Imperial University and the civil service examinations themselves. Entry to the Imperial University was limited to the sons of officials whose performance was outstanding at school. The civil service examinations, on the other hand, was open to all "recommended men" *(juren)*, those who had passed qualifying examinations anywhere in the empire. Both graduates of the Imperial University and candidates successful in the civil service examinations, which were held regularly in the capital, could take the palace examinations, the final arbiter of merit. According to the grades awarded in the palace examinations, scholars received appointment as officials in the metropolitan or provincial administration.

The strictest precautions were taken at every stage in order to ensure fair and honest results, though it has to be admitted that cheating was never entirely stopped. In each provincial capital, there was a permanent examination compound, subdivided within and isolated from the outside world by a high wall. The thousands of cells in which the candidates stayed, during the two days a qualifying examination lasted, were under the observation of soldiers stationed in watchtowers. Since a soldier who discovered a book or any piece of paper with writing on it was awarded a measure of silver, the scrutiny remained very stringent throughout the examination. The only movement allowed was the passage of servants replenishing water supplies and removing human waste. When a candidate became tired, he could lay out his bedding and take a cramped rest. But a bright light in a neighbouring cell would probably compel him to take up his brush again, in an attempt to answer the complicated literary questions set. It is likely that each candidate would have learned by heart the 431,286 characters of the Confucian canon and the five classics. Overwrought and exhausted, as well as conscious of the sacrifice his family had already made for such a detailed preparation, many a candidate was subject to nightmares or worrying day-dreams. There are records of candidates going completely insane under the pressure. A contributory cause must have been the belief that the examination compound alone was a place where the ghosts of wronged individuals could seek revenge. Scholars who had disastrously dabbled with the affections either of servant girls or married women were often taken screaming from thir cells. Above all else, the straitjacket of the curriculum brought about a conformity of thought, an unquestioning acceptance of the will of the imperial house.

For those who failed to become an official, in the late empire the most lucrative as well as the most honourable career available, there was a lasting sense of inadequacy.

In 1469 there were only 100,000 civil and 80,000 military officials in the imperial service. During the Ming and the Qing dynasties competition became steadily worse with the passage of time, in the late eighteenth century the odds against succeeding in the palace examinations becoming as high as 3000 to 1. Yet belief in the efficacy of this arduous selection procedure died hard, even when a candidate such as Hong Xiuquan had failed four times in the qualifying examinations. The ploughed Taiping revolutionary leader in 1843 angrily declared: "Let me give examinations to scholars instead of the Manchus."

The accession of emperor Yong Le (1402–24) was a very violent start to an otherwise remarkable reign. According to the Histories, he "behaved with the utmost cruelty and barbarity to those who had been loyal to his unfortunate nephew, and pursued them with the utmost savagery . . . He also ordered that all relatives, both by the father's and the mother's side, should be seized and executed . . . At length, wearied by this wholesale butchery, and finding no more prominent subjects on which to wreak his vengeance, he stayed his hand." As suspicious and vindictive as ever Hong Wu had been, Yong Le is still remembered as a ruler who restored China to its former glory. Even before he usurped the throne, his swift action in 1396 had foiled a Mongol counter-attack, when he marched beyond the Great Wall and caught the enemy before a full concentration of tribesmen could take place.

Although it was not until Yong Le was on the throne that serious attention was given to foreign affairs, there were a number of significant developments before the first Ming emperor died in 1398. Whilst Yunnan was annexed around 1382, an army had to be maintained in the southwest because the Mongol invasions of Burma and Thailand had left those countries in a state of turmoil, and Chinese intervention was needed in Burma, which under the Ming empire remained a dependency with a client king. The incorporation of Yunnan was permanent, despite a series of bitter revolts, and for the acquisition of this independent-minded province the Ming

Fig. 69 A seal presented to a ruler of a Tibetan tribe by one of the early Ming emperors, whose foreign policy was dictated by the need for secure frontiers. Judicious alliances with border peoples was a long-standing Chinese practice, however

had Kubilai Khan to thank. Until the Mongols drove through it in a manoeuvre to outflank the remaining forces of the Southern Song, the inhabitants of the Yunnan plateau had fought off all foreign invaders. In the Tang court its envoys were always given precedence over those sent from Japan. For the Ming dynasty, though, the depredations of Japanese pirates were a worry, and from 1387 a network of fortifications had to be built along the eastern and southern coasts. These defensive measures were of little avail against small, fast-sailing squadrons, as it was impossible to garrison the whole coastline. Although unrest in Japan after 1467 led to a falling away of raids, the impression was left in the Chinese mind that all foreigners who arrived by ship were both unreliable and pugnacious, a belief soon confirmed by the advent of European buccaneers.

But the threat from the sea was in the Ming empire never more than an annoyance. Reverses on land caused the downfall of the dynasty in 1644, though even then the

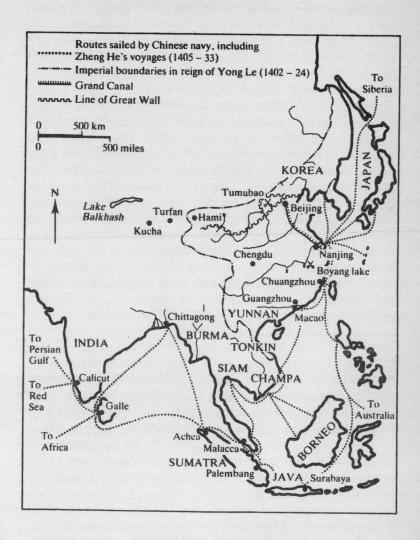

Routes sailed by Chinese navy, including
Zheng He's voyages (1405 – 33)
Imperial boundaries in reign of Yong Le (1402 – 24)
Grand Canal
Line of Great Wall

0   500 km
0   500 miles

N

To Siberia

KOREA

JAPAN

Lake Balkhash

Turfan

Hami

Tumubao

Beijing

Kucha

Chengdu

Nanjing

Boyang lake

Chuangzhou

Guangzhou

YUNNAN

Macao

Chittagong

BURMA

TONKIN

To Persian Gulf

INDIA

SIAM

CHAMPA

Calicut

To Red Sea

Galle

To Africa

To Australia

BORNEO

Achea

Malacca

SUMATRA

Palembang

JAVA

Surabaya

Fig. 70 The Ming Empire

Manchu invaders gained power only by carefully exploiting the confusion of a prolonged civil war. Under Yong Le the might and splendour of the empire was unmatched by any other state in East Asia, so that only Tamerlane, the fierce Central Asian conqueror, might have challenged the Ming, had he not died in 1404 on the northwestern border of China. In 1407–8 imperial forces invaded Tonkin, present-day north Vietnam, following a request by the son of its murdered king. The death of this prince in the fighting brought about annexation, the Histories relate, "since a search made for other heirs to the throne proved fruitless". As in the Former Han period, the country was again divided into commanderies and administered by provincial officials. Personally Yong Le dealt with the Mongols, who regained some of their strength after their withdrawal from China: the spoiling blow delivered in 1396 had slowed down their reorganisation, but a further campaign was necessary by 1408. The failure of this expedition, in which 50,000 Chinese soldiers were massacred, persuaded the emperor to take matters into his own hands. The Histories say

> Next year the Emperor himself led an army of 500,000 men into Mongolia and obtained a great victory over the combined forces of the Mongols in the western part of the country. He then marched eastwards and engaged another large army, when success again attended him. Afterwards he returned to Beijing, his army laden with plunder, where he rewarded those who had shown conspicuous valour during the campaign.

A direct result of these victories was the revival of Chinese influence in the "Western Regions", where a number of small states had come into existence after the fall of the Yuan empire. The most important one, based upon the city of Hami, remained under Ming sway until it was occupied in 1473 by the neighbouring city-state of Turfan.

At the same time as imperial forces campaigned in Indo-China, Yong Le dispatched a great fleet under the command of the grand eunuch Zheng He to cruise the islands of South-East Asia and the Indian Ocean. Brought up in the Muslim faith, Zheng He had come to imperial notice by the distinguished service he rendered in the suppression of rebellion in his native province of Yunnan. In 1404 he was promoted to be the superintendent of the office of eunuchs, and after overseeing the construction of the new fleet that Yong Le had ordered, Zheng He was appointed principal envoy and commander-in-chief of all expeditions to the "Western Ocean". This was the first occasion on which a palace eunuch was given military command.

Between 1405 and 1433 the Ming dynasty mounted seven major seaborne expeditions which caused the authority and power of the Son of Heaven to be acknowledged by more foreign rulers than ever before, even distant Egypt sending an ambassador. The renown of the empire was increased by these voyages in which the foremost navy in the world paid friendly visits to foreign ports; and states which accepted the suzerainty of Beijing were guaranteed protection and gifts were bestowed on their kings. "Those who refused submission", the Histories tell us of the first expedition, "they over-awed by a show of armed might. Every country became obedient to the imperial commands and, when admiral Zheng He turned homewards, sent envoys in his train to offer tribute. The Emperor was highly gladdened, and before very long commanded Zheng He to go overseas once more and scatter largesse among the different states. On this second expedition, the number who presented themselves before the throne grew even greater." The epoch of these expeditions comprised the heroic years of the Ming empire, before reverses in Tonkin forced the occupying Chinese forces to evacuate the province in 1427, and the disastrous defeat at Tumubao in 1449, when emperor Ying Zong was taken a Mongol prisoner, resulted in the contraction of the northern frontier to the line of the Great Wall.

The maritime expeditions had a dual purpose. As indicated in the Histories, their first concern was to reassert

Chinese authority in southern seas after the expulsion of the Mongols. Advances in nautical technology had given Chinese squadrons command of these waters even before the Southern Song emperors were the first rulers in the world to establish on a permanent basis a national navy. In 1237 this navy could boast a combat force of twenty squadrons with 52,000 men; its main base was on the Yangzi river, close to the site of modern Shanghai, while a second anchorage in Hangzhou bay protected the capital. Vessels had armour plating and were armed with small cannon, mines and gunpowder bombs. There can be no doubt that they would have deployed on the numerous rivers of south China as another Great Wall, thereby hindering the Mongol advance. The build-up of a naval arm so as to overcome the Southern Song gave Kubilai Khan in turn the means of launching his own adventures overseas: 4400 ships were sent to attack Japan in 1281 and, twelve years later, an expeditionary force was carried to Java in 1000 ships. It would seem, therefore, that rulers who welcomed Zheng He were acknowledging a return to the more peaceful maritime relations prevailing before the Mongol conquest of China.

The second purpose of the voyages was the restarting of a system of state trading, first introduced to protect the precious metals of the empire. The import of luxury items such as ivory, drugs and pearls had been a severe drain on the limited supply of silver available, and a regulation issued in 1219 specified the commodities to be used in place of cash to pay for foreign imports—silk, brocades and porcelain. The last became the chief item of exchange during the Ming dynasty, and porcelain was used in places as far away as East Africa and north Borneo. They were welcome gifts from the Son of Heaven, who received in return luxury goods and commodities sought after at court. The sultan of Malindi, for example, sent an embassy to China in 1415 with exotic gifts, among them a magnificent specimen of a giraffe for the imperial zoo. At the gate of the palace Yong Le personally received the animal, together with a "celestial horse" and a "celestial stag"; the giraffe was regarded as "a symbol of perfect virtue, perfect government and perfect harmony in the Empire and the Universe". To mark his appreciation the ambassadors were conducted all the way home to East Africa on the fifth voyage of 1417–19.

The Ming expeditions were very different in character from those of the Portuguese: instead of spreading terror, slaving, and planting fortresses, the Chinese fleets engaged in an elaborate series of diplomatic missions, exchanging gifts with distant kings from whom they were content to accept merely formal recognition of the Son of Heaven. The greed and intolerance of the conquistador was entirely absent. No greater contrast could be drawn between the peaceful trading of Zheng He at the great city of Calicut, in south-west India, and the atrocities practised there in 1502 by Vasco da Gama. There was no Chinese equivalent of the Portuguese habit of sailing into an Indian port with corpses hanging from the yards. On only two occasions did Zheng He resort to the force of arms. In 1406 he crossed swords with a pirate chief who attempted to surprise his camp at Palembang: the buccaneer was duly returned to China for punishment, since he hailed originally from Guangdong province. Eight years later, again on the island of Sumatra, Zheng He was ordered by Yong Le to restore a deposed sultan to the throne of Semudera.

Archaeological evidence for Zheng He's pacific diplomacy comes from Sri Lanka, where a stele, dated 15 February 1409, has been found with a trilingual inscription. The Chinese text explains how the voyages were intended to announce the mandate of the Ming to foreign powers, the inscription ending with a list of the presents offered to the Buddha: gold, silver, silk, porcelain and so on. Here we have a Muslim ambassador from China dedicating gifts to a Buddhist monastery in the Indian Ocean from the Son of Heaven, the One Man of Confucian ethic. More fascinating still is that the other two inscriptions do not translate the Chinese one. The Tamil text praises Tenavari-nayanar, an incarnation of Vishnu, while the Persian invokes Allah and the great saints of

Islam. Such urbanity has nothing in common with the fanaticism of the Portuguese.

On his first voyage, in 1405, Zheng He took 317 ships to Java, Sumatra, Malacca, Sri Lanka and India; 27,870 men in all were under his command. The exact limits of his exploration are hard to determine, but a reasonable supposition would be that reconnaissance squadrons reached the southernmost extremity of Africa, touched the northern coast of Australia, and sailed widely in the Pacific. On the death of Yong Le in 1424 voyages were suspended, and in spite of the seventh expedition of 1431–3, the era of maritime exploration and diplomacy came to an end. Perhaps the last voyage was Zheng He's finest navigation in that he called at Jedda on the Red Sea and extended Chinese influence in Arabia, then cruised

Fig. 71 An articulated barge loaded with mines and explosives. This late sixteenth-century drawing indicates a continuing Chinese interest in naval power, albeit on rivers and lakes

along the African coast, his foremost ships going far to the south of Malindi. Shortly after his return to China in 1433, Zheng He died at the age of sixty-five.

The death of the great admiral coincided with a gradual turning away from the sea, for by 1525 it was an offence to own or build craft with two or more masts. Not all the reasons are apparent for this momentous alteration of policy, which left a power vacuum in the Indian Ocean and the China Sea—into which Vasco da Gama and Europe unwittingly sailed. A combination of circumstances seems to have been responsible. The scholar-officials, strongly against the maritime expeditions from the beginning, were even more strongly opposed to the prestige Zheng He and the eunuchs derived from their success. They were also becoming less profitable as trading ventures and the cost of mounting them pressed hard on the imperial exchequer. But not to be overlooked are the improvements that Song Li had made to the Grand Canal, henceforth the focus of Chinese navigation. Inland craft replaced ocean-going junks in the sixteenth century as the anti-maritime policy reached its height. Although there was a later recovery of mercantile shipping, the rundown of the imperial fleet was dramatic and irreversible, so that naval architecture petrified during the Qing dynasty, when a deliberate policy of indifference to sea power exposed China to the imperial ambitions of nineteenth-century European nations.

Even more significant than Zheng He's voyages was the decision taken by Yong Le in 1421 to remove the capital from Nanjing to Beijing. Overruling opposition to the move in a more imperious manner than the Shang king Pan Geng would have thought feasible, Yong Le ordered his capital to be laid out within a city wall measuring 23.5 kilometres in length. This wall followed the plan of the former Mongol capital, Kanbula, except that it was about two kilometres shorter at the northern end and about half a kilometre farther extended towards the south. What Yong Le accomplished in moving the capital northwards was a return to the rectangular grid plan of the classical Chinese city, which had reached its perfection in seventh-century Chang'an, the seat of the Tang dynasty. It was a definite reaction from the sprawling, irregular cities of south China, and notably the temporary Southern Song capital of Hangzhou.

Despite considerable rebuilding during the present century, the chessboard pattern of Beijing is still apparent, with the division of the city into distinct quarters. At the centre is the imperial palace, the Purple Forbidden City *(zijincheng)*, a literary allusion to the pole-star. The imperial palace was considered the centre around which the empire gravitated, just as the pole-star was the centre of the celestial world. Arranged in accordance with the pole-star and the adjoining constellations, the Purple Forbidden City has a north/south orientation, all its principal terraces and openings facing south. The middle of its three sections was most important because it contained the great ceremonial buildings of state. Enclosed by a moat and a high wall, not quite one kilometre square, and divided internally into numerous compounds and courtyards by lesser walls and buildings, the Purple Forbidden City has its official place of entry in the Meridian Gate *(wumen)*, thought by some commentators to be the finest architectural unit in China. Erected in 1421, re-erected in 1647 and restored in 1801, this monumental gateway comprises an open rectangle, the sides projecting 92 metres towards the south and forming at both ends a bastion upon which pavilions are placed. The central building, 126 metres in length and 20 metres in height, is crowned by a double roof and pierced by five vaulted tunnels. The impression of grandeur and solidity is strengthened by the use of gorgeous colours: the walls are built of brick coated with plaster; the wooden pillars of the pavilions are covered with thick lacquer and painted bright vermilion; the roofs are laid out with glazed yellow tiles; and the staircases and balustrades are made of white marble. Set dramatically against the sky, the Meridian Gate is a reminder of the restoration of the empire under the early Ming rulers. The approach is from Tiananmen square, whose great expanse in the late 1960s formed the

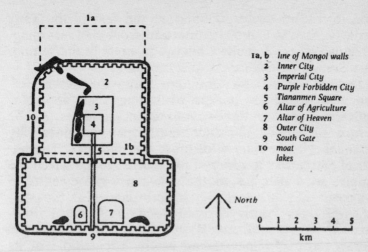

1a, b   *line of Mongol walls*
2   *Inner City*
3   *Imperial City*
4   *Purple Forbidden City*
5   *Tiananmen Square*
6   *Altar of Agriculture*
7   *Altar of Heaven*
8   *Outer City*
9   *South Gate*
10   *moat*
    lakes

Fig. 72 Schematic plan of Ming Beijing, showing the line of the Mongol defences. The decision of Yong Le to move the capital northwards from Nanjing caused later Ming emperors great difficulties because of the rising power of the Manchu tribesmen beyond the Great Wall

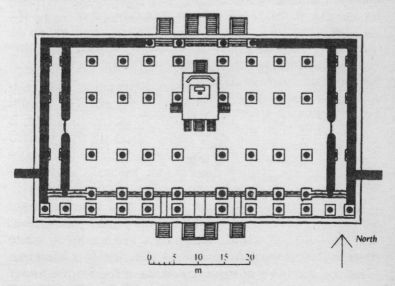

Fig. 73 Hall of the Supreme Harmony, Beijing, with the imperial throne

venue for rallies of Red Guards, an echo of which today is still visible there in the tomb of Mao Zedong.

The Meridian Gate gives access to a vast flagged court across which in a wide curve from east to west flows a small river. The five bridges spanning its undulating course lead to the pavilions of the Gate of Supreme Harmony *(taihemen)*, beyond which stand the buildings used for imperial audiences. The dragon throne on which the emperor sat is in the Hall of Supreme Harmony *(taihedian)*, one of the three big ceremonial chambers in the palace. It stands on a high dais and is approached by three flights of steps.

Close to the Purple Forbidden City were other areas reserved for imperial use. While Coal Hill—named according to tradition because an emergency supply of coal was stored there by one of the Yuan emperors—served as an immediate recreation and pleasure ground, so did the numerous temples and pavilions dotted on the islands and shores of the three lakes lying to the west of the palace. Most of these buildings were erected by the Qing dynasty, though White Pagoda Mountain *(baitashan)*, in the middle of the northern lake, has been identified with Kubilai Khan who, according to Marco Polo, moved a live forest of trees in order to plant this artificial eminence. Kubilai Khan had embraced Buddhism under the influence of Tibetan advisers.

Two sacrificial altars attended by the Son of Heaven are still situated south of the Purple Forbidden City on either side of what was the southern gateway of the outer Ming city. Emperor Yong Le performed the sacred rites as the One Man on a single site in the vicinity, but about 1530 it was determined, after a thorough historical investigation by a commission of scholars, that separate altars should be built not only for Heaven and Earth but also for the Sun and Moon as well as other spiritual powers. Within one large enclosure stand the Altar of Heaven *(huanqiu)*, a circular three-tier terrace nearly five metres in height, and the well-known Temple of Heaven *(tiantan)*, a circular edifice with a triple roof of blue tiles. In this majestic building the emperor offered prayers during the festivities on the turn of each year. Nearby is the Altar of Agriculture *(shejitan)*, whose sacrifices were connected with the spring ploughing and were directed at the securing of good harvests. Beneath the architectural use of monumental terraces here, as in the layout of the Purple Forbidden City, lay an ancient religious tradition in north China that stretched back to the primitive mounds dedicated by the earliest tillers of its loess soil. The oldest known terrace-altar associated with palatial buildings is the Shang one recently excavated at Zhengzhou: it dates from at least the fifteenth century BC.

Final testimony of the pains Yong Le took in establishing Beijing as a capital worthy of a great empire is found today in the valley containing the imperial Ming tombs. Since it was believed that the prosperity of the dynasty depended on keeping the ancestral spirits in a state of contentment (which meant undisturbed graves and regular worship) Yong Le gave orders that a propitious place be located for his own tomb as well as his successors near the new capital. In Nanjing the menu for sacrifice to deceased members of the imperial house had already been altered by Hong Wu, who felt that the dishes traditionally on offer would not suit the taste of his peasant ancestors. But only in Beijing were detailed plans laid for the after-life of the entire dynasty. Protection of the new imperial cemetery, situated about 50 kilometres northwest of the city, was entrusted to a garrison of soldiers, which patrolled the outer ramparts and guarded each tomb as soon as it was built. Guardian families *(linfu)* were then settled within the necropolis, their duties being its general maintenance as well as the supply of the ingredients used by the officials responsible for sacrifices. Present-day names recall the Ming tomb each village was originally founded to serve. The largest and best preserved mausoleum belongs to Yong Le himself; he was buried there in 1424, along with the remains of his empress who had died in Nanjing two decades earlier. Completely restored in the 1950s, this tomb *(changling)* has a series of formal buildings and gardens in front of the funeral mound, which is planted with oaks.

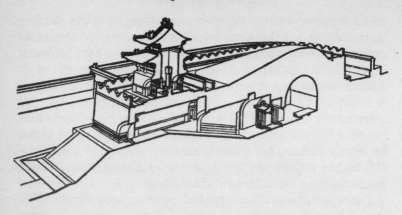

Fig. 74 Cross-section of Ci Xi's mausoleum, near Beijing. The Qing dynasty followed the Ming pattern of imperial burial as established by Yong Le. Ci Xi was buried in 1908

The new city of Beijing and extensive maritime reconnaissance indicate the higher productivity of the empire and, consequently, the extent to which China had climbed out of the deep economic trough at the end of the Yuan dynasty. No matter the splendour of the capital however, the choice of a site so close to the Great Wall was to prove a strategic handicap for later emperors. Hardly had Yong Le designated Beijing as the capital in 1421, when he was compelled to wage another campaign against the Mongols. Although the cost of these continuous wars were to become a serious burden on the empire, there could be no question of any relaxation of vigilance with an enemy less than 100 kilometres away from the seat of government. The Grand Canal, an official noted, was like a man's throat: if it was unable to supply southern tax-grain for a single day, the capital would die. This lifeline did not fail, but its operation permanently tied up 15,000 boats and 160,000 soldiers.

The disaster in Tumubao in 1449 was the turning point for the Ming dynasty. The inability of the victorious Mongol tribesmen to take advantage of a battle in which the emperor Ying Zhong was captured reveals the extent of Chinese recovery, yet the event also signals a decline in the vigour of the dynasty after the reigns of the early emperors. Resoluteness on the part of senior officials ensured that an attack on Beijing was driven back, after a ferocious engagement in the suburbs, but this saving of the dynasty from extinction was not followed by any increase in civil service power, since emperors soon forgot that Ying Zhong's humiliation had been brought about by Wang Zheng, his eunuch mentor. Emperor Wu Zong (1506–20) placed his trust in Liu Jin and seven other eunuchs, who were termed the "Eight Tigers" because of the lack of mercy they showed to their opponents. The scale of corruption was revealed on the fall of Liu Jin in 1510, when it was found that the eunuch had amassed untold riches in the abuse of his position at court. Ineffectual government was aggravated, too, by a number of crises in the sixteenth century: these were renewed pressure along the northern frontier, the onset of major epidemics, and recurrent famines.

New work undertaken on the Great Wall by 1600 had turned it into a more sophisticated and formidable defensive fortification than its Han and Tang predecessors. But for the first time in history China fell behind other countries in technology and science, a rude shock for the imperial armies when in 1592 they exchanged fire in Korea with the Japanese invasion force under the command of Toyotomi Hideyoshi, whose superior guns were based on the Portuguese matchlock. Though Ming soldiers were equipped with cannon and explosives, hard wood rather than copper or iron was the material from which hand-guns were made, suggesting an underlying weakness in metallurgy. In the last decades of the Ming dynasty the services of Jesuits in the casting of guns were much appreciated. Whilst it was the work of Adam Schall von Bell (died 1665) in astronomy that won him a high reputation and position at court, this versatile missionary was in 1636 commanded to start a foundry for the making of cannon and, in spite of his reluctance to fulfil such an unpriestly task, he found it impolitic to disobey.

Edicts prohibiting trade with foreigners ceased after

1567 and Chinese vessels were allowed to sail from Zhangzhou in Fujian province. In 1514 the first Portuguese ships had put into Guangzhou, but the violent and ungovernable behaviour of their crews soon led to serious clashes, which were not contained until nearby Macao was leased in 1553 as a trading base. Command of the seas passed within half a century to the Dutch, who in 1622 launched an attack on Macao. Beaten off with heavy loss by the defenders, the Dutch turned their attention to other parts of the Chinese coast, repeating the outrages of the Portuguese. To the dismay of the Chinese, English vessels then appeared and behaved in a similar manner, although one of the Cornish adventurers who bombarded Guangzhou in 1637 was impressed enough by what he saw to keep an illustrated diary. He wrote: "This Countrie May bee said to excell in these particulers: antiquity, largenesse, Ritchenesse, healthynesse, Plentiffullnesse. For the Arts and manner of government I thinck no Kingdome in the world Comparable to it, Considered altogether."

One foreign visitor who made a very favourable impression on a number of senior officials was the Jesuit missionary Matteo Ricci (1552–1610), despite his introduction at court in 1598 by the eunuch party. Once he realised that in China priests did not enjoy the degree of respect bestowed on them in Europe, Ricci abandoned the clothes of a Buddhist monk for those of a scholar. He was also prepared to tolerate religious practices like ancestor worship, which further endeared him to those brought up to believe in the teachings of Confucius. It was from Jesuit descriptions of the empire, including the extensive diary kept by Ricci, that influential thinkers and writers in the West, such as Leibniz and Voltaire, obtained a tantalising glimpse of an alternative civilisation. They thought that China had a model form of government because of the absence of hereditary privilege and a powerful clergy, unlike Europe in the eighteenth century.

It is a paradox that the mission of Matteo Ricci should overlap that of Yunqu Zhuhong (1535–1615), the out-

Fig. 75 Yunqu Zhuhong, the outstanding Buddhist cleric of the late empire. He was largely responsible for giving the faith the form it has today

standing Buddhist cleric of the Ming dynasty, who entered the monastic order at the age of thirty-two, one year after the death of his mother. Having studied under various masters, he travelled to south China where the beauty of the landscape around Hangzhou persuaded him to found a new monastery. There he reformed monastic discipline, which had grown lax with the decline of Chan Buddhism. Monks who had never gone through the transforming experience of enlightenment were nevertheless

willing to denigrate morality—as though they had become Chan saints themselves. Zhuhong therefore saw a
sense of moral seriousness as the essential counter-measure.
It could take the form of strict observance of monastic
rules in the case of a monk, or social philanthropy in the
case of the lay devotee. For Zhuhong the compelling
question was how to preserve the faith in a secular age.

Monks were too interested in the pursuits of scholars—
calligraphy, painting and poetry—and too prepared to
accept donations from the laity, who in turn believed that
providing for the material comforts of monks was all that
they needed to do. Both were enjoined to contemplate
the basic tenets of Buddhism and to refrain from the
killing of sentient beings. Instead of viewing human relationships and social obligations as obstacles to personal
salvation, Zhuhong regarded them for lay devotees as the
appropriate means to salvation. Only those who chose
the monastic path had to reject the world; the rest could
find enlightenment through filial piety and loyalty to the
throne. Chan indifference to the method of release had
been brought to its logical conclusion, but Zhuhong in his
Record of Self-Knowledge (Zizhi Lu) left no one in doubt
over what actions were required to approach this state of
bliss. One of the altruistic and compassionate deeds expected of the layman was "to carry a sick person encountered in the street back home for rest and treatment".
Although the lay movement Zhuhong inaugurated at the
end of the Ming may be seen as the final "Confucianisation"
of Buddhism, it remains true that the concern for suffering, and especially that imposed upon animals, which was
injected into popular morality through the good deeds of
those involved effectively rounded out the humanitarian
outlook of the Chinese people.

The drawing together of Buddhist traditions into a
comprehensive system, essentially Zhuhong's achievement,
had a parallel in contemporary literature and science.
The gigantic *Yong Le Encyclopaedia* was compiled in
four years by 2000 scholars; on completion in 1407, its
11,095 volumes were judged to be too numerous for a
printed edition, a misfortune for us because the main

collection of hand-copied rolls perished when British troops sacked the Summer Palace in 1860. The encyclopaedia, in which sections from books all over the empire were copied, was a reflection of intellectual attitudes amongst the scholars returned to office under the Ming. They were preoccupied with the past. Though this antiquarian emphasis led directly onto the new disciplines of philology and phonetics, with a consequent reassessment of the authenticity of many ancient texts, the intellectual revival in China contrasts with the scientific aspects of the European Renaissance, and appears strangely anti-scientific in the context of the previous millennium of technological advance pioneered by the Chinese. Even the great codification of herbs by Li Shizhen (1518–93), the *Outline of Herbal Medicine (Bencao Gangmu)*, represents no more than a summation of previous pharmaceutical knowledge. It was in fact recognised as the definitive work on Chinese medicine because it surveyed all existing knowledge up to the middle of the sixteenth century.

More originality, however, was evident in two comparatively new fields of composition—the play and the novel. As in painting, the exclusion of so many scholars from an official career under the Yuan emperors provided scope for experimentation beyond traditional forms. Mongol delight in drama must have proved a stimulus, especially as the emperors were avid theatre-goers, but surviving texts hardly reveal features which suggest outside additions to native material. While drama, or rather opera, was a Chinese development, in the works staged in the northern provinces, there appeared a new highly colloquial idiom suited to the play as well as the novel. Some subjects were even a favourite of both: the fantastic adventures of the monk Xuan Zhang on his famous pilgrimage to India had already been enhanced by generations of productions before Wu Chengen (1500–82) wrote *Journey to the West (Xiyou Ji)*, possibly the most widely read book in Chinese literature. The knockabout humour and frank speech of this novel may surprise Western readers, not least because the wisdom of honest laughter has long been appreciated by the Chinese as the most

Fig. 76 A literary gathering in a garden. The "ink boy" is making sure that the scholar about to compose verse will not have to pause once he dips his brush. After a seventeenth-century painting

potent weapon to deploy against religious fanaticism. Two other historical romances of immense popularity were Luo Guanzhong's *Romance of the Three Kingdoms (Sanguo Yanyi)* and *Outlaws of the Marsh (Shui Hu Chuan)*. Written in the late fourteenth century, these novels touched a chord in the popular mind that is still resonating in the People's Republic, since *Outlaws of the Marsh* is said at the time to "have enthused the masses and angered the ruling class". Less esteemed now is *Golden Lotus (Jin Ping Mei)*, a novel of manners published anonymously at Suzhou in 1610. Moved by its candour Lu Xun (1881–1936), the earliest practitioner of the modern novel in China, remarked how in "variety of human interest no novel of that period could surpass it".

During the Mongol conquest, most of the Chinese painters had lived in the Yangzi river valley; this remained so in the Ming epoch. The rift between court and scholar-painters, voluntarily living away from the capital, was widened into a gulf under the stimulus of private patronage, as the owners of large estates gathered together collections of Song and Yuan masterpieces along with the works of contemporary artists. Whereas Ming court painting lost its vitality, conforming more and more to historical stereotype, the literary painters *(wenren)*, who traced their origins back to Wang Wei in the Tang period, cherished their independence in the provinces and sought to extend the recent achievements of Yuan landscape painters such as Huang Gongwang (1269–1354) and Ni Zan (1301–74). Both these voluntary exiles from the Mongol capital had strong connections with Daoist quietism: Huang Gongwang wandered through mountains and valleys, while Ni Zan spent most of his life on a houseboat amid the lakes of Jiangxi province. The inspiration of their lives informed the work of leading Ming painters such as Shen Zhou (1427–1509) and Wen Zhengming (1470–1559), who dwelt in the countryside near the city of Suzhou.

Perhaps the most characteristic product of the Ming is its decorated porcelain, the famous "blue and white" *(ginghuaci)*. Painting in underglaze blue was introduced during the Yuan dynasty, but only in the fifteenth century did fine quality porcelain become common. The Chinese method of manufacture used a single firing. Pigment was applied to the unglazed body, the whole was covered with glaze, and the piece then fired, so that the complete fusion of all the materials resulted in an unequalled brilliance and luminosity. Although some of the porcelain made at the Jingdezhen kilns in Jiangxi province found their way abroad, the prime purpose of production was the supply of wares for the court, the massive order placed in 1433 for 433,500 pieces giving a measure of imperial patronage.

Corruption under the eunuch advisors of the late Ming emperors simply added to the financial difficulties of the imperial exchequer, already over-burdened with the enormous expenditure of the court. Increased taxation drove

Fig. 77 A Ming provincial commander-in-chief, a soldier of the same rank as Wu Sangui. The complicated civil war following the death of Chong Zhen in 1644 gave the Manchus their chance of conquest

the ordinary people into open rebellion, the province of Shaanxi rising as a whole in 1627 after a very severe drought. Ming government troops succeeded in defeating the uncoordinated rebel armies, even when they moved into other provinces, but no sooner had one uprising been crushed than another sprang up elsewhere. Particularly persistent was the rebel leader Li Zicheng, whose organisation spread through the important provinces of Henan and Hebei. In 1641 his followers attacked and seized Luoyang, where the imperial granaries and the storehouses of the rich were thrown open to the starving populace. Though Kaifeng and several other large cities in the Yellow river valley held out against him, Li Zicheng felt strong enough in 1643 to declare himself first emperor of the Shun dynasty and in the following year boldly march on Beijing. As there was little resistance from government forces, the rebels easily took control of the outer city of the capital, and in despair the last Ming emperor Chong Zhen (1628-44) hanged himself in the palace gardens on Coal Hill.

THE QING DYNASTY (1644-1911)

The Ming dynasty fell almost by accident. The Manchus did not conquer China on their own: it was conquered for them by the complicated civil war which followed Li Zicheng's usurpation. The initial lack of resistance to his march on Beijing can be explained by the need to defend the line of the Great Wall against Manchu blows. Ever since Nurhachi (1559-1626) defeated the Ming army responsible for the defence of what today is Liaoning province at the battle of Sarhu in 1619, imperial forces had been concentrated along the northern frontier. The confidence that Nurhachi's leadership gave to the Manchus not only cost the Ming dynasty the initiative in the long struggle but also tied up most of its available military power during a period of prolonged peasant unrest. The combination of famine, epidemics, rebellion and disgruntled frontier generals was just

Fig. 78 A seal belonging to the "South Ming" forces of one of the imperial princes who tried to resist the Manchus in the far south of China. Dating from 1648, it was found in Guizhou province

enough to let the Manchus found the Qing dynasty in 1644.

Although Li Zicheng (1605–45) was a man of little education, his abilities as a commander were manifest and the domination of the Ming court by the eunuchs encouraged the feeling that a change of imperial house might not be disadvantageous, providing it was a native one. People recalled how the first Ming emperor had been a peasant and how the vigorous policy he inaugurated had contained the problem of encroachment from the steppe. Under a strong new dynasty the empire would be able to cope with the rising power of the Manchus, now dominant beyond the Great Wall.

A factor not taken into full account by Li Zicheng was the susceptibilities of the general responsible for defending the gates in the Great Wall immediately north of the capital. This man, Wu Sangui, had a grudge against the Shun emperor, since his favourite concubine had been forcibly enrolled in the imperial harem. Seeing that other frontier commanders were considering a counter-attack, Wu Sangui reached an agreement with the Manchus and opened the gate at Shanhaiguan, "the pass between the land and the sea". Whatever he might have hoped from this pact, the abandonment of the main road between

Manchuria and China was a fatal error, for upon it the Ming system of northern defence hinged.

Fearing that Wu Sangui would defy his authority but unaware of the alliance the general had made with the Manchus, Li Zicheng marched to Shanhaiguan "with an immense army to conquer the last enemy that he supposed he had to meet before the empire was securely his own". The Histories add that to "strengthen his position Li Zicheng brought with him the father of Wu Sangui as well as the son of the last Ming emperor". The former was led in front of the frontier fortress, where he implored his son to surrender, and thus save his life. When Wu Sangui declared that he was a loyal supporter of the Ming, his father was executed before his eyes, an event that made him become more than ever "fully determined to defeat the rebels". In the ensuing battle, which took place during a fierce storm, the decisive moment came as "20,000 iron breast-plated Manchu horses madly galloped

Fig. 79 Ming soldier with a multiple gun behind a protective shield. The Ming army possessed better weapons than the Manchus in 1644

into the rebel host." Unnerved by the unexpected attack, the rebels broke ranks and fled, following the example of Li Zicheng.

While Wu Sangui pursued the hated Li Zicheng westwards, the Manchus took advantage of the power vacuum in Beijing to instal their seven-year-old king as the first Qing emperor Shunzhi (1644-61). Related to the Jin tribesmen who had ruled north China from 1125 to 1212, the Manchus had grown in strength by adopting settled agriculture and ironworking from the empire, whose bureaucratic administration they had imitated too. In 1644 they possessed neither the manpower nor the firearms necessary to subdue all the provinces; their "conquest" therefore depended upon the Chinese, whose slowness to rally to Wu Sangui must account for failure of his own revolt against the newly installed Qing dynasty (1673-83).

For the first thirty years the authority of the Qing emperor was restricted to north China. The rest of the empire was under the control of Wu Sangui and other military figures who supported a variety of Ming pretenders. Had Wu Sangui raised the banner of rebellion earlier, the Manchus might have been driven out altogether. By the time the people of the southern provinces were disposed to rise, there was an energetic Manchu ruler on the throne, Kangxi (1662-1722). With the aid of loyalist Chinese commanders, Kangxi asserted his authority over south China, the last Ming centre of resistance on Taiwan falling in 1683. Not previously under Chinese jurisdiction, the Manchus incorporated the island into the empire, thanks to the services of Dutch transports.

Under the direction of Kangxi and his immediate successors, the resources of China combined with Manchu military ambitions to annex the outlying territories that now form part of the People's Republic. Before their entry to China, the Manchus had already subjugated Korea and Inner Mongolia: the remainder of Mongolia was conquered in 1697, when Kangxi personally won an overwhelming victory at Urga. Turning westwards, Qing armies next overran Turkestan (before 1700), Tibet (1720) and Zungharia (1757). Manchu expansion on the steppe proved a lasting strategic benefit to China because it ended the ancient menace of nomad raiders, although this extension of borders was to cause conflicts in the nineteenth and twentieth centuries with the Russians who were simultaneously occupying other parts of Central Asia and Siberia. The southern frontier was strengthened through the renewed submission of Burma and Vietnam; even in the Himalayas a rare defeat inflicted in 1792 on the Ghurkas caused Nepal to acknowledge for a while the suzerainty of the Son of Heaven. Internally, the Qing government took a firmer line with minority peoples living within the empire. The Miao, who inhabited the less accessible parts of Yunnan and Guizhou provinces, lost between 1726 and 1731 their separate administration under hereditary chieftains and came for the first time under the direct control of the provincial officials.

Emperor Qing Kangxi was a model ruler. In 1684 he visited the shrine of Confucius at Qufu in Shandong province, a pilgrimage first undertaken by a Chinese emperor in 72, when Han Ming Di offered sacrifices to the Sage of Lu as one "who had given good laws to the people". There the Manchu ruler heard the ritual music and listened to lectures on the classics; he was shown the famous collection of precious objects and had pointed out to him the place where a descendant of the philosopher had hidden the classics when the First Emperor burned the books. But scholars knew that they need have no fear of Kangxi's intentions, because his admiration of Chinese culture was genuine and profound. Lacking a distinctive tradition of their own, the Manchus were obliged to identify with the Confucian orthodoxy which underpinned the authority of the One Man. This antiquarian tendency soon generated an encyclopaedic movement that far outstripped anything done by Ming scholars: the hallmark of their Qing successors was perspiration rather than inspiration. Although in Yuan Mei (1716–79) the dynasty was blessed with a distinguished poet as well as an expert on cookery, and in *A Dream of the Red Chamber (Hong Lou Meng)* at least one outstanding novel, the last epoch of the Chinese empire was devoted to making

Fig. 80 The last day of the Lantern Festival, from a Qing woodcut. The adoption of Chinese culture by the Manchu conquerors led in time to the loss of their own language and customs

collections of masterpieces belonging to the past rather than the creation of new works. In the nineteenth century the danger for China was to lie in the ultra-conservative tendency within the uncritical respect the Manchus had for tradition. Then, an alien dynasty clung adamantly to the customs of the past when the only hope for the country as a sovereign state was in adaptation to the conditions of the modern world. Under the Qing, Chinese culture became stultified.

Although scholars living in south China had to admit the cultivated outlook of the Manchu emperors, their dislike for the regime was never lessened by imperial patronage of learning and so the southern provinces remained dissident, a potential for renewed unrest whenever conditions allowed. Just as the Ming revival had begun there, the disturbances which emphatically marked

Qing decline in the nineteenth century and pointed to national renewal after the end of the empire all started south of the Yangzi river. It is sometimes overlooked that both the Taiping revolutionary movement (1851–66) and the Long March (1934–5) began in the southern provinces.

Southern hostility to the Manchus derived from a very different experience of "conquest". The entrance afforded by the gate at Shanhaiguan meant for the population in north China a more or less peaceful take-over of power, unlike the devastation of the south caused by Wu Sangui's long rebellion. The benefits of the new regime were felt in the northern provinces, too, because the Manchus preferred to retain Beijing as the capital for the reason it was near their homeland. Not a few southerners thought the wealth of south China was being drained northwards for the sake of a foreign house, despite the rapid cultural assimilation of the Manchus through the acquiescence of the northerners. There is indeed truth in the view that sees the establishment of the republic in 1912 as the culmination of southern agitation against the Qing.

A real cause of grievance was the operation of the official examination system. It was decreed that one-half of the posts in the civil service should be reserved for Manchus, and one-half left to the Chinese. Since the vast majority of the 250 million Chinese alive at the beginning of the Qing dynasty had their homes in the southern provinces, the practice of holding separate examinations for north and south China, at Beijing and Nanjing respectively, served only to exacerbate the problem. Candidates who converged on the examination compound in Nanjing represented three-quarters of the empire's population, yet they competed for a quarter of the official posts. As a consequence, the southerners who qualified tended to be the most intelligent members of the civil service, while Manchu officials, almost certain of their posts from birth, had no need of exceptional talents to gain office. The corollary was that many able and ambitious southerners who experienced repeated failure often went from disappointment to desperation, and from des-

Fig. 81 In spite of southern hostility to the Manchu domination, the first half of the eighteenth century was a peaceful and prosperous period for China. Scholars debarred from office took advantage of their freedom to travel and write guidebooks, the classic version of which appeared in 1857, entitled *An Illustrated Guide to Mount Emei*. This is one of its illustrations of the famous Buddhist mountain in Sichuan province

peration to revolt. The Taiping rebellion, which permanently crippled the Qing dynasty, was started by one such disappointed candidate.

It was near the close of Qianlong's reign (1736–96) that the flawed nature of the empire was recognised by Lord Macartney, the first British ambassador to China. "The government as it now stands", he wrote, "is properly the tyranny of a handful of Tartars over more than three hundred millions Chinese . . . Superiority animates the one, depression is felt by the other. Most of our books confound them together, and talk of them as if they made only one nation under the general name of China; but whatever might be concluded from any outward appearances, the real distinction is never forgotten by the sovereign who, though he pretends to be perfectly impartial, conducts himself at bottom by a systematic nationality, and never for a moment loses sight of the cradle of his power."

That the polite but indifferent reception accorded to

Fig. 82 "A systematic nationality" is what Lord Macartney believed that Qianlong exercised to maintain Manchu supremacy. This late Qing seal graphically demonstrates the division: it predates the visit of the first British ambassador to China

the British trade mission in 1793 was grounded on a deliberate policy of exclusion Lord Macartney was in no doubt. The sheer extent of the empire—its size, resources and population—might be blamed for encouraging Qianlong to ignore economic developments outside of China, but there was a danger in self-satisfaction, not least he noted because "a nation that does not advance must retrograde and finally fall back to barbarism and misery". Though Lord Macartney was astute in connecting the exclusion policy with the maintenance of Manchu supremacy, and especially fear of what effect outside contact would have on the Chinese, the reluctance of the emperor to end restrictions on international trade tallied with a tradition going back to Ming times. Scholar-officials could not object to the decree of 1757, which ordered all foreign trade to be transacted at Guangzhou. Keeping troublesome foreigners in a semi-official limbo at a port remote from the capital seemed a reasonable compromise, even if there was bound to be a certain amount of congestion. And genuine anxiety about the activities of the "ocean devils" *(yang guizi)* cannot be discounted. Father Amiot, a Jesuit long resident in Beijing, told Lord Macartney that his embassy "would have met with fewer problems at the outset if it had arrived before the imperial government had been alarmed by the news of great troubles in Europe, the inhabitants of which are indiscriminately considered by them as of a turbulent character." A direct consequence of the wars arising from the French Revolution is recorded in the Histories, for the British occupied Macao in 1802 and again in 1808, lest the French attack this Portuguese holding. When the Chinese protested the second time, "the English admiral made use of threats against the Guangdong authorities, and even went so far as to make an armed demonstration, but fearful of doing injury to trade, he did not proceed to hostilities".

For the East India Company, the greatest trader at Guangzhou, the arrangement was very frustrating and caused severe financial difficulties. As the export of tea and silk continued to expand yet the import of British manufactured goods remained constant, the Company found itself unable to obtain sufficient silver to cover the deficit, and so it had lobbied for a freer approach to Chinese markets. The failure of Lord Macartney's mission either to establish diplomatic relations or negotiate a trade treaty led ultimately to the Anglo-Chinese War of 1839–42, known as the First Opium War.

It was an inevitable collision of two governments whose views were totally different: two diametrically opposed social and economic systems met head-on. Brushing aside the setback of Lord Macartney's embassy, London had sent out other ambassadors in order to reach an agreement with Beijing. But in 1816 Lord Amherst was unable to achieve anything at the Qing court, whilst in 1834 Lord Napier discovered that even his arrival at Guangzhou was deeply resented. After his approaches to the local Chinese authorities had been rebuffed, and a few shots exchanged between his frigates and the shore batteries there, Lord Napier retired to Macao and died shortly afterwards. The recommendation in his report that the island of Hong Kong be acquired as a naval and commercial base influenced later British strategy, however.

The expiration of the East India Company's charter in the same year soon produced a situation where conflict

Fig. 83 The Qing Empire (1644–1911), showing territorial losses

arose. Thereafter trade was in the hands of private merchants and the British government ceased to accept any responsibility for its transaction, and in particular the growing commerce in opium. The influx of this drug from India, where the East India Company had deliberately stimulated production as an alternative to payment in silver, caused such great concern to emperor Dao Guang (1821–50) that in 1839 he dispatched a special commissioner, Li Zexu, with instructions to stamp out the whole business. The action which Li Zexu took was to destroy the opium stocks without compensation, and to insist that European merchants promise to end the traffic in the drug. The British merchants were uneasy about this suppression and the murder of a Chinese by a group of drunken British and American sailors added to the tension. When none of the men involved in the fatal incident was handed over for justice, Li Zexu ordered that supplies be withheld from all foreign shipping. A clash then occurred at Kowloon, casualties were sustained by both sides, and the British were formally excluded from the city of Guangzhou.

In retaliation a British expeditionary force of twenty ships arrived off Macao with 4000 British and Indian troops. After attacking Guangzhou in 1840, the force received further soldiers from India, and then sailed northwards inflicting heavy damage on coastal towns and cities. Since Qing forces had little defence against the superior fire-power of the invaders, the emperor was obliged to accept in 1842 the Treaty of Nanjing, which opened up the ports of Guangzhou, Xiamen, Fuzhou, Ningbo and Shanghai to international trade, and ceded the island of Hong Kong to Britain as a sovereign base. Particularly obnoxious to Chinese sentiment was the "most-favoured-nation" clause, which established the divisive principle of extra-territoriality. The total immunity this gave British residents from Chinese law was deeply resented, especially when they carved out privileged enclaves in the Treaty Ports. Chinese alive today can recall the sign which once hung on the entrance of a park in Shanghai: "Dogs and Chinese Not Allowed".

The sordidness of the First Opium War, and its aftermath, still casts a shadow over China's relations with the West. It is not forgotten how the Royal Navy in its glorious sweep up the Yangzi river preceded a flotilla of opium ships, despite Gladstone's condemnation of the drug trade in the House of Commons. As he rightly pointed out, the British government of the day had only to prohibit the cultivation of the poppy in India to curtail the miseries of addiction. Of the hostilities between China and Britain he declared "a war more unjust in its origin, a war more calculated in its progress to cover this country with permanent disgrace, I do not know, and have not read of." Yet even Gladstone was able to manage his conscience in such a way that in a debate of 1870 he could contend that opium had become a commercial commodity through the imposition of an import duty. What he chose to overlook was that this concession had been wrung from an unwilling China in the Treaty of Tianjin (1858) after the further intervention of gunboats. Like most nineteenth-century politicians, Gladstone was deeply impressed by the powerful impact of a modest naval force on the tottering Qing dynasty. European dominance, as then expressed in industrial technology and expanding capitalist activity, seemed a natural progression in world history. A similar opinion was held by the British electorate, who returned Lord Palmerston with a thumping majority just before the outbreak of the Second Opium War (1856–8).

The shock of capitulation to such a small expeditionary force in 1842 was enormous, for the fragility of the Qing empire was demonstrated to the world. It signalled that China was besieged, and an easy target for any industrial power bent on aggression. The siege can be said to have lasted until our lifetimes, since only through the foundation of the People's Republic in 1949 has the country recovered enough strength to deter modern predators. The 1985 agreement reached with Britain over the return of Hong Kong represents much more than a diplomatic triumph for Deng Xiaoping: it is a tacit admission by Europe that China has returned to its rightful place on the world stage.

The dynastic weakness that made China vulnerable to foreign assault also decreased the empire's resistance to internal rebellion. A harbinger of the disorders of the nineteenth century was the "White Lotus" rising in Shandong province. The origins of this sect—which believed that the coming of the future Buddha Maitreya was at hand and that a descendant of the Ming dynasty was about to drive out the Manchus—can be found in the twelfth century, but significantly its fame had been established in the popular movements of the 1340s against the Mongols. In 1774 Wang Lun, a leader of one of the

Fig. 84 A Miao woman. Unrest among the Miao tribal people of southwestern China was but one of the signs of dynastic weakness in the eighteenth century. Other revolts broke out in places as far apart as Taiwan and Gansu province

"White Lotus" sects, raised the first major rebellion of the late Qing and temporarily threatened the passage of grain-tax along the Grand Canal. Savagely suppressed though this rising was in Shandong, unrest steadily spread through the other provinces of the empire: the Muslims of Gansu rose in 1781, a revolt broke out on Taiwan in 1786, and in 1795 in the far south-west the Miao people took up arms in protest at excessive labour demands on public works. Further outbreaks of disorder fermented by members of the "White Lotus" in the final years of the eighteenth century were a sure indicator of impending dynastic decline.

Behind the growing instability of the empire stood an economic crisis which was worsened by population growth. Under the Qing dynasty the Chinese people increased from 200 million in the seventeenth century to 417 million in 1851, after which census returns were disrupted by the Taiping rebellion. Although New World crops like maize, peanuts and potatoes were introduced and there was an expansion of the area under cultivation, the agricultural economy barely kept pace with population growth. No agricultural boom occurred like the one experienced in south China under the Southern Song dynasty and farming tended more and more towards food grain production at the expense of commercially valuable crops such as cotton. The single largest handicraft industry in China during the Qing dynasty—cotton manufacture—was plagued with shortages of raw materials as demand for food accelerated. Unlike Britain, which between 1741 and 1775 tripled its consumption of New World cotton and absorbed excess population into manufacturing activities, the self-imposed isolation of China from international trade left little room for adjustment. Commerce and industry had to manage within an economic system proving itself to be less and less satisfactory, while demographic pressure on land brought about a subdivision of farms into small and uneconomic units.

At first, there were sufficient resources to meet the needs of an elaborate state and a large population, but even by the time of Qianlong's rejection in 1794 of Lord Macartney's overtures on trade, this balance was tipping towards disaster. The imperial exchequer had already been obliged to devise schemes for supplementary revenue, since few of the provinces could meet their full taxation targets each year. Court extravagance, official corruption, and tax evasion amongst wealthy landowners only added to the burden placed on the poor, many of whom were driven to banditry, if not outright rebellion. Absentee landlordism must account for the pent-up hatred and the fury released in the peasants by the disturbances, since we know that many wealthy families preferred to live in towns and cities where there were opportunities to make profits in moneylending, commerce and urban real estate. Relations in the countryside were frequently reduced to the cash nexus, a situation which allowed the local moneylender or pawnbroker to become very important indeed. The selling of degrees between 1816 and 1830 did little to endear the Qing dynasty to Chinese scholars, although these honorary qualifications gave no entitlement to an official position. Hints at corruption within the civil service examination system were to be confirmed in 1858, however. That year emperor Xian Feng (1851–62) discovered how the use of certain code-words allowed examiners to identify favoured candidates, whose poor papers could then be substituted with those deemed to have passed. Punishment was severe. Offending examiners were beheaded, dilatory examination administrators banished to remote provinces, and the graduates who tried to cheat lost all the qualifications they had previously gained. Sensational as the purge was, and even effective in combating dishonesty for a while, the atmosphere in the examination compound grew more hopeless and corrupt as the empire visibly declined. The abolition of the whole system at the beginning of this century was a foregone conclusion after the failure of the Hundred Days of Reform in 1898. The final examinations held in 1904 were an irrelevance in a world patently dominated by foreign knowledge and technology. The stultification of the official Chinese outlook under Qing conservatism had cost the country dear, not least because China's slowness to modernise was turned into a serious military weakness by the 1872 decision of the Meiji government to open Japan to European and American influence. The first East Asian country to adapt to modern conditions, Japan embraced the imperialist ambitions of the European powers it so diligently copied too.

To deal with internal disorder the Qing emperors turned to regional militias formed by local gentry, and allowed some of these militias to develop into real armies. This step they were very loath to take, but the abject state of purely Manchu units, whose fighting abilities had been sapped by generations of garrison duty, left the embattled throne without any choice. The new armed forces, largely separate from official control and under Chinese command, remained loyal to the dynasty and put insurrection down, sometimes with foreign help. One of the powerful new army commanders was Li Hongzhang (1822–1901), who patronised in 1865 the establishment in

Shanghai of a factory for making rifles, guns and ammunition. He also lent his support to steamship navigation, mining and textile mills. His advocacy of modern technology as a means of making China strong was not without its problems. Apart from the nervousness of the throne and the xenophobia of most landowners, Li Hongzhang had to reconcile the adoption of foreign ways with traditional values: "Western learning for practical purposes" *(xixue wei yong)* and "Chinese learning for the fundamentals" *(zhongxue wei ti)*.

The only previous borrowing from abroad the Chinese had ever made on any scale was from India, when they accepted the Buddhist faith. As astute scholars saw, there were dangers to the Confucian state in the wholesale import of Western-style factories. The dilemma was succinctly put by Liu Qihong, a member of the first permanent mission China sent in 1876 to the West. Noting how steamships, railway trains, mines and roads were "mutually related", he wrote in his diary: "One thing will lead to another, and we will not be able to refuse them." So profound was the change involved in modernisation that it would be impossible for China to accept only what it wanted from abroad and reject the rest.

A not dissimilar argument over "bourgeois liberalism" in early 1987 was to cause the downfall of prime minister Hu Yaobang. Not even his Long March credentials were enough to save Hu Yaobang from the accusation that the economic reforms he sponsored had weakened the People's Republic, the student agitation over the winter months being cited as unwelcome imports of capitalist behaviour. Its citizens at the time of his resignation were reminded in the official press of the bullying suffered by China during the nineteenth century, when the first attempt to benefit from foreign knowledge occurred. Quoted were these words of Mao Zedong: "Imperialist aggression shattered the fond dreams of the Chinese about learning from the West. It was very odd—why were the teachers always beating the student?" The implication was that Deng Xiaoping's programme of modernisation could work only within the framework of Chinese socialism.

The driving force for change under the late Qing was the upheaval caused by the Taiping rebels, who defied the imperial authorities from 1851 to 1866. Zeng Guofan (1811–72), a large landowner in Hunan province, not only raised and equipped a first-rate militia army but more he set up in 1861 an arsenal in Anhui province so as to sustain the imperial counter-attack. With other militia commanders such as Li Hongzhang, he eventually wore down rebel resistance in the southern provinces, the centre of the uprising, although not before as many as 50 million people had died. The costly defeat of the Taipings gave a respite to the weakened Qing dynasty but the throne's reliance on the military, coupled with the imposition of further embarrassing treaties, paved the way for a more radical revolution that overthrew the empire itself. On one hand, it produced Yuan Shikai and a generation of warlords; on the other, tales of the heroic struggle put up by the Taiping rebels moulded the character of Dr Sun Yatsen, who as a boy cherished the nickname "Hong Xiuquan the Second".

The Taiping Heavenly Kingdom, which Hong Xiuquan (1814–64) declared in 1851, countenanced revolutionary ideas in respect of land reform, the liberation of women, and attitudes to foreigners. A tragedy for the Taipings, in spite of their professed Christian belief, was the coldness of the majority of the Europeans living in China, especially those with commercial interests at stake or missionaries anxious over differences concerning doctrine. The Taipings soon learned that the Europeans were neither co-religionists nor allies against the Manchus. Drawing on Protestant tracts and the visions he experienced after disappointment in the civil service examinations, Hong Xiuquan preached the overthrow of the Qing dynasty and the conversion of the Chinese people to Christianity. His Society for the Worship of God *(Bai Shang Di Hui)* achieved astonishing successes against government troops, acted as a magnet for oppressed peasants, and by 1853 he made its capital Nanjing. Though failure to march straight on to Beijing probably cost the Taipings eventual victory, their control of the populous southern provinces led to a

Fig. 85 Taiping revolutionary banner. One of the standards carried by a division of the forces belonging to the Heavenly Kingdom

long and bitter struggle, which was ended only by an alliance between the British and the Qing governments. Foreign vessels and foreign troops sealed the fate of this unexpected Christian movement, the price of this aid being the further concessions wrung from the empire in the Treaty of Tianjin (1858) and the Convention of Beijing (1860). Following incidents in Guangdong, an Anglo-French force had begun operations in 1857, bombarding coastal settlements as it sailed northwards. This gunboat diplomacy was completed by Lord Elgin, who arrived with orders to resort to "the most violent measures of coercion and repression on the slenderest provocation". Unhappy though he professed to be over this pugnacious role, Lord Elgin overcame his finer feelings while in Beijing and ordered in 1860 the destruction of the Summer Palace as a reprisal for the deaths of several British envoys, and in the process destroyed a large portion of the imperial collection, including precious books, paintings and other works of art.

The Russians also took advantage of Qing difficulties to appropriate vast territories along the Amur river. The dismemberment of the empire then proceeded apace: Burma in 1885 passed into British hands, Vietnam the same year into French, and after a short campaign Japan in 1895 seized Korea, the Liaoning peninsula and the island of Taiwan.

The crushing victories achieved by the Japanese on land and sea should have been enough to convince the Qing court that modernisation was overdue. Minute in comparison with the empire, Japan had shown its potency and there were scholars ready with constructive suggestions for innovation. When the Treaty of Shimonoseki was signed with Japan in 1895, Kang Youwei (1858–1927) led 1200 scholars who had passed the provincial examinations and were then in Beijing for the palace examinations to submit a memorial to emperor Guang Xu (1875–1908), opposing the treaty and requesting immediate political reform. Reinterpreting Confucius in order to justify change, Kang Youwei proposed in essence the substitution of constitutional monarchy for traditional autocracy. Though this memorial failed to reach the throne, the would-be reformer's activities received strong support in south China, where greater familiarity with foreign goods and ideas only increased the exasperation felt at the dilatoriness of Beijing. A native of Guangdong, Kang Youwei had visited Hong Kong in 1879 and seen "Western learning" in action.

Convinced that change was necessary, Guang Xu gave his confidence to Kang Youwei and a series of edicts announced the reform of the civil service examinations, the establishment of Western-style schools, the modernisation of the armed forces, and economic measures, including central planning, modern banks, the opening of mines and construction of railways. It looked as if China was about to follow the example of Japan. Then, almost without warning the Hundred Days of Reform came to an abrupt end in September 1895, when the empress dowager Ci Xi (1835–1908) staged a palace coup with the aid of Yuan Shikai's modernised New Army. An arch-conservative, Ci Xi did more than anyone to prevent change, using a network of spies and informers inside and outside the imperial palace. Her rallying of the conservatives, Manchu and Chinese alike, effectively set the scene for the outburst of xenophobia known as the Boxer rebellion (1900). For reasons of his own, Yuan Shikai allowed the imprisonment of the emperor on one of the islands adjacent to the Purple Forbidden City. Because of possible reaction from the West (which was thought to be sympathetic to reform), Ci Xi did not dare to execute Guang Xu at once, but thereafter it was obvious that the Qing court would oppose any fundamental change in Chinese society and serious revolutionary activity concentrated on the extinction of both the dynasty and the empire. In place of Kang Youwei's constitutional monarchy, the vision of the future became Dr Sun Yatsen's republic.

The height of folly was the encouragement Ci Xi gave to the Boxers. About 1898, the members of a secret society called the "Righteous Harmonious Fist" *(Yi He Tuan)* enlarged their sacred boxing to include attacks on Christian missions and foreign importations such as telegraph lines. Pressure from British and American representatives in Beijing compelled the Qing court to send soldiers from the New Army to suppress the Boxers in Shandong province, where the recent concessions of Weihaiwei (to Britain) and Qingdao (to Germany) had started the anti-foreign agitation; but not even the ruthlessness of Yuan Shikai could prevent the movement spreading throughout the north-east and drawing into its ranks members of the conservative gentry. Seeking to use the Boxers for her own purposes, Ci Xi decided to allow imperial troops to help in their assault on the Legation Quarter in Beijing. One had no need of a crystal ball to foresee that the consequence of the Boxer rebellion would be a punitive expedition of soldiers drawn from all the countries with diplomatic staff in China. Despite the modern guns of the Dagu forts, an international squadron forced a passage upriver to Tianjin, where a relief column was disembarked and made ready to capture Beijing.

The fall and looting of the capital underscored the bankruptcy of the Qing dynasty. The peace terms Li Hongzhang negotiated were all that could be expected: massive reparations, punishment of war criminals, permanent garrisons of foreign soldiers in Beijing, and a 5 per cent import tariff. Had it not been for the declaration of an Open Door policy proposed by the United States in 1899 and 1900, whereby China was to remain an open market, there is every reason to believe that the spheres of influence of the various imperial powers would have gradually developed into colonial possessions. As it was, the Russians stayed on in Manchuria for five years, till total defeat in the Liaoning peninsula during the Russo-Japanese War (1904–5) and revolution at home persuaded St Petersburg that President Theodore Roosevelt was right in advocating non-intervention.

Again, modernised Japan had shown the way. Not only did the victory over Russia confer the Chinese territory the West had denied her in 1895, but more important it demonstrated that a properly equipped oriental country could beat an occidental one. Pressure for change in China became irresistible, and the execution of Guang Xu in 1908, ordered by Ci Xi from her deathbed, created a power vacuum that was swiftly filled by forward-looking republicans who advocated an entirely new constitutional framework. Everything favoured revolution, with the result that uprisings in the provinces of Sichuan and Hubei swiftly triggered a national rebellion that swept away the empire and allowed Dr Sun Yatsen to be sworn in on 1 January 1912 at Nanjing as the first president of the provisional government of the Chinese Republic.

PART III

POST-IMPERIAL
CHINA

6

THE REPUBLIC

The Impact of Modern Times (1912–49)

THE END OF EMPIRE (1911–12)

Although the number of modern factories in China increased from the 1870s, the economy as a whole remained impervious to modernisation before the foundation of the republic in 1912. Xenophobia played a part in the reluctance of the Chinese to purchase foreign manufactured goods, but as a British trade report of 1866 pointed out, it was not the sole reason for the poor sales of pieces from Lancashire mills. The report noted:

> Cotton is grown extensively in China, and the people weave it into a coarse, strong cloth which is better suited to the wants of the peasants and working men than the more showy but less substantial product of foreign machinery. The customers of British manufacturers in China are not the bulk of the people but only those who can afford to buy a better looking but less useful article.

Clearly the empire was no backward economy. It had an elaborate system of production and distribution, albeit founded on handicraft industries, that left no vacuum for the foreign traders in the Treaty Ports to fill. The empire could manage without technological innovation, the emperor shopping around for major items of manufacture, such as the quick-firing Krupps guns which in 1900 had delayed the international relief squadron at the Dagu forts. The political upheavals from 1851 onwards have tended to blind some commentators to the resilience of the traditional economy, which in decline though it surely was did not hit rock bottom till the late 1920s—the aftermath of the warlord era. Where, for instance, entirely new products were introduced into the economy, such as cigarettes and kerosene, Chinese businessmen rapidly handled their distribution and in the case of the former had by 1915 acquired a stake in the market as producers using local materials.

The Treaty Ports were peripheral, although the scale of their parasitic functions as centres of financial speculation and international commerce, was not economically insignificant for the reason that the empire was so vast and populous. At the time of the First Opium War (1839–42), Shanghai already handled a volume of shipping equal to that of London. But only Manchuria under the colonial rule of Japan was to experience accelerated development during the republic. Eccentric and thinly populated prior to 1900, the five provinces that constituted the original Manchu homeland were a relative frontier, an easy area for planned Japanese investment. The method of change elsewhere was more indirect: modernisation came from the educational activities of the missionary societies and the self-help movements of those Chinese who found employment in Western-style enterprises. In the final decades of the empire the pace of change had been deliberately slowed by the empress dowager Ci Xi, who clung to the fond hope that the Qing dynasty could survive without any concession to modern times. She fully approved of the decision to dismantle China's first railway line, built in 1876 to connect Shanghai and Wusong, after people living nearby complained that "fire-carriages" *(huoche)*, were disturbing the peace of the land.

Nevertheless, railways were to be the trigger for the national uprising that led to the abdication of the last

Fig. 86 Imperial predators, a French cartoonist's view of the final years of the Chinese empire

Qing emperor Xuan Tong (1909–12). In spite of Ci Xi's stubborn conservatism right up to her death in 1908, a network of trunk lines was in the process of construction before the end of the empire and the defence of provincial interests in its development become a case of grievance, when the imperial government decided to hand over individual lines to foreign companies in return for loans. The decree of May 1911 seizing the Guangzhou/Hankou and Sichuan/Hankou railways not only alienated provincial investors but soon inaugurated a mass protest movement in Sichuan, Hunan, Hubei and Guangdong provinces. In August a rally attended by tens of thousands of protestors at Chengdu set the pace by calling strikes among workers and students and urging peasants to withhold their taxes. By September the governor of Sichuan province considered that strong measures were necessary and he ordered the execution of numerous people in Chengdu. This action only prompted an armed insurrection which within a few weeks had merged with the anti-Qing uprising at Wuchang, one of the three cities comprising modern Wuhan, the capital of Hubei province. Here in October the accidental discovery of a plot by the authorities, and the arrest of republican activists, compelled an all-out rebellion by civilians and members of the armed forces alike. Within three days the rebels had occupied Hanyang and Hankou, the other two cities of Wuhan.

As news of this success spread, republican sympathisers organised risings throughout the southern provinces, with the result that two-thirds of the empire had repudiated the Qing dynasty by the time Nanjing fell in early December. Most of the Manchu garrisons in the provinces were already massacred. Where provincial governors remained at the head of their troops, they did so through making common cause with the revolutionaries, from whom they may have meant to break free at the earliest opportunity. At first the court underestimated the strength of the uprising but, as soon as reports showed its true proportions, a desperate expedient was adopted. In November Yuan Shikai received full power to deal with the situation, a task the general had patiently awaited in retirement.

Slowly Yuan Shikai reasserted imperial authority north of the Yangzi river, eventually arranging a ceasefire with the rebels, who on 1 January 1912 had set up a provisional government at Nanjing with Dr Sun Yatsen as president. The agreement reached between the two sides exactly suited Yuan Shikai's personal ambitions, since Dr Sun Yatsen promised to step down in favour of the general, once the Qing emperor had been induced to renounce the throne and declare the establishment of a republic. In February the young ruler obliged and Yuan Shikai was declared president by a unanimous vote of the provisional assembly in Nanjing.

It is easy now to regard the republicans as naive. At the time there was no real alternative to collaboration with the only Chinese military leader possessed of a modernised army. The hostile attitude of most foreign powers hardly helped: throughout October a dozen British, American, Japanese, German and French warships had remained at the alert, anchored in the Yangzi roads off Wuhan. The rapid progress of the revolution precluded intervention on behalf of the beleaguered Qing dynasty, but it did not stop credit being offered to Beijing against further concessions. Nor were foreign envoys slow in advocating Yuan Shikai's nomination as soon as constitutional change became inevitable. On 7 September 1909 the Beijing correspondent of *The Times* had lamented "the deplorable weakness of the central government, where since the fall of Yuan Shikai, there seemed no man competent or willing to assume responsibility". On 12 February 1912 the European powers could congratulate themselves on the return of this "strong man" to China's helm. Towards the close of the republican period similar arguments were advanced to justify continued support for another soldier, Jiang Jieshi (Chiang Kaishek, 1887–1975), even after it became obvious that he no longer commanded the respect of the Chinese people.

It is also sad that Europe preferred to recognise the regime Yuan Shikai ran at Beijing as well as float the enormous loans necessary to finance his military forces, when the original Nanjing revolutionaries, whom they chose to ignore, were such uncritical admirers of Western democratic institutions. However, this was *la belle époque,* when a self-confident and optimistic Europe, sustained by industrial technology and world-wide colonial empires, felt certain of its superior judgement concerning the deceased Chinese empire. Even so, there existed among Dr Sun Yatsen's supporters a belief that Yuan Shikai was in sympathy with the republican ideal. In the event Yuan Shikai was astute enough to retain the support of most foreign powers and out-manoeuvre politically the Guomindang, as the party of Dr Sun Yatsen became known from 1912. A problem for the early republicans was the absence of any understanding in China of what was involved in the working of democratic institutions. Their own lack of popular support was observed by a British correspondent during the 1913 election. He concluded that

the election of members, whether of the National Parliament or of provincial assemblies, is absolutely unreal . . . In Newchang, which is a town of some 100,000 inhabitants, the election of a parliamentary

representative took place while I was there. Thirty-
five voters recorded their votes, and of those thirty-
five the majority were employees in the office of
the local administrator. The public took no part
and exhibited no interest in the proceedings.

Between the republicans, who were led by overseas Chinese and men driven abroad by the Manchus, and the
majority of the Chinese people, there was only one point
of agreement: the correctness of overthrowing the Qing
dynasty. Dr Sun Yatsen himself was a typical revolutionary. Poverty in Guangdong province had caused him in
1879 to join his elder brother who was building up a
successful business in Honolulu. He received a Western
education, then studied medicine in Hong Kong, before
in 1893 returning home. Trouble with the Qing authorities, and an exclusion order from Hong Kong, led to a
sojourn in Japan, the United States and Britain. During
his stay in London he read widely in the British Museum
and evolved his three principles of nationalism, democracy and socialism. He also achieved notice in 1896 when
the *Globe,* a newspaper inclined to liberal causes, publi-
cised his detention in the Chinese embassy, to which Dr
Sun Yatsen had been lured. Moving his base of operations to Japan, he founded in 1905 the Chinese Revolutionary League *(Zhongguo Tong Meng Hui),* which issued
propaganda against reformists such as Kang Youwei and
fermented revolts in the southern provinces.

Support for these revolutionary activities came from
the overseas Chinese community, whose members had
migrated mainly from the provinces of Fujian and Guangdong. These settlers engaged in mining and farming,
besides starting industries and trading ventures in towns.
Encouragement of Chinese immigration was the policy of
the Brooke family, the "White Rajahs" of Sarawak, a
principality in Borneo obtained in 1841 from the sultan of
Brunei. Its second largest town, Sibu, was nicknamed
"New Fuzhou" because of the influx of farmers from
Fujian province. Large concentrations of migrants had
appeared earlier in the British settlements of Penang,

Malacca and Singapore. When Stamford Raffles occupied Singapore in 1819 there were only 120 Malays and 30 Chinese inhabiting an obscure fishing village. Two years later, the architect of British imperialism in the archipelago was gratified to observe that the Chinese population of the colony had risen to over 1000, some of whom had come directly from the port of Xiamen. The British belief in the presence of a large Chinese community as a proof of prosperity laid the basis of the present state of Singapore, with more than 2 million citizens of Chinese origin. Though envied for their new-found prosperity by the local inhabitants, and even the object of savage persecution by the Spaniards in the neighbouring Philippines, the Chinese migrants usually steered an independent course, maintaining their own culture and declining involvement in local politics. They still looked upon China as their homeland and gave aid to Dr Sun Yatsen in the struggle against the Manchus, a political allegiance which Jiang Jieshi inherited when he assumed the leadership of the Guomindang in 1925.

Once the last Qing emperor had abdicated in February 1912, Yuan Shikai set about preparing his personal bid for the throne, though he seems to have recognised that his title might need to be king rather than emperor. To consolidate his position as chief warlord, he had to weaken the local militia under the Guomindang's influence, undermine the confidence of elected-representatives, and increase his own military strength. In 1913 he dismissed the governors of Jiangxi, Anhui and Guangdong provinces, swiftly putting down the so-called "Second Revolution" which the Guomindang declared against him. Dr Sun Yatsen was forced once again to flee abroad. When a year later Yuan Shikai declared the Guomindang an illegal organisation and substituted presidential dictatorship for parliamentary rule, his subversion of the constitution caused no ripples in international circles. Western acquiscence was particularly galling to Liang Qichao (1873–1921), a disciple of Kang Youwei and an admirer of European civilisation. He bitterly said that the president "did not know the difference between a man and a beast.

All he knows about human beings is that they fear weapons and love gold, and it is by these two things he rules the country. For four years, there has been no politics in Beijing except the ghostly shadows of a knife and a piece of gold. By bribery and terror, he has enslaved the people".

But all was not to go according to Yuan Shikai's plan. The outbreak of the First World War removed Europe's restraining hand on the Japanese, who occupied the German-leased territory of Qingdao and adjoining parts of Shandong province. Then, in January 1915, Japan presented the "Twenty-One Demands", whose purpose was the reduction of China to a virtual protectorate. With no hope of support from the European powers, now locked in total war, Yuan Shikai was obliged to accept the least offensive demands. To a large number of Chinese the agreement of the president, however reluctant, was the final betrayal by a man who had successively betrayed the reforming emperor Guang Xu (1898), the child-emperor Xuan Tong (1912) and the republic (1913).

So in a general atmosphere of distrust, as one province after another declared its independence from Beijing, Yuan Shikai announced at the beginning of 1916 his new dynasty of the Great Constitution *(Hong Xian)*. Yet both his political skill and his luck had deserted him, for this usurpation of imperial authority was opposed not only by the republicans but even more importantly by other warlords. The words that Kang Youwei, the leader of the 1898 reform movement, addressed to Yuan Shikai summed up the general sentiment. He wrote:

What law is there under your rule? You think that since the republic was created by you, it can be abolished by you? You are a conjuror who regards the rest of us as ants and termites completely at your disposal. The changes of the recent years have left no impression whatever on your conscience.

Reverses on the battlefield soon brought an end to Yuan Shikai's reign. In March 1916 he abandoned his imperial pretensions in order to retain the presidency, but the game was up and he died in the following June after a nervous illness caused by disappointment. The closest Yuan Shikai ever got to becoming the One Man was celebrating the New Year in 1916, when the ambitious warlord was conveyed to and from the Temple of Heaven in an armoured car.

THE WARLORD PERIOD (1916–28)

Although Japanese agents played a role in his downfall, lesser warlords had no need to look beyond Yuan Shikai's own career in order to appreciate the effectiveness of strategic disobedience. His legacy to the ailing republic was a host of military rulers who had never been officers of the regular army; these opportunists, whom he had nominated or accepted as the provincial authorities in order to reduce the influence of the Guomindang, were able to tap local resources and act independently after the chief warlord disappeared. It was Yuan Shikai's personal eminence that had permitted a comparatively peaceful transition from empire to republic: the political revolution was contained within the continuity of the military establishment. The twelve years of warlord rivalry after 1916 revealed the actual extent to which the country had disintegrated.

Warlord armies fought one another for economic prizes and the ferocity of their internecine struggle grew as the armies captured the means of improving their weaponry. The greatest prize of all was Beijing, since the European powers refused to recognise any other administration as legitimate. Financial motives were behind this persistence, for their loans were financed by customs duties which they collected in the name of Beijing. In 1917 one warlord even attempted to restore the ex-Manchu emperor, but the intervention of other warlord armies sent him swiftly back into retirement. All that this move, and the later Japanese restoration of Xuan Tong as head of the puppet state of Manzhouguo, achieved was to discredit still further the imperial system. Caught in the collapse of the old order, Puyi (the personal name of emperor Xuan Tong) found himself as little more than the quarry of competing forces. With warlords, large and small, fighting over the resources of the provinces, conditions steadily deteriorated. The troops themselves were ruffians in uniform, ex-bandits and the dregs of society; not even the remnant of Yuan Shikai's New Army could claim the distinction of having seen action against a foreign foe: they were garrison troops whose commanders turned their garrison areas into private estates. The most common methods of extortion included a squeeze on central government taxes, local trade, and the rents due from peasants. Drainage and irrigation schemes not surprisingly fell into disrepair and communications were often dislocated. What capital there was in the countryside fled into speculative ventures in the Treaty Ports. The ordinary people, plagued by soldiers, bandits and famine, suffered dreadfully. "There are districts", a British commentator wrote in 1931, "in which the position of the rural population is that of a man standing permanently up to his neck in water, so that even a ripple is enough to kill him."

Much of the country fell within the sphere of influence of one colonial power or another, and foreign troops were stationed widely within China to guard their interests. The Japanese were so aggressive that in 1919 a surge of patriotic protest compelled the Beijing government to withdraw its delegation from Versailles without signing the peace treaty. The May Fourth Movement, spearheaded by students from Beijing University, was a spontaneous reaction to the news that Japan had been awarded the ex-German holding of Qingdao. Ignoring official warnings, 3000 students demonstrated in Tiananmen square, expressed their concern at the American legation, and then burned down the houses of pro-Japanese ministers. The impact of the demonstration upon China was out of proportion to its size: in towns and cities meetings were held and a boycott of Japanese goods inaugurated. The American philosopher John Dewey, then a lecturer at Beijing University, wrote in a letter home: "To think of kids in our country from fourteen on, taking the lead in starting a big clean-up reform movement and shaming merchants and professional men into joining them—this is sure some country!"

The May Fourth Movement was a watershed in the history of modern China. It raised political consciousness among students and workers in the urban areas, thereby stimulating discussion about the problems facing the republic. Dr Sun Yatsen had always argued that three stages were necessary in its development: the phase of struggle against the empire, the phase of educative rule, and the phase of truly democratic government. In the Beijing student demonstration the republic had at last found educators capable of advancing understanding under an authoritarian regime. The lightning effect their views had on contemporary opinion also indicated that the traditional role of the scholar as the upholder of public morality was by no means dead. Repression of student activities soon followed; in Tianjin Zhou Enlai (1898–1976) was imprisoned for six months along with other graduates. Even before Zhou Enlai set out for France later in 1920, he had become deeply interested in Marxism and pondered the possibility that it might provide a solution to China's ills. It was, however, another young thinker who perceived how the brutality of military rule was preparing conditions for the next stage of the revolution, that of the peasants. This was Mao Zedong (1893–1976), one of the founding delegates of the Communist Party of China in Shanghai on 1 July 1921.

The social and political turmoil of the warlord period was captured in the caustic satires of Lu Xun (1881–1936), who led a literary revolution by adopting the common language for his stories and novels. The crusade for reform had started with an article by Hu Shi (1891–1962). While a student at Columbia University, he sent an article entitled "Suggestions for a Reform of Literature" to *New Youth (Xinqingnian)*, a magazine founded in Shanghai in 1915 that became the mouthpiece of the younger intellectuals. Hu Shi advocated the adoption of *baihua*, or vernacular Chinese, as the national medium of communication and told writers that they should not hesitate to use colloquial words and expressions. "In the history of change in speech and writing," he asserted, "generally the common people are the reformers and the scholars and the writers the conservatives." His target was the literary style associated with the imperial examination system, the old preserve of the scholar-officials, whose mode of speech *(kuanhua)*, had served as the lingua franca of administration. On his return to China in 1917 Hu Shi was appointed professor of philosophy and chairman of the English department at Beijing University, where together with like-minded teachers he strove to advance the vernacular, despite accusations by offended colleagues that the reformers used the "cant of street vendors and rickshaw pullers". Hu Shi countered with the argument that the general trend of Chinese literature had been its periodic appropriation of sub-literary forms of popular entertainment: folk song, drama and fiction. For this reason he recommended as subjects for the new writer "factory workers of both sexes, rickshaw pullers, inland farmers . . . domestic tragedies, marital sorrows, the position of women, the unsuitability of educational practices". Official resistance was overcome by the patriotic agitation of the May Fourth Movement, and in 1920 by government decree *baihua* was introduced into elementary schools.

Two characters out of Lu Xun's amazing gallery of figures are sufficient to bring the collapse of the old order into focus. The first is the displaced student Kong Yuji, literally "Confucius himself". Educated without success for the abolished imperial examinations, Kong Yuji is reduced to begging and stealing in order to satisfy his craving for wine. The narrator of the story notices only the emaciated student when he hears him remark to a waiter that "the lower part of the character used for a certain dish can be written in four different ways". The narrowness of his literary studies had set Kong Yuji's mind in such a way that he could never forget the complexities of etymology and switch his attention to the new learning. Too proud to turn to commerce and too weak for physical labour, this pathetic victim of an outmoded system of education simply faded away on the edges of the republic, just as the imperial examinations themselves ceased to have any relevance in the modern world. Equally tragic, although more humorous, is Ah Q, a bone-headed odd-job man who envies his social superiors and emulates their worst behaviour. His insignificance makes swanking difficult: as the village butt, he cannot find a victim to bully himself and he retreats into a make-believe world of "moral victories" *(jingshen sengli)*. The epitome of the ineffectiveness of China and the well-to-do people running the republic, Ah Q's progress of self-deception and deceit appealed to many readers in 1923, the year Lu Xun attained recognition through the publication of this tale. The supreme irony is the execution of Ah Q, failed bandit and revolutionary, by means of an imported machine-gun.

With the various warlords fighting among themselves and seizing each other's territories, Dr Sun Yatsen made an attempt in 1921 to found an independent government in Guangdong province. But the European powers steadfastly refused any financial or diplomatic support, and a serious outbreak of fighting in the ensuing year compelled him to hurriedly quit Guangzhou for Shanghai. Thoroughly disillusioned with the colonial policies of the West, Dr Sun Yatsen came to the view "that the one real and genuine friend of the Chinese Revolution is Soviet Russia". In Shanghai he met a senior Russian emissary, Adolph Joffe, who explained that Soviet policy towards China was based on the abrogation of the treaties which the tsarist government had imposed on the tottering Qing dynasty. This admission of past unfairness so impressed Dr Sun Yatsen that he began to wonder if Western democracy could ever be a solution to China's problems, when countries such as Britain and France were only too willing to exploit internal weaknesses. As a result of this contact, members of the Chinese Communist Party were allowed to join the Guomindang as "individuals" and plans were laid for a new revolution to crush the warlords and reunite the country as a socialist state.

The government and the army were to be left in the hands of the Guomindang, while the Communists concentrated on propaganda and mass organisation. To increase the military efficiency of the revolutionary forces, Jiang Jieshi was sent to the Soviet Union for training and on his return he became the first commandant of Huangpu Military Academy, near Guangzhou. Previously trained in modern techniques in Japan, the course of advance studies with the Red Army enabled Jiang Jieshi to train a generation of famous generals—Guomindang and Communist. His appointment also gave him a chance to build up a personal following within the Guomindang, so that after the death of Dr Sun Yatsen in 1925 he assumed the leadership of the Northern Expedition against the warlords.

At Huangpu the relations between the Communist advisers and the Guomindang military experts were generally amicable. The diplomatic skills of Zhou Enlai may have contributed to this unity of purpose, since in 1924 he was recalled from Europe and appointed as its political director. At the same time for the Chinese Communist Party he was given the task of overseeing political activities in Guangdong and Guangxi provinces. Events were nonetheless moving in a direction favourable to revolution. On 30 May 1925, two months after Dr Sun Yatsen's death, a crowd of students was fired upon with some fatal casualties by a police detachment belonging to the International Settlement in Shanghai. They had taken to the streets in protest at brutalities already perpetrated on striking workers in a Japanese-owned mill. That these young people could be shot down without any redress aroused indignation at the freedom of action foreign residents claimed in China under treaties signed by the Qing emperors. Extra-territoriality became the focus of widespread agitation and early in 1926 Jiang Jieshi judged that the moment for moving against the compliant military had come. Resistance in the southern provinces was slight, as warlords found their armies melted away before the heat of revolutionary ardour. By the summer Jiang Jieshi had reached the Yangzi river and the great cities of Wuhan, Nanjing and Shanghai were all occupied, but the victorious march northwards brought the Communists and Guomindang into open conflict, as the landlords and businessmen backing Jiang Jieshi were terrified by the bitter social conflict being stirred up by Mao Zedong in the countryside and Zhou Enlai in the towns.

On 26 March 1927 Guomindang troops were ordered to cooperate with the underworld toughs in attacking the rebellious Shanghai workers, although a general strike held firm for nearly three weeks. Then on 12 April a concerted assault was launched on trade union offices by gangsters, who had been secretly assembled in the International Settlement and the French Concession. Most of the leaders perished in resistance or were instantly shot when taken prisoner. By a quirk of fate Zhou Enlai escaped the massacre, which in subsequent days engulfed thousands of activists. Henceforth the Chinese Communist Party and the Guomindang were bitter enemies, despite the Japanese invasion of China which produced in the late 1930s a second united front.

GUOMINDANG RULE (1928–37)

In 1928 Guomindang forces entered Beijing. Although the Japanese tried to obstruct the final stage of the Northern Expedition, Jiang Jieshi's army bypassed Japanese units in Shandong province, following the route of the Hankou/Beijing railway, and easily drove out of the city the army of the Manchurian warlord Zhang Zoulin. His assassination by the Japanese, who blew up the armoured train in which he fled, may not have been so opportune for the Guomindang as at first appeared. Eight years later it was his son, Zhang Xueliang, commander of the anti-Communist expedition in Shaanxi province, who devised the Xi'an Incident, when at the point of a gun Jiang Jieshi agreed to a truce with the Communists and the formation of a united front against Japan. The "Young Marshal" Zhang Xueliang was assisted in this conspiracy by another Guomindang general, Yang Hucheng. Later Zhou Enlai, the Communist negotiator at Xi'an in 1936,

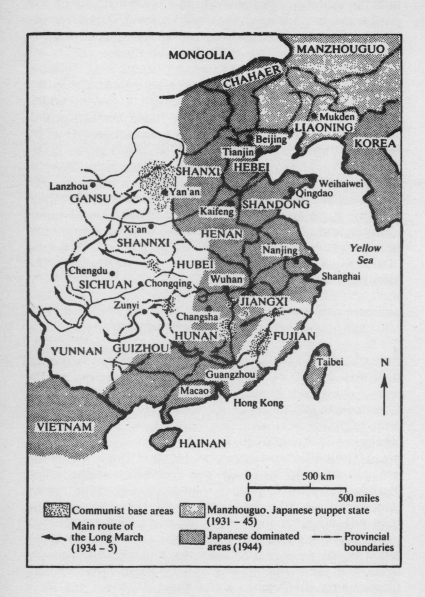

Fig 87 China (1934–45)

unofficially adopted Yang Hucheng's son after Jiang Jieshi had the general executed during the final days of his power on the Chinese mainland. Zhang Xueliang remained in prison on Taiwan until 1962. The kindness shown by Zhou Enlai after the Communist victory in 1949 was unknown in top Guomindang circles, where a legacy of warlord rivalry still lingers on today. For Jiang Jieshi's success in 1928 had depended on the eventual support of two other powerful military commanders. From Shaanxi province the forces of Yan Xishan (1883–1960) had also converged on Beijing, while from further west aid was sent by Feng Yuxiang (1882–1948), the so-called "Christian General".

Feng Yuxiang was strongly anti-Communist and had supported Jiang Jieshi's campaign in 1927 against the Chinese Communist Party. His support then, and in the final push to Beijing, earned him the post of vice-president in the Guomindang administration, which Jiang Jieshi established at Nanjing. This did not prevent Feng Yuxiang from retaining his own political and military base in the northern and northwestern provinces, from which he even launched attacks on Guomindang forces in 1929 and 1930. No less independent was Yan Xishan, whose progressive outlook allowed some industrialisation to occur in Shanxi province. His methods of social control, including the study of his own thoughts, were partly inspired by the Communists and partly anticipated them. An uneasy balance of power between Jiang Jieshi, Feng Yuxiang, Yan Xishan and Zhang Xueliang (who took over the Beijing area) typified Guomindang rule. Not only were the northern generals concerned to free themselves from Jiang Jieshi's ever-growing influence and to assert greater independence, but other military adventurers tried also to take advantage of their intrigues, even in the southern provinces. Jiang Jieshi outwitted them all, with the assistance of the Shanghai financiers who raised his foreign loans, but there was no peace: from the early 1930s the Communists emerged as a real threat in the south, and after 1928 the Japanese tightened their grip on large parts of north China. In 1931 the latter were able to take over the whole of Manchuria and rename it Manzhougou, "the Manchu homeland".

By the capture of Beijing in 1928 Jiang Jieshi had obliged the European powers to acknowledge Guomindang rule, notwithstanding initial fears that he might still be inclined to Communism. The attitude of the British was not extraordinary. On the one hand they accepted the international status of the Chinese Republic; on the other, there existed a strong desire to treat China as an unorganised or dependent territory. Thinking clung stubbornly to the gunboat policies of Lord Palmerston. The Treaty of Tianjin (1858) had guaranteed treaty powers the right for their warships to visit inland ports and the Admiralty took full advantage of the possibility of stationing vessels along the navigable length of the Yangzi river. The last gunboat in the Yangzi River Flotilla, HMS *Sandpiper*, was launched as late as 1933. If a British firm had labour troubles or passport holders were in jeopardy, a gunboat would be sent to the locality as a precautionary measure. To overawe the Chinese it was customary for ships of the Royal Navy to salute each other with seventeen- or twenty-one gun salutes. A commander-in-chief once boasted to the Shanghai Chamber of Commerce that the officers and men in the Yangzi River Flotilla exceeded the total number of fellow countrymen employed in trade pursuits on that waterway. In September 1927 some of these sailors took part in a bombardment which left between 50 and 2000 Chinese dead at a settlement near Wuhan. Britain's ambivalence about the republic was adroitly used by Japan to lend a degree of respectability to its own aggression.

Whilst Jiang Jieshi was ready to press the European nations on the vexed issue of extra-territoriality, which the Foreign Office in London thought it advisable to concede, he avoided offering direct resistance to the increasing Japanese threat. Instead, he concentrated on "extermination drives" against the Chinese Communist Party, which after a number of abortive urban risings in the late 1920s had moved its operations into the countryside. Although urban movements in Guangdong and Hunan provinces had been ruthlessly crushed in 1927, another series of expensive failures were necessary in 1930 before different tactics could be officially adopted. Already in 1928 Mao Zedong and Zhu De (1886–1976) had withdrawn to the hinterland in order to secure an effective base on the Hunan/Jiangxi provincial borders. There Mao Zedong came to the conclusion that the impoverished peasantry would be able to wage protracted war from revolutionary bases situated in remote areas, not least because it was at places where the control of the Guomindang was weakest that the spark of revolution could be lit. His own optimism was expressed in the famous phrase "A single spark can start a prairie fire".

More than any other Communist leader Mao Zedong saw that China's plight was unique. The country differed from outright colonies in that it was controlled by several foreign powers and not just one alone, a situation which was extremely painful and humiliating, but which offered plenty of scope for successful revolutionary activity because the imperialists could never adopt a common approach. He wrote in 1930 to Lin Biao (1907–71):

Imperialism . . . needs more urgently than ever to struggle in China. As this struggle becomes more intense the contradictions between imperialism and China as a whole, and among the imperialists themselves, develop within China's boundaries at the same time; consequently there arises in China's ruling classes chaotic wars that spread and intensify with every passing day, while the contradictions among them grow.

Thus the lack of a strong central authority and the concentration of imperialist influence in the cities made the rural hinterland a promising area for revolution. Unauthorised by Comintern, the rural "soviets" of Mao Zedong were condemned by the Central Committee of the Chinese Communist Party in Shanghai as "rightist", especially as by implication they appeared to regard industrial workers, the sacred proletariat, as auxiliaries of the peasants.

The disastrous uprisings of 1930, ordered by Comintern, finally persuaded Mao Zedong that the only strategy was "encircling the cities with the countryside". He was now convinced that the city remained the instrument of governmental control, as it had traditionally been from the reign of the First Emperor onwards. Looking back on these difficult years in 1939, Mao Zedong said "the ruthless economic exploitation and political oppression of the peasants by the landlord class forced them into numerous rebellions against its rule . . . It was the class struggle of the peasants, the peasant uprisings and the peasant wars that constituted the real motive force of historical development in Chinese feudal society". What the Chinese Communist Party had to do was lead the peasant masses in their historic mission: the democratic forces of the countryside would rise to overthrow the bureaucratic feudalism supported by the cities, be it imperial or republican.

Against the ideology of the Communists there was little Jiang Jieshi could convincingly deploy, except the argument that the unreadiness of the Chinese people for democracy forced the Guomindang to rule on their behalf. Because a fully democratic system had to be regarded as a long-range goal, it was said that a period of dictatorship represented the only feasible form of government. Jiang Jieshi himself showed little sympathy for democratic ideals and naturally inclined towards an authoritarian approach. He once remarked: "I believe that unless everyone has absolute trust in one man, we cannot reconstruct the nation and we cannot complete the revolution." To many foreign observers the Generalissimo, as Jiang Jieshi was styled, seemed a stronger and more consistent Yuan Shikai; he ended the chaotic conditions of the warlord era, a return to which business interests argued would bring irrevocable ruin to trade and endanger the substantial investments already made in the Chinese economy. They chose to overlook the uglier aspects of Guomindang rule. Scant notice was taken of the political terrorism of the Blue Shirt Society, a parallel of the

Italian Black Shirts and the German Brown Shirts, while the spoils of office, the vast fortunes amassed by senior members of the Guomindang, went almost unremarked, even though it was known that Jiang Jieshi personally used the craft of the Opium Suppression Superintendence Bureau to traffic in the drug. In a moment of candour the Generalissimo admitted in 1930 that "not only is it impossible to find a single party headquarters which administers to and works for the welfare of the people, but all are stigmatised by the most reprehensible practices, such as corruption, bribery, and scrabbling for power".

The admission indicated how cut off the Guomindang was from the mass of the population. Following the 1927 split with the Chinese Communist Party and the subsequent suspicion of any remaining Guomindang members who wished to organise the people and improve their lot, this gap is hardly surprising, although it was made more dangerous politically by the lack of discrimination shown in recruitment to top appointments. Jiang Jieshi was obliged to take note of the preferences of powerful military commanders and compromise over many provincial appointments, but he compounded his difficulties by failing to instil a sense of public duty in these new administrators and to supervise closely their activities once they were in post. The result was an extensive military bureaucracy that was devoted to its own enrichment.

A fundamental weakness of the Guomindang was an uninspiring ideology. The three principles of Dr Sun Yatsen—nationalism, democracy and socialism—never became a clarion call for the Generalissimo's followers. Jiang Jieshi embraced Christianity in 1927, yet his regime was not Christian: he admired the nineteenth-century loyalist Zeng Guofan and quoted the precepts of Confucius, though he repudiated the imperial system. Once Jiang Jieshi had become supreme, he expected complete loyalty from his subordinates and unquestioning obedience from the Chinese people. To what end he led the country, to what kind of future, few could be certain. Worst still, blind nationalism seemed bankrupt when in

practice it meant appeasement of the Japanese. Internecine conflict, first with the warlords, then with the Communists, consumed the strength of the republic and
depleted its scarce resources: of the total government
expenditure in 1929 nearly 50 per cent was spent on war.
Jiang Jieshi, the well-to-do farmer's son, outdid all his
military contemporaries in the most turbulent period of
late Chinese civilisation.

A large proportion of this military expenditure went on
the five offensives Jiang Jieshi launched against the Communist base areas in the southern provinces of Hubei,
Hunan, Jiangxi and Fujian, before Mao Zedong and his
rural revolutionaries in 1934 had to break out on their
famous Long March. The first two, in 1930 and early
1931, employing 300,000 troops, 200 heavy guns and 100
aeroplanes, were repulsed by a guerrilla strategy then
being developed by Mao Zedong, Zhu De and Lin Biao.
The third encirclement, directed by the Generalissimo
himself, was interrupted by the Mukden Incident in September 1931, when Japan took advantage of alleged disturbances to seize Manchuria and install the ex-Qing
emperor, Puyi, as puppet ruler of a new state called
Manzhouguo. The actual cause of Japanese intervention
was Zhang Xueliang, who in 1930 occupied Beijing in the
Guomindang interest, suppressing a revolt against Nanjing
by local military commanders. This action was displeasing
to the Japanese, who wished to check the growth of Jiang
Jieshi's authority, which was then spreading over the
whole country. There can be no doubt that the Japanese
forces stationed in Manchuria had decided that Zhang
Xueliang was a threat to their ambitions and must be
driven south of the Great Wall.

Pretending that the Chinese had tried to blow up a
railway line south of the city of Mukden, Japanese units
took control of all the five provinces of Manchuria, including the northern ones bordering on Russian Siberia.
The railway was Japanese, taken from the Russians in
1905. But we are now aware that this "incident", like the
alleged clash in 1937 at the Marco Polo bridge south of
Beijing, was devised by the Japanese army as a pretext

for further expansion. The 1930 naval conference in London, which aimed at the limitation of navies, had worried the military faction in Tokyo, not least because the throne took civilian advice and accepted its recommendations. As a result, they decided to initiate a series of extra-legal military adventures in China which culminated in the entry of Japan into the Second World War.

The Japanese government neither received detailed information about military intentions nor actions; after a significant number of civilian members of the government were assassinated by "patriots" in the mid-1930s there was no question that the Japanese army had taken over. The military, heirs to the warrior ethic of the samurai, came to dominate political life in Japan and look upon China as a field for unrestricted activity. Occupation of Manchuria led Japan to withdraw from the League of Nations in 1933 and enter the Anti-Comintern pact with Germany and Italy three years later. Although the unexpected Nazi–Soviet agreement in 1939 temporarily stunned Japanese public opinion, Hitler's sweeping victories in Europe led in September 1940 to a strengthening of ties between Germany, Italy and Japan. The take-over of Manchuria had also given the Japanese a border with Russia, and even led in 1939 to a severe reverse over a frontier dispute at Nomonhan, but almost until the close of the Second World War Tokyo and Moscow remained in a state of strained neutrality.

Jiang Jieshi was unable to turn a blind eye to Japanese expansion forever. Violent agitation compelled him to offer resistance in Shanghai. Responding to a boycott of Japanese goods, in January 1932, Tokyo had sent into the city via the International Settlement an expeditionary force of 4000 marines. When these soldiers tried to drive Chinese guards away from the border of the concession, they faced a sustained counter-attack. To the general amazement of China and the world, the Guomindang forces stationed in Shanghai were still fighting the invaders a month later, by which time the Japanese had committed 30,000 men. After thirty-four days of indiscriminate bombing and atrocity, Japan obliged Jiang Jieshi to accede to a humiliating peace—he had to agree to stop the anti-Japanese protest that had by then become nationwide.

"The history of modern China", Mao Zedong acutely remarked years afterwards, "is the history of imperialist aggression." The continued siege of the country had been the historical prerequisite for revolutionary change. But in the early 1930s Mao Zedong's advocacy of the opportunities which foreign aggression gave to revolutionary movements in the countryside was by no means accepted as correct by the Chinese Communist Party. It would be rash to assume that all the southern base areas were then under his control. Each rural soviet enjoyed a high degree of autonomy and there was little co-ordination between them, even in the worst days of the encirclements. To many of their inhabitants they were rather temporary refugees from Guomindang repression than the active centres of revolution envisaged by Mao Zedong. Although the remarkable victories Zhu De and Lin Biao achieved over the besieging Guomindang forces in the first two encirclements led to a growing confidence, the Jiangxi base area where Mao Zedong resided could have fallen in 1931 had not the Mukden Incident diverted Jiang Jieshi's attention first to Manchuria, then Shanghai. It was not until the Long March was underway that Mao Zedong became in 1935 chairman of the Chinese Communist Party at the Zunyi conference in Guizhou province, and his ideas concerning rural revolution were subsequently adopted as the basis of victory against both the Japanese and the Guomindang.

Mao Zedong's disregard of Comintern pressure to abandon guerrilla warfare and openly defend the borders of the base areas was not simply a matter of military caution. He gained nothing from major battles which ended with Guomindang forces retreating in defeat. He depended on capturing guns and ammunition to keep his own soldiers supplied, and additionally the large number of prisoners who elected to enlist in the Communist ranks was always a bonus. Some 3000 Guomindang captives had changed sides after the repulse of the first encirclement alone. Their defection was a sign that the reluctance of

Jiang Jieshi to resist Japanese encroachment was already
having a serious effect on the morale of Guomindang
units. They would have also contrasted the lack of compassion in the orders they had received with the code of
behaviour expected from Communist soldiers. First laid
down in 1928 by Mao Zedong, the military code insisted
on a sense of responsibility previously unknown among
Chinese armies. As re-issued to the People's Liberation
Army in 1947 it read:

The three main rules:
1 Obey orders in all your actions.
2 Don't take a single needle or a piece of thread from
   the people.
3 Turn in everything captured.

The eight points:
1 Speak politely.
2 Pay fairly for what you buy.
3 Return everything you borrow.
4 Pay for anything you damage.
5 Don't hit or swear at people.
6 Don't damage crops.
7 Don't take liberties with women.
8 Don't ill-treat captives.

That the peasant-farmers would appreciate such behaviour
was so obvious a fact as to be entirely ignored by
Guomindang commanders, who allowed their troops to
forage mercilessly. "Our principle", Mao Zedong said,
"is that the Party commands the gun and the gun must
never command the Party."

Peasant resistance to the Japanese invaders after the
start of the Sino-Japanese hostilities in 1937 arose from a
similar indifference to suffering. Certain senior Japanese
officers in China seemed to have realised the disastrous
effects of bad discipline: documents captured in Hubei
province in 1939 contain a report of a speech made by a
general to his officers. This divisional commander said
that, unless the Imperial Japanese Army could improve

its behaviour towards the civilian population, defeat would be inevitable. No improvement occurred throughout the long struggle in China, not least because the dreaded Kempetai, a Japanese equivalent of the Gestapo, was sufficiently powerful to engage in racketeering without check. Looting, rape and indiscriminate killing was the lot of provinces overrun by Japanese troops. One part of Shaanxi province which changed hands between Japanese, Guomindang and Communists coined the saying, "Japanese, too many deaths; Guomindang, too many taxes; Communists, too many meetings."

Notwithstanding this expression of fatigue over political education, there is no doubt that the Communist experience in the countryside was a pleasant surprise for many peasants. Again the moderating influence of Mao Zedong was evident in the method used to redistribute land. He argued that there should be as little disruption as possible. Existing arrangements were to be adapted by trimming the larger holdings rather than any wholesale reallocation of land, lest agricultural output suffer in the process. Not only was this approach more realistic than the anti-rich peasant line then being pushed by Comintern, as a consequence of Stalin's drive against the kulaks in the Soviet Union, but even more it was based on a profound understanding of the outlook of the Chinese peasant. Mao Zedong knew how attached a family could become to its plot of land, a sentiment almost as strong as the one binding it to the ancestral tombs. Whilst other would-be Communist leaders went to study abroad, he had chosen to remain at home and analyse contemporary conditions. In July 1936 he told Edgar Snow, the first Westerner to receive an interview: "I felt that I did not know enough about my own country, and that my time could be more profitably spent in China."

The wisdom of Mao Zedong's position on land reform was unrecognised at the time. Nor was his advice heeded in the military sphere after the fourth Guomindang encirclement in 1933 was frustrated by conventional battles. It was held that a prolonged rural struggle was unnecessary when positional warfare offered an immediate chance of victory. What Mao Zedong so clearly understood was the cost of such a strategy, for once Jiang Jieshi received intelligence of this tactical change he ordered a massive concentration of forces to meet the challenge. In order to ensure that the engagement would be decisive, and settle once and for all the rivalry between the Guomindang and the Communists, the Generalissimo constructed forts and blockade lines so as to deny the base areas supplies and prevent a break-out. As a result, the fifth encirclement so entrapped the Communists that at the end of 1934 total defeat stared them in the face.

Breaking out of the closing trap was the only resort. On 16 October 1934 the Long March began, an epic of human endurance. In 370 days the Communists covered 8000 kilometres; of the 100,000 men who fought their way through the encircling Guomindang lines only 20,000 survived the march. It was force of circumstances rather than deliberate planning that made the journey so long. Withdrawal to the north-east corner of Guizhou province was the first objective, a move covered through a rearguard action mounted by scattered guerrilla bands, largely comprising men unable to travel a great distance because of wounds. But continued harassment from Guomindang forces soon made it plain that the Communists needed an overall plan. This was devised at the Zunyi conference in January 1935, when Mao Zedong was acknowledged as the leader of the Chinese Communist Party. Taking up his slogan "Go north and fight the Japanese", the conference agreed that they should head northwards to Yan'an, the only remaining base area in the north of Shaanxi province. It was no accident that Mao Zedong emerged from political eclipse at the very moment the Japanese army began to advance again. The possibility that Jiang Jieshi might reach a general settlement with Japan was a daunting prospect for the Communists, against whom joint action by the Imperial Japanese Army and Guomindang forces had been suggested by Tokyo. When the Generalissimo indicated no great reluctance over extending diplomatic recognition to Manzhouguo or granting "autonomy" to Hebei and Chahaer provinces, the

Chinese Communist Party became very alarmed and embraced Mao Zedong's nationalist approach. Although Jiang Jieshi's friendliness towards Berlin and Rome may have been intended as a counterbalance to Tokyo, the motives of the Italians were just as predatory as the Japanese. The only major European power to have missed gaining a territorial stake in China, Mussolini's Italy financed aerodromes in the provinces of Jiangxi and Fujian as footholds in any future dismemberment of the country.

Summing up the Long March from the comparative safety of the Yan'an soviet, Mao Zedong commented:

> We say the Long March is the first of its kind ever recorded in history, that it is a manifesto, an agitation corps, and a seeding-machine . . . For twelve months we were under daily reconnaissance and bombing from the air by scores of planes; we were encircled, pursued, obstructed and intercepted on the ground by a big force of several hundred thousand men; we encountered untold difficulties and great obstacles on the way, but by keeping our two feet going we swept across a distance of more than 20,000 *li* through the length and breadth of eleven provinces. Well, has there been in history a long march like ours? No, never. The Long March is also a manifesto. It proclaims to the world that the Red Army is an army of heroes and that the imperialists and their jackals, Jiang Jieshi and his like, are perfect nonentities. It announces the bankruptcy of encirclement, pursuit, obstruction and interception attempted by the imperialists and Jiang Jieshi. The Long March is also an agitation corps. It declares to approximately two hundred million people of eleven provinces that only the road of the Red Army leads to their liberation. Without the Long March, how could the broad masses have known so quickly that there are such great ideas in the world as are upheld by the Red Army? The Long March is also a seeding-machine. It has sown many seeds in eleven provinces, which will sprout, grow leaves,

blossom into flowers, bear fruit and yield a crop in future. To conclude, the Long March ended with our victory and the enemy's defeat.

The Generalissimo could never accept such a verdict, and Guomindang forces were therefore moved in 1936 against the Yan'an base area. In the cities of Xi'an and Lanzhou arrangements were made to accommodate over 100 bombers. As the bombs were stockpiled ready for operation, rumour spread that the majority contained poison gas. This campaign, Jiang Jieshi asserted, would be the final encirclement.

The expeditionary commander was less sure. While Zhang Xueliang disliked the trend of Guomindang policies, his Manchurian troops could hardly be expected to welcome a fierce guerrilla campaign when Japanese soldiers were freely looting and raping their native provinces. What neither the commander nor his men could understand was the Generalissimo's readiness to oblige Japan in suppressing outbursts of nationalist feeling. When Zhang Xueliang was unable to secure the release of prominent civilians arrested by the Guomindang police for their anti-Japanese views, he told Jiang Jieshi that his "cruelty in dealing with the patriotic movement of the people is exactly the same as that of Yuan Shikai". But the Generalissimo gravely underestimated the strength of feeling amongst all ranks of the northern armies and arrived at operational headquarters in Xi'an to expedite the war. On 12 December 1936 Jiang Jieshi found himself the prisoner of Zhang Xueliang and Yang Hucheng, commander of the Shaanxi army. Two events had tipped the scales towards mutiny. The first was the signing of the Anti-Comintern pact between Germany, Italy and Japan, which led Mussolini to establish diplomatic relations with Manzhouguo. Infuriated by Guomindang nonchalance towards this move, Zhang Xueliang told his officers: "This is absolutely the end of the Fascist movement in China!" Secondly, the offensives launched by both Zhang Xueliang and Yang Hucheng during the early summer had been decisively repulsed by the defenders of the Yan'an base area. Many prisoners fell into Communist hands and were converted to the idea of a second united front against Japan before being released. For homesick Manchurians the appeal of a slogan as "Fight back to Manchuria" was very potent indeed. They had been serving in exile since the Japanese take-over of 1931, following the Mukden Incident.

Zhou Enlai had already proposed the cessation of hostilities and by October Manchurian units were no longer engaged in the field. Other Guomindang forces made desultory attacks on Communist positions, but it was no secret in Xi'an that the favoured line was resistance to further Japanese encroachment. Into all this, Jiang Jieshi flew. At gun point he was forced to conclude a truce with the Chinese Communist Party, which was represented at the negotiations by Zhou Enlai. Then an agreement was signed by which the Communists acknowledged the Nanjing government, but were allowed to establish their own autonomous regime in Yan'an. Both parties pledged themselves to resist Japan.

THE SINO-JAPANESE WAR (1937–45)

The pledge was soon to be honoured. In July 1937 the Imperial Japanese Army, after provoking a minor incident near Beijing, seized that city and then attacked Shanghai as well. The fighting this time could not be restricted to a few places, but soon developed into a full-scale Japanese invasion of China.

For the Chinese Communist Party the start of hostilities came as more than a welcome relief. It was agreed that Guomindang armies would meet the invaders in positional warfare, while Communist forces infiltrated behind the Japanese lines, waging a guerrilla campaign and organising local resistance. Communist regiments dissolved into battalions and companies, and trickled into the unpacified countryside: by the beginning of 1938 they were operating on the shores of the Yellow Sea, nearly 1000 kilometres from Yan'an. Revolutionary activity was

thus able to spread over large areas of north China,
especially after Jiang Jieshi was forced to withdraw into
Sichuan province and establish a wartime capital at
Chongqing in late 1938. The growth in national self-
awareness, rudely stimulated as it was by Japanese atrocity, can be judged in the increased numbers joining
Communist units. This upsurge raised the regular forces
under Mao Zedong's command from about 90,000 in 1937
to 880,000 in 1945; militia strength on the Japanese surrender is estimated to have topped 2 million. More telling perhaps are the statistics showing the political control
of the Chinese Communist Party, since from the original
1.5 million inhabitants of Yan'an the total number of
people living in Communist dominated areas rose to well
over 90 million.

As Mao Zedong predicted to Edgar Snow in 1936 the
defeat of Japan would mean "that the Chinese masses
have awakened, have mobilised, and have established
their independence". That the great welling up of national consciousness involved in this victory took on a
revolutionary vigour is a tribute to Mao Zedong's vision
of the Sino-Japanese conflict as part of a larger struggle
against Fascism. His revolutionary optimism remained
unshaken throughout the Second World War. He wrote
during his stay in Yan'an that the war would "decide the
fate of mankind" (1941), "produce a more progressive
world and a more progressive China" (1943), and change
"the consciousness of the whole world" (1945). Perhaps
his tendency always to take a broad view, coupled with
an unrivalled knowledge of conditions in China, gave
Mao Zedong this assurance in stark contrast to the low
morale of the Guomindang. Certainly it allowed him to
perceive that all the forces of change in the country
which had been gaining strength under the republic were
becoming what Edgar Snow termed a "rip tide".

Japanese army leaders may have believed in 1937 that
Jiang Jieshi would not really resist; that north China at
least would be yielded to them, and that a settlement
could be enforced which left the Nanjing government as
defenceless client state. They do not seem to have ex-

pected a widespread campaign arising immediately from the exchange of shots in July at the Marco Polo bridge. Although Chinese resistance ended in the defeat of the Guomindang armies, the Japanese Imperial Army in China had insufficient men to engage in the conventional battles necessary to dispose of these regular forces as well as deal with the partisan activities of Communist irregulars behind their lines. By the time the Japanese were ready to turn their attention to the countryside of north China it was too late: in October 1938 they found that it had been organised against them and the irregular units supported by the peasant-farmers were a serious foe. The Communists had been able to provide a body of men with long experience of guerrilla warfare against an enemy with superior weapons and to offer the advantages of a co-ordinated strategy. In the united front groups (*lianhe zhenxianzu*) that were set up in order to administer the countryside they also facilitated unity by not pressing for radical land reform but accepting the principles of Dr Sun Yatsen, which fixed rents at a reasonable level and gave the tenant a degree of security without denying the landlord's ownership.

From a distance the initial phase of the Sino-Japanese war looked to many observers an overwhelming Japanese victory. Jiang Jieshi's crack troops were decimated in a brave, though militarily futile, defence of Shanghai from August till November 1937. With a war imminent in Europe, the British tolerated the Japanese violation of their treaty rights in the city and even maintained a stiff upper lip when the the British ambassador's car was machine-gunned from the air. Nanjing itself fell in December, and for several weeks suffered an orgy of atrocities. But the Japanese did not have everything their own way, for in Shandong province the invaders sustained a heavy reverse before overcoming resistance in January 1938. Progress southwards was also slowed by the "scorched earth" tactics of retreating Guomindang commanders, who took the appalling step of breaching the Yellow river dykes. This inundated several provinces, killing millions of peasants and rendering great stretches of land impassable. To avoid capture Jiang Jieshi had already transferred his capital to Wuhan, on the middle course of the Yangzi river, but this had to be abandoned in October 1938 when the Japanese struck inland. In remote Chongqing the Generalissimo finally settled down with the shattered remnants of his forces.

The Guomindang were soon effectively cut off from the outside world. By means of a number of landings the Japanese took control of the whole coast of China and fought their way along railways until they had secured the major towns and cities. Jiang Jieshi had the support only of the agriculturally rich province of Sichuan, and of the scarcely developed provinces around it. Strenuous measures had been made to move factories westwards, but their capacity when back in production was inadequate for a defensive war against industrial Japan. Even the Burma Road could not meet his needs, although Tokyo was alarmed enough by this supply route to compel Britain to close it temporarily in the autumn of 1940. The fall of France and the evacuation of the British Expeditionary Force from Dunkirk persuaded the Japanese to make demands, especially as they believed that Britain and the United States were primarily responsible for the maintenance of Chinese resistance. Winston Churchill did not like bowing to this pressure at all, and was relieved to be able to tell the Americans that the closure would coincide with the three months of the rainy season, a period during which traffic largely stopped anyway. Vichy France, on the other hand, readily agreed to the passage of Japanese troops through Indo-China and the use of airfields north of Hanoi.

By 1940–1, the Sino-Japanese war had become an endurance test in which the Japanese were trying to deny China outside support and the Chinese were hoping to exhaust the invaders in the field and indirectly to ruin Japan's economy. How critical the economic factor became in 1941 is evident in the December attack on Pearl Harbor, which brought both Japan and the United States into the Second World War. This surprise assault on the United States Pacific fleet was the last step in the military opportunism that had begun a decade earlier in Mukden. That it involved the United States was inevitable because an Open Door policy meant, in reality, continued aid for the Guomindang government in Sichuan province. Especially frustrating for Japan was the American reaction to the take-over of French Indo-China in July 1941, a trade embargo which endangered its oil supplies. Since Japanese oil stocks were estimated to be inadequate for the three years that were reckoned as necessary to complete the conquest of China, the oilfields of the Dutch East Indies seemed a tempting prize, along with the rubber plantations and tin mines of Malaya—too tempting for the Japanese war party which was increasingly baffled by the refusal of the Chinese to submit. So the Pearl Harbor attack was intended to weaken American power in the Pacific and allow Japanese forces an uninterrupted sweep through East Asia.

On paper the strategy of the Imperial Japanese Army in China was perfect. Japanese troops controlled the entire coast and all the centres of industry; they occupied the richest provinces of the country, with the exception of Sichuan, and although the countryside was lightly held, there seemed to be only guerrilla forces to oppose their will. Jiang Jieshi had ceased active operations and was content to remain in his mountainous stronghold at Chongqing. With the cities and communications firmly under control, Japanese military leaders felt that they could wait until a paralysis of the Chinese economy resulted in surrender. What they overlooked were the changes that were taking place behind the scenes.

The Chinese Communist Party was becoming a powerful influence, especially after clashes between Guomindang and Communist guerrilla detachments in Shandong, Hubei and Shaanxi provinces led in early 1940 to the establishment of its supremacy over all the occupied areas in north China. Mao Zedong even tried to extend his growing authority by slipping Communist units across the Yangzi river. When in 1941 Jiang Jieshi reacted forcibly to this intrusion into the southern provinces, the last vestiges of the unity of purpose forged at Xi'an five years before disappeared. The message to the Chinese people was clear: they had to choose between Mao Zedong and Jiang Jieshi, between an active opponent of Japan and a survivor from the warlord era. The contrast was made all the more clear by the defection of Guomindang soldiers to the Japanese side and their employment against Communist guerrillas. The suspicion that Jiang Jieshi was merely awaiting the outcome of the war, and hedging his bets by allowing some of his troops to change sides, was hard to deny.

Jiang Jieshi's reluctance to engage the Japanese in battle was obvious to his American supporters by the beginning of 1944. Vice-President Henry Wallace was sent to Chongqing to see what could be done to increase the Chinese war effort, but he had only to ask American advisers there to realise that the Generalissimo was saving his strength for a showdown with Mao Zedong. The best Guomindang troops, furnished with the latest American equipment, were deployed near the Yan'an base area. The same conclusion had already been reached by the Communists, who reconciled themselves to an armed struggle once Japan was defeated. Because of his warlord outlook, Jiang Jieshi was unable to see that building up a modern army was not enough to hold China. Idleness weakened the morale of Guomindang soldiers just as energetic resistance to the Japanese strengthened the resolve of Communist irregulars. As the latter received no outside supplies and had to survive on captured guns and ammunition, their successful actions indicated an iron will that was not likely to be bent by imported firepower. General Joseph Stilwell, chief American military adviser in China until 1944, said that the government at Chongqing was typified by "greed, corruption, favouritism, more taxes, a ruined currency, terrible waste of life, callous disregard of all the rights of men". This inability on the part of the Guomindang to reform itself and take the lead in a second united front made the triumph of Communism in China virtually unavoidable: at the very least it ensured that on the surrender of Japan in September 1945 the Chinese Communist Party alone could make a patriotic appeal.

THE TRIUMPH OF COMMUNISM (1946–49)

The shaky foundations of Jiang Jieshi's support were not apparent outside China. The Chinese Communist Party had waged an unknown campaign in the northern provinces, while the Generalissimo had been praised in Allied wartime propaganda as the determined opponent of the Japanese, bravely holding out in beleaguered Chongqing. American diplomats and military advisers could not be unaware of the ramshackle administration and army that Jiang Jieshi led, but the reports they sent back to Washington were not intended for general consumption, and anyway their criticisms would not have squared with accepted attitudes towards China in the United States.

Ever since the 1900 declaration of the Open Door policy, which according to American legend had saved the country from the clutches of European imperialism, the fortunes of China had a special place in the outlook of many citizens. Had not Dr Sun Yatsen been a follower of Western democratic traditions? Surely Jiang Jieshi was his legitimate successor, and not that Soviet puppet Mao Zedong. Such attitudes were reinforced by the effectiveness of Madame Jiang, whose American education allowed her to more than smooth the difficult relations between the Generalissimo and his impatient advisers. In 1939 she had penned for the New York-based *Liberty Magazine* this telling sentence: "Eighty per cent of Japan's war supplies come from America and 90 per cent of the aviation gasoline which was used by Japan in her ruthless bombing was American." In contrast Madame Jiang pointed out, the Soviet Union had already extended to China more credit for the purchase of materials than either Britain or the United States. The "China Lobby" was a powerful pressure group in Washington long before it was obvious that Guomindang forces were no match for Communist ones. Once this fact could not be disguised in the civil war of 1947–9, lobby members stepped up their pressure on the administration to succour Jiang Jieshi and prevent a "Red China". They were unable to accept the assurance of the Secretary of State

Dean Acheson that "the unfortunate but inescapable fact is that the ominous result of the civil war in China was beyond the control of the Government of the United States". Perhaps this inability to face reality is not so surprising when it is recalled that within six months of the foundation of the People's Republic on 1 October 1949, Senator Joseph McCarthy would announce to the world that he had a list of numerous Communists "known to the Secretary of State" who were still working and making policy in the State Department. A balanced assessment of Chinese politics was hard to find in Washington during the uncertain atmosphere which preceded McCarthy's witch-hunt.

Civil war could not be avoided as long as Jiang Jieshi thought that he would win. Initially he had expected American forces to land on the southern coast and move northwards against the Japanese. Behind the shield of the United States Army he would have been able to consolidate his own position, before striking at the Chinese Communist Party. It was, therefore, a bitter disappointment to him when the success of the campaigns in the Pacific caused the United States to alter its strategy from a landing on the Chinese mainland to a plan of island hopping until the Japanese islands themselves were reached. This change relegated Jiang Jieshi to the periphery of the war and made available to the Guomindang far less military supplies than he had anticipated. In the event, the dropping of atomic bombs on Hiroshima and Nagasaki in August 1945 caught everyone by surprise.

The war in East Asia was suddenly over, but the problems created by the Sino-Japanese conflict remained unsolved. The Guomindang were bottled up in the west of China, while the Communists controlled the northern provinces apart from the cities and towns with Japanese garrisons. To whom these soldiers should surrender proved an immediate point of dispute.

The reconciliation of Jiang Jieshi and Mao Zedong had been a policy of the United States since late 1944, when Patrick Hurley arrived from Washington with instructions to bring the Guomindang and the Communists into a coalition government. General Hurley even visited Yan'an in the November of that year—much to the annoyance of Jiang Jieshi—but this immaculately dressed soldier quickly decided that the interests of the United States were best served by preventing the collapse of the Guomindang. He may have deliberately suppressed the proposal of Mao Zedong and Zhou Enlai in January 1945 that they should go to the White House to discuss China's future. The message never got through, and the political isolation of Yan'an was thus confirmed. Had the American representative in Chongqing been more sympathetic to the Chinese Communist Party at this time, or had a landing of US troops led to active co-operation with Communist forces against the Imperial Japanese Army, then it is not impossible that Jiang Jieshi would have been prevented from acquiring so easily a monopoly of Western support.

The Chinese Communist Party openly admitted to Hurley its fears of a bloody civil war in China, once the Japanese surrendered. In the face of considerable criticism in Yan'an, Mao Zedong argued that there were good reasons for talking to US officials. Between the peoples of China and the United States, he maintained, there were "strong ties of sympathy, understanding and mutual interest. Both are essentially democratic and individualistic. Both are by nature peace-loving, non-aggressive and non-imperialistic". Such views caused Stalin to dub the Chinese Communist Party as "margarine Communists". He even told American visitors that they were "not as good" as Jiang Jieshi. This preference for the Guomindang was not unconnected with Stalin's presentiment that in power Mao Zedong would be difficult, if not impossible to deal with. The rural revolutionary had already exhibited more independence than Moscow could tolerate, whereas the Generalissimo at the head of a weak China offered greater scope for manipulation in the post-war world. For this reason the Soviet Union extended loans, on favourable terms compared with those advanced by Britain and the United States, to Chongqing and sent virtually no aid directly to Yan'an. Perhaps the remark Mao Zedong had made to Edgar Snow in 1936 still rankled with Stalin: the chairman of the Chinese Communist Party had said that "we are certainly not fighting for an emancipated China in order to turn the country over to Moscow!"

The pragmatism of Mao Zedong and Zhou Enlai in January 1945 was unusual even by the prevailing standards of war-time co-operation between Communist resistance movements and the Allies. That they were prepared to offend Russia by visiting the United States reveals how isolated the Yan'an base area really was. As far as is known face-to-face talks with Stalin were never considered. Apart from the ideological differences between Moscow and Yan'an, there was the memory of perennial conflict with China's northern neighbours to cool any enthusiasm for a close Soviet embrace. Although the Soviet Union had told Dr Sun Yatsen that the old tsarist treaties were open to renegotiation, the chaotic conditions of the early republic allowed the moment to pass and therefore a danger still existed of serious differences over the northern border in the future. A stunned world was to hear in March 1969 of major clashes between Chinese and Russian troops at Zhenbao, north-eastern Manchuria. Further engagements provoked the Soviet Union into hinting at a nuclear strike, notwithstanding an announcement by the People's Republic in October that two more successful nuclear tests had just been carried out in Xinjiang. These border clashes were in part China's reaction to the Soviet invasion of Czechoslovakia during the previous year, because it was believed in Beijing that the Russians were very unhappy about the ideological implications of the Great Proletarian Cultural Revolution (1966–9). They also sprang from excessive defensiveness, arising out of the acute domestic unrest stirred up by Red Guards. No invasion of the People's Republic appears to have been planned by the Russians, but the fact that the Chinese Communist Party became involved in such a border crisis at all indicates a legacy of profound distrust stemming ultimately from Yan'an days.

Yet the coolness between Moscow and Yan'an was

missed by the Americans in 1944–5. Jiang Jieshi was able to prevent US aid from being given to the Chinese Communist Party and to slow US equipment going to the Viet Minh, Ho Chi Minh's resistance movement to the Japanese in Vietnam. As a result of the Generalissimo's eminence in the eyes of Washington, the popular resistance movements in both China and IndoChina were destined to become anti-American.

Given the lack of esteem accorded to the Chinese Communist Party by the Allies, there could be no question that Japanese forces in China had to surrender to the Guomindang. This decision was finally sealed by the signing of the Sino-Soviet Treaty on 15 August 1945. In return for railway rights in Manchuria and naval facilities on the Liaoning peninsula, essentially the privileges enjoyed by the Russians before the Russo-Japanese War of 1905, Moscow recognised the Chongqing government as the sole government of China. Recognition was one thing, however; control of the country was another. As President Truman admitted in his *Memoirs:*

> In reality it would be only with the greatest difficulty that Jiang Jieshi could even re-occupy South China. To get to North China, he would need an agreement with the Communists, and he could never move into Manchuria without an agreement with the Communists and the Russians. It was impossible for Jiang to occupy Northeast China and South Central China with the Communists in between the rail lines. It was perfectly clear to us if we told the Japanese to lay down their arms immediately and march to the seaboard the entire country would be taken over by the Communists. We therefore had to take the step of using the enemy as a garrison until we could airlift Chinese National (Guomindang) troops to North China and send Marines to guard the seaports. So the Japanese were instructed to hold their places and maintain order. In due course Chinese troops under Jiang Jieshi would appear, the Japanese would surrender to them, march to

the seaports, and we would send them back to
Japan. The operation of using the japanese to hold
off the Communists was a joint decision of the
State and Defense Departments of which I approved.

Few decisions taken at the close of the Second World
War backfired so badly. Its military and political conse-
quences were equally disastrous to Jiang Jieshi and
Truman.

Even from a strategic viewpoint the rushing of Guomindang troops to northern cities made little sense. With the
Communists in effective control of the northern provinces other than Japanese-garrisoned cities, Jiang Jieshi
simply inherited the military difficulties of the Japanese
Imperial Army. Had he chosen to secure the southern
provinces first, and at the same time tried to reassure the
peasants by introducing a measure of land reform, then
the Generalissimo might have been able to push northwards without peril. Guomindang forces were instead
seen to ally themselves with the defeated Japanese and
with those Chinese units which had co-operated with the
invaders. While Dean Acheson might protest that US
military personnel were in China "not for the purpose of
any Chinese faction or group," the assistance rendered to
Jiang Jieshi seemed oddly like direct intervention. Also
the misconduct of US servicemen in Beijing, where the
rape of a girl student caused nationwide protests, served
to increase resentment against the imposition of Guomindang rule. But most galling of all was the continued use
of Japanese soldiers, long after the official end of the war
in East Asia. This is how one American diplomat recorded his own bewilderment in a diary entry for 27
December 1945:

I still don't understand about the Japanese. Officially they are disarmed, but the fact is they never
seem to be. In Shanghai fifteen thousand still walk
the streets with their full equipment. In Nanjing the
high Japanese generals are bosom buddies of the
Chinese. In the north tens of thousands of Japanese

soldiers are used to guard railroads and warehouses and to fight Communists. If you ask what all this is about the answer is either a denial or in more candid moments, 'Shhh, we don't talk about that.'

The contrast between the opposing sides, the Guomindang and the Communists, could not have been more dramatically demonstrated than in their attitudes to the defeated enemy.

The presence of American troops supporting Jiang Jieshi—there were 143,000 in China by early 1946—was as aggravating to Mao Zedong as the unhelpful stance of the Russians, who from August 1945 till April 1946 occupied Manchuria. The Soviet Union could have passed its resources to the Chinese Communist Party, but Russian soldiers were ordered to dismantle and remove to Siberia the industries built up there by the Japanese before handing over the cities to the Guomindang. Thinking that Mao Zedong was unlikely to win the forthcoming civil war, Stalin plundered the industrial plant and urged Yan'an to reach an accommodation with the Generalissimo. What the Soviet leader failed to realise was the lack of appetite amongst the Chinese for a conflict waged on Jiang Jieshi's behalf. "When marching through Shanghai", an American consul was to note in 1947, "recruits have to be roped together. There have been repeated incidents where groups brought here attempted to escape and were machine-gunned by guards with resultant killings."

American attempts at mediation failed during 1946. Despite a partial embargo on the sale of US weapons to the Guomindang, it was obvious to his American advisers that nothing would restrain Jiang Jieshi. But since even official support for a coalition between the Guomindang and the Communists was construed by the "China Lobby" in Washington as "selling China down the river," scope for diplomatic manoeuvre was restricted almost to the point that hardly existed. Jiang Jieshi could persue his military goals, even if they were fatefully reminiscent of the warlord era. As his top priority was control of the northern cities, and in particular the industrialised ones of Manchuria, he dispatched his best troops to act as their garrisons, There can be no doubt that he over-stretched himself, although US marines relieved the Guomindang of many guard duties until well into 1947. The tactics of the People's Liberation Army (*Renmin Jiefangjun*), as the Communists now styled their forces, were quite different; units were withdrawn from many cities, including Yan'an, and efforts were directed at consolidating its position in the countryside, from which blows could be delivered at Guomindang concentrations without the risk of large-scale engagements.

The winter of 1947–8 was not without its difficulties for the Chinese Communist Party in the northern provinces. Land reform measures were discovered to be too ex-treme in many places and from spring 1948 newly "liber-ated" areas were treated with circumspection. Landlords were still executed or imprisoned, so that their traditional hold over village life was broken forever, but wealthier peasants lost less land than some radicals would have wished. A new experience for villagers was the voice they acquired in their daily affairs. Yet though the problems faced by Mao Zedong in implementing land reform were worrying, they had nothing in common with the calamity which the return of Guomindang rule brought Jiang Jieshi. Those parts of China under his control suffered govern-mental incompetence and corruption, rampant inflation, and economic collapse. Guomindang expenditure on the civil war would have outrun American aid without the wholesale peculation that riddled its administration, from the Generalissimo's family downwards. As, later, Tru-man sadly commented in retirement, they "were all thieves".

By the end of 1947 the military situation of the Guomindang was becoming precarious in Manchuria, where Lin Biao brilliantly commanded an army of 300,000 men, comprising Chinese, Manchurian and Mongolian irregulars. To the world Jiang Jieshi had trumpeted ear-lier in March the fall of Yan'an, the war-time capital of the Chinese Communist Party. What he preferred not to advertise was that only a few Communist training units

were encountered in the base area, for the good reason
that the People's Liberation Army had shifted its theatre
of operations to the north-eastern countryside.

The capture of Yan'an was a hollow victory. The strategy of "encircling the cities with the countryside" was
having both a military and a political effect on Jiang
Jieshi's fortunes, not least because falling morale amongst
his own soldiers caused an increasing rate of desertion to
the Communist side. But even as late as September 1948,
just before the Guomindang collapse, the Generalissimo
still possessed substantially more troops and far superior
equipment than his opponent.

Offensives launched by the Communists at the beginning of 1948 confirmed that the turning-point of the civil
war had been reached. The surrender of isolated Guomindang garrisons was their target. These fell steadily from
the spring onwards, but the psychological moment occurred on 2 November, when the city of Mukden surrendered and Manchuria passed into Communist hands.
470,000 Guomindang troops were lost. While Jiang Jieshi
put a brave face on the disaster, commenting that "the
loss of Manchuria . . . relieves the government of a burden . . .and allows it to concentrate its war effort to the
south of the Great Wall", the military situation was far
beyond repair as advanced Communist formations had
entered the Yangzi river valley. Already a decisive battle
was taking place in Jiangsu province at Xuzhou, an important junction on the railway to Nanjing. The engagement, which lasted for sixty-five days, ended on 10 January
1949 in an overwhelming Communist victory. The Guomindang never recovered from the losses it sustained at
Xuzhou: 600,000 men.

On 20 April the People's Liberation Army swept across
the Yangzi river, its field artillery near Nanjing crip-
pling the British frigate *HMS Amethyst* for "a violation
of Chinese waters". The incident marked the close of
the gunboat era, though Jiang Jieshi's refuge on the
island of Formosa was soon protected by the US Seventh
Fleet. The triumph belonged to the countryside, where

as an American diplomat noted, "the Communists, perhaps as much through necessity as wisdom, are penetrating the villages and finding a response where for a long time no one has cared what happened or who thought what."

7

THE PEOPLE'S REPUBLIC

The Modern Miracle (1949 onwards)

"THE CHINESE PEOPLE HAVE STOOD UP!"

Thus Mao Zedong explained the establishment of the People's Republic on 1 October 1949. The peasant-farmers had passed the Mandate of Heaven to the Chinese Communist Party, whose authority was challenged only in Hainan, Tibet, Taiwan and a few offshore islands. What he chose not to explain publicly during the moment of triumph was the opposition it had had to face from the Soviet Union. As Mao Zedong remarked thirteen years afterwards:

> They did not allow China to make revolution. This was in 1945, when Stalin tried to prevent the Chinese revolution by saying that we must collaborate with Jiang Jieshi. Otherwise the Chinese nation would perish. At that time, we did not carry this into effect, and the revolution was victorious.

There can be no doubt that the dropping of atomic bombs on Japan had deeply worried the Russians. "Many were frightened," Zhou Enlai clearly recalled, "even Stalin was mentally shocked, and was concerned about the outbreak of the Third World War."

It is difficult to recapture the uncertainties of the late

1940s, when neither the Soviet Union nor the United States were able to distinguish between genuine anxiety and political opportunism. In Washington few appreciated that the devastation wrought by the Germans in Russia caused Stalin to become preoccupied with the defence of Eastern Europe, even to the extent of discouraging the Communist movement in China. The Russian leader totally misunderstood American intentions and, by adopting a tough line in negotiations, helped to justify anti-Soviet fundamentalism in the United States. Everything Churchill said of an "iron curtain" descending across Europe in his celebrated speech at Fulton, Missouri, on 5 March 1946, seemed to be confirmed in Czechoslovakia after the 1948 takeover. Its repressive Communist regime showed the way for the other countries in Eastern Europe and reinforced attitudes of intolerance in American public opinion that were deftly exploited by the "China Lobby". The Republicans, denied national power for over a decade, were not slow to take up the idea of Stalin as a controller of a monolithic world movement, a Communist threat to be met wherever his agents were at work. That Tito's Yugoslavia would not automatically toe the Kremlin line was discounted as a sign of independence, just as doctrinal differences between Stalin and Mao Zedong were regarded only as theoretical arguments. President Truman's election for a second term in 1948 actually coincided with the start of the Cold War between the United States and the Soviet Union. Growing anti-Communist pressures in the country were too powerful for the White House to resist, even though the Democrat incumbent had already told Congress that "it must be the policy of the United States to support free peoples who are resisting attempted subjugation by armed minorities or by outside pressures". But as Truman was amazed to discover, his own doctrine of active support abroad was thought to be too weak at home.

Despite the efforts of President Truman's personal representative George Marshall from late 1945 onwards to prevent a civil war in China, Jiang Jieshi was able to turn American public fears about "the Reds" into a blank cheque payable to the Guomindang account. General Marshall's pessimism about his military prospects the Generalissimo felt he could safely ignore, for the United States would never permit a Communist victory. Although he was right in predicting intervention, Jiang Jieshi must have been disappointed that the role of the US Seventh Fleet was essentially defensive, a gunboat screen around his refuge on the island of Taiwan. He had, however, the satisfaction of seeing the Korean War put a stop to any accommodation between the United States and the People's Republic. The invasion of South Korea by forces belonging to North Korea on 25 June 1950 effectively blocked the entry of Beijing to the United Nations Organisation for more than two decades. Not until October 1971 would the People's Republic overcome the two-thirds margin that the United States succeeded in making necessary for its membership to be approved. Then the General Assembly voted 76 to 35 to expel the representatives from Taibei and seat those from Beijing.

While the United States claimed that Mao Zedong was a tool of the Russians and the Guomindang on Taiwan were manning a bastion of the Free World, a number of countries did offer the People's Republic immediate recognition in 1949. The first non-Communist state to establish diplomatic relations was Burma on 9 December. The same month this example was followed by India, Pakistan, Sri Lanka, Norway, Britain, Denmark, Israel, Finland, Afghanistan and Sweden. Upon hearing that London had recognised Beijing, Madame Jiang remarked bitterly in a radio broadcast that Britain had "bartered the soul of a nation for a few pieces of silver". Diplomatic recognition was in reality an acceptance of the political situation after the civil war.

CHINA AND RUSSIA

On 16 December 1949 Mao Zedong went to Moscow to sign with Stalin a thirty-year treaty of "friendship, alliance, and mutual aid", which was supplemented by two agreements. The first settled a timescale for the rundown of Russian forces in the Liaoning peninsula, where they had been stationed at two ports following the agreement reached between Stalin and Jiang Jieshi in 1945, as well as arranging for the simultaneous handing over of connecting railway lines. In return the Chinese recognised the independence of the Mongolian People's Republic, a region incorporated in the empire only by the Qing dynasty. By the second agreement, the Soviet Union gave the People's Republic a five-year loan of an amount equivalent to US $300 million. Some settlement may have been reached about the Japanese equipment looted by the Russians in Manchuria as well. For Mao Zedong the treaty was advantageous, although the question of the tsarist borders was excluded and, pending a peace treaty with Japan, the Russians reserved the right of naval access to a Liaoning port. With relations between the People's Republic and the Soviet Union placed on a friendly footing, the Chinese sense of betrayal over the Russian occupation of Manchuria could begin to be forgotten. A satisfactory account of this episode has yet to be written, but several explanations have been advanced to explain Stalin's lukewarm attitude towards the Chinese Communist Party at the close of the Second World War. It may be that Stalin was concerned to recover Russian privileges in East Asia, lost through the Russo-Japanese War of 1904–5. At the Yalta conference in February 1945 the United States and Britain had accepted the claims of the Soviet Union without even consulting Jiang Jieshi. Another possibility, that Moscow understood conditions in China as little as did Washington and London, has the historical evidence of Stalin's persistent urging of a Guomindang-Communist coalition government, much to the annoyance of Mao Zedong. Moscow seemed to cling to a view of Chinese politics more suited to the 1920s: no account was taken of the Yan'an experience of the Chinese Communist Party, nor the extent of Guomindang disintegration during the idle years in Chongqing. As Stalin saw it, the Communists were restricted to the countryside with little chance of carrying the revolution from village to town and city. The decision to loot factories would have been reached in the expectation of stalemate in China. Anxious that the Guomindang, and their American allies, should be denied the industrial power built up by the Japanese in Manchuria, Stalin may have seen the issue as one of security for the Pacific states of the Soviet Union.

There is, however, another explanation which credits Stalin with a dog-in-the-manger attitude to the Chinese Communist Party. Moscow was aware of the doctrinal aberration of Mao Zedong's thought, a fundamental divergence of view on revolutionary potentiality in the non-industrial world dating from the days of southern base areas. Though Mao Zedong was careful never to break completely with Moscow, the Chinese Communist Party received almost no assistance in its struggle against the Imperial Japanese Army or the Guomindang forces. When on 3 February 1949 the People's Liberation Army marched into Beijing, foreign observers in the Legation Quarter, through which the Communists deliberately routed their triumphal entry, were surprised to find that the column contained neither Russian weapons nor Russian advisers. As Derk Bodde, a Fulbright fellow, noted in his diary:

> I missed the first contingents of infantry and cavalry, as well as part of the motorised units. But in what I did see, lasting about an hour, I counted over 250 heavy motor vehicles of all kinds—tanks, armoured cars, trucks of soldiers, trucks mounted with machine-guns, trucks towing heavy artillery. Behind them followed innumerable ambulances, jeeps, and other smaller vehicles. As probably the greatest demonstration of Chinese military might in history, the spectacle was enormously impressive. But what made it especially memorable to Americans was the fact that it was primarily a display of *American* military equipment, virtually all of it captured or obtained by bribe from Guomindang forces in the short space of two and one half years.

That he was witnessing "the beginning of a new era in Chinese history" the observer was quite sure, not least because there could be no doubt "that the Communists come here with the bulk of the people on their side". Mao Zedong had won the civil war unaided by Russia, but he was to learn that the price for future aid, financial and technical, entailed less ideological freedom than he could stomach. Perhaps in stripping Manchuria of its modern industries Stalin was trying to ensure that a Communist Beijing would have no scope for independence, since it was highly unlikely that any other foreign power would help in restoring the Chinese economy.

Although it was therefore hard for the People's Republic to achieve a close alliance with the Soviet Union, neither Stalin nor Mao Zedong could afford to fall out publicly. Moscow intended that heterodox Yugoslavia should find no allies within the socialist bloc and so the request by Beijing for assistance with reconstruction did not fall on deaf ears. Nonetheless, the views of Mao Zedong on atomic weapons may have already disturbed the Kremlin. To counter pessimism he had told Anne Louise Strong, an American reporter visiting Yan'an in 1946, that "the atomic bomb is a paper tiger used by US reactionaries to scare people. It looks terrible, but in fact it isn't. Of course, the atom bomb is a weapon of mass slaughter, but the outcome of a war is decided by the people, not by one or two new weapons." This point was to be used by the Russians after the estrangement between Moscow and Beijing as an accusation that the Chinese were willing to run the risk of a nuclear war because of a belief that they more than others would survive it. Mao Zedong's perspective on the international situation was different, however, since he rejected Stalin's fear that local wars in East Asia would increase political tension to such an extent that another world war must result. The events since 1945 have proved Mao Zedong correct in that relations between the Soviet Union and the United States have been able to accommodate liberation movements in the Third World.

Mao Zedong always argued that contradictions within

the West itself were sufficient to prevent an alignment of all capitalist countries against the Soviet Union. These contradictions arose from class differences within each country as well as the rivalry and competition which necessarily existed between the capitalist countries themselves. While he was aware of the American commitment to the status quo in East Asia, Mao Zedong foresaw that even its vast resources could not sustain indefinitely client regimes engulfed by "a people's war".

For China post-war East Asia was very unsatisfactory indeed. It was unfortunate for relations with the West that the Americans, as successors to the Japanese, created a sphere of influence which included areas that China had traditionally controlled or possessed. Unperceived in Washington was the pattern of influence in East Asia prior to the European colonial era, when the Chinese empire through the tributary system had maintained close ties with many adjacent peoples, contributing significantly to the advancement of their cultures. Countries such as Vietnam and Korea had remained intimately connected with Chinese civilisation as late as the nineteenth century. Thus the presence of American forces in a ring of bases around the eastern and southern borders of the People's Republic was seen by Beijing not only as a continuation of imperialism but more the denial of China's traditional role in the East Asian community of nations.

As a result of this sense of unjust containment, the intervention of Chinese "volunteers" in the Korean War (1950–3) represented a response to both the Allied drive towards the Manchurian frontier and the anti-Chinese stance of the United States. Conflict broke out in Korea during the campaign of the People's Liberation Army in Tibet, a Qing dynasty conquest that had remained beyond Chinese control for most of the twentieth century. In 1936 Edgar Snow had learned from Mao Zedong that Tibet and Xinjiang "will form autonomous republics attached to the Chinese federation". But the invasion of Tibet and the restoration of Chinese influence in Central Asia was overshadowed in November 1950 by China's entry into the Korean War. "Volunteers" from units of the People's Liberation Army first clashed with American troops in Korea the previous month, when they achieved tactical surprise by a sudden crossing of the Yalu river. Their swift disengagement lends support to Beijing's contention that this action was intended to alert the United States to the possibility of a fullscale Chinese attack, if America and its allies (including Britain) failed to evacuate North Korea.

Although the origins of the Korean conflict are still obscure, there are no grounds for supposing that Mao Zedong approved of the original North Korean attack. Conventional war was not the method he would have chosen to solve the problem of a divided peninsula, because it could prove exhausting and dangerous with active American support for South Korea. Whether North Korea acted alone or received Russian encouragement is unknown, but it was apparent that the People's Republic took the counter-attack under General Douglas MacArthur seriously enough to put its own forces in the field. What may have added to Mao Zedong's fear was the espousal of Taiwan, which President Truman ordered the US Seventh Fleet to protect as soon as the North Korean invasion began. He made it clear that he could accept the reconquest of South Korea, but not the loss of North Korea, any more than the United States had been able to tolerate the original invasion. Should the whole of the Korean peninsula have fallen under American sway, then Mao Zedong thought that Washington might be tempted to launch Jiang Jieshi on an attempted reconquest of China itself with full military support.

Although Truman had ordered MacArthur not to undertake military action close to the Korean borders with China and the Soviet Union, the American commander ignored his instructions and allowed US soldiers to take up positions on the Yalu river, which marked the frontier with the People's Republic. The Chinese reaction was unexpectedly successful, driving MacArthur's troops in headlong flight down the peninsula; leading formations of the People's Liberation Army under Lin Biao entered

Seoul in January 1951. The Allied army then rallied and pushed the Chinese back to the 38th parallel, the dividing line between the two Koreas. This recovery cost màny lives, because Lin Biao's successor, Peng Dehuai, fought a very skilful withdrawal. By employing stealth and flexible tactics the People's Liberation Army overcame technological inferiority, yet even the euphoria in China could not disguise the limits of success against a more modern and mobile foe than Jiang Jieshi's army. Two more years of severe fighting resulted in moderate UN advances, and finally led to a peace settlement in 1953 which gave South Korea slightly more territory than it had held when the war began in 1950.

The Korean War was costly to China. Apart from the heavy casualties sustained on the battlefield, the conflict drew scarce resources away from domestic reconstruction and increased the dependence of the People's Republic on Russian aid, besides strengthening the "China Lobby" in Washington. But intervention in Korea had rallied the Chinese people around the new regime in a way that might not have been possible without it, for the country was exhilarated by the ability of the People's Liberation Army to stand up to General MacArthur and other foreigners who talked of invading China. So much so that the opposition of Peng Dehuai (1898–1974) to the Great Leap Forward in 1959 caused Mao Zedong considerable embarrassment. On his return from a seven-week tour of the Soviet Union and Eastern Europe, Peng Dahuai boldly informed Mao Zedong in a letter that the failure of the Great Leap Forward necessitated a change of economic direction. In the ensuing struggle Peng Dehuai was dismissed as Minister of Defence, a post he had held from 1954, and Lin Biao was appointed to replace him. Even if the condemnation reflected Soviet views on the subject and was linked with military cooperation, Mao Zedong decided that China could afford to pursue its own policies without the Kremlin's permission. The other hero of the Korean War was therefore asked to assume responsibility for national defence, but only until 1971 when Lin Biao was killed in an air crash apparently escaping to the

Soviet Union. This dramatic end probably resulted from his criticism of Mao Zedong's strategy of normalising relations with the United States: both Korean veterans may have become too identified with the Russians for their own safety.

The Korean War had given Mao Zedong no reason to like the Soviet Union. Whereas Stalin seems to have been supportive of North Korea's decision to start the conflict, he left the Chinese to shoulder the burden of the North Korean repulse almost unaided, as little extra was given to the People's Republic in the way of military equipment or financial support. The Russians had already committed themselves to assistance with 211 major projects and thousands of experts were seconded to China, but there was never any question that the money they made available for this development would have to be repaid, which indeed it was over a decade from China's growing trade surplus. Differences between Moscow and Beijing remained hidden then from general view until 1956, three years after the death of Stalin. The initial programme of the Chinese Communist Party provided no scope for doctrinal dispute: starting in 1950, land reform closely followed the Russian model with the expropriation of landlords. Though it was discovered that landlordism was not as extensive as under the tsars—in the northern provinces approximately 70 per cent of the land was worked by owners—the redistribution of property did result in the loss of life, perhaps as many as 2 million dying in the upheaval. But the Chinese Communist Party benefited from land reform, because rural change gave rise in each village to a core of peasant activists and even those villagers who had no real understanding of the policies being implemented were grateful for the land they received. As in the towns and cities, the pace of socialist reform was geared to maintain output at a reasonable level.

By 1955 the Chinese Communist Party was ready to move from private property to socialist ownership as a basis for the economy. As in Soviet Russia, the first step was the setting up of rural cooperatives in order to begin large-scale production methods backed by better equipment and fertilisers, but in contrast to Stalin's collectivisation programmes of the late 1920s and early 1930s the transition in the Chinese countryside was achieved without violence; the differences of wealth were small enough to permit the use of persuasion and so few peasants were enrolled in cooperatives against their will. The change brought about an expansion in food production but the improved diet of the peasant-farmer accounted for most of this increase and the amount of grain collected by the state, through taxes and compulsory purchase, remained stationary.

Mao Zedong therefore determined that a shake-up was necessary. In 1956–7 he lifted some of the restrictions on public expression, urging the people to "let the hundred schools contend, let the hundred flowers bloom", a reference to the contending philosophic schools of the Warring States period. Through the expression of constructive criticism, he hoped, would come a tremendous release of latent energy that the Chinese Communist Party could harness to accelerate China's economic progress. The period of relaxation known as the Hundred Flowers was the first occasion on which Mao Zedong demonstrated his belief in the necessity of a permanent or continuing revolution. For he insisted "that which is correct always develops in the course of struggling against that which is wrong. As mankind in general rejects an untruth, a truth will be struggling with erroneous ideas. Such struggles will never end. This is the law of Marxism." So the key to unlock a socialist future was psychological change, the renewal of enthusiasm amongst party members and people alike. Even Liu Shaoqi (1898–1969) echoed this principle during the Great Leap Forward when he said: "The present task is to effect a thorough and systematic readjustment in the relationships between people, rooting out the capitalist and feudal survivals of bygone days and building new socialist relationships." Along with other senior Communists, Liu Shaoqi disapproved of the Hundred Flowers episode and took advantage of the economic difficulties caused by the Great

Leap in 1959–60 to reduce the power of Mao Zedong. It could be said that the cultural turmoil that raged between 1966 and 1969 was an attempt by Mao Zedong to regain control.

The differences between Mao Zedong and Liu Shaoqi were highlighted by the torrent of complaints that poured forth in 1956–7. Although Mao Zedong was taken aback at the depth of many educated people's dislike of the regime, withdrawing on 8 June 1957 the licence to criticise, he was more disturbed by the general reluctance of the Communist bureaucracy itself to accept criticism. He found many of the officials whom Liu Shaoqi was prepared to defend both arrogant and inflexible. They were simply a modern version of the scholar-bureaucrats of the old imperial civil service. Since the empire also possessed a tradition of public management rather than large-scale private enterprise, there existed a danger that these officials might revert to a Confucian scale of values, owing as much loyalty to the family as the state. Unless a "proletarian viewpoint" emerged as a value of judgement, the intellectuals running the apparatus of the state and the growing industrial sector could be tempted into "bourgeois thinking", or they could slip back into the hierarchic attitudes of the imperial official. The problem was partly related to size, membership of the Chinese Communist Party having risen from 1.2 million in 1945 to 17 million in 1961. As a slogan put it during the Great Proletarian Cultural Revolution (1966–9), people needed to "follow the Yan'an way".

The years 1956–7 were also the years in which Nikita Khrushchev denounced Stalinism as a way of modernising the Soviet system. Detainees were released from labour camps and a degree of free expression permitted, indeed anticipating the relaxation in China. But there any comparison stops. The Chinese Communist Party was outraged that Khrushchev should assault Stalin's memory without consultation or even warning it in advance. Nor did the results of the "anti-doctrinaire tide" in Eastern Europe impress Beijing, for in November 1956 Soviet troops had to invade Hungary in order to prevent an abandonment of Communism, a last-minute device which to Mao Zedong smacked of Russian incompetence. "In Hungary," he said, "a section of the people, deceived by domestic and foreign reactionaries, made the mistake of resorting to acts of violence against the people's government, with the result that both the state and the people suffered." As foolhardy in his view was Khrushchev's advocacy of peaceful coexistence with the West and the revisionist notion that capitalist countries could achieve a transition to socialism without undergoing a revolution.

In East Asia the chief enemy of the People's Republic was still the United States, then underwriting any and all anti-Communist governments. To remind Washington that the Chinese civil war was never finished, the People's Liberation Army began in September 1954 shelling offshore islands still held by the Guomindang a few days before the South-East Asia Treaty Organisation was set up in Manila. The zealous American Secretary of State, John Foster Dulles, responded by announcing a military pact with Taibei, no mean reaction to what Peng Duhuai had said was a manoeuvre "to call your attention" to the fact that Taiwan and the islands are Chinese. Two years later Suez also cast doubt on the acquiescence of Britain and France in their diminished world role, although Mao Zedong could not have failed to notice how it was President Eisenhower who aborted their invasion of Egypt.

More serious for Sino-Russian relations was that the orientation of the Soviet Union towards the industrial part of the world blinded its leadership to the value of the Chinese experience for revolution amongst the underdeveloped nations. This ideological rift widened in 1958 when Mao Zedong launched the Great Leap Forward and rejected the Russian model of economic development, claiming that communes would be a short-cut to full Communism. The reluctance of Moscow to sustain Beijing in a second off-shore island crisis during the same year only encouraged an independent foreign policy, which seemed fully justified as the Americans and the Russians edged towards an arms control agreement. Had not the Soviet Union already reneged on a promise to help China acquire atomic weapons? Was not Khrushchev now "revising, emasculating, and betraying" Communism? So it appeared in early 1960 when China and Russia finally split and, at a month's notice, Khrushchev withdrew all technical assistance and cancelled all financial aid.

CULTURAL REVOLUTION (1966–76)

The prelude to the unprecedented upsurge of revolutionary activity in the late 1960s was the Great Leap Forward. In 1959–60 the Chinese Communist Party accepted Mao Zedong's decision to cut its links with the Soviet Union, but the failure of the Great Leap Forward raised serious questions about his leadership and Liu Shaoqi took over the position of head of the government. There was by no means a decisive swing away from the revolutionary course that Mao Zedong was attempting to steer, if only for the reason that almost all top party members had shared in 1958 his enthusiasm for rapid economic advance; yet Mao Zedong's authority was so reduced that the policies introduced at the beginning of the 1960s were not at all to his liking. Following the death of Mao Zedong in 1976, there has been a reassessment of his political career in China and current opinion would regard the Great Leap Forward as the first serious example of Mao Zedong's lack of realism. With hindsight it is easy to see how his prestige was great enough in 1959 to carry the Chinese Communist Party with him, despite Peng Dehuai's telling remark about "hotheadedness". Because remedial measures were not immediately taken and the Great Leap Forward ran on to late 1960, the Chinese economy suffered a major setback, which indirectly proved to be the trigger for more extensive disruption during the Great Proletarian Cultural Revolution that Mao Zedong started in 1966 as a psychological great leap.

In order to understand the agitation stirred up by this second revolution, as well as its aftermath in the early 1970s, we need to consider the original purpose of the Great Leap Forward, which was part of Mao Zedong's unfolding thought. For he was one of those rare individuals who seemed to reverse the usual effects of growing old—that is, he became more revolutionary as the years passed. At the time of the Great Leap Forward his willingness to take risks in accelerating economic and political change was undisguised. He dared to ignore the warnings of Russian advisers and rely on a direct appeal to the enthusiasm of the peasants because they "want change, want to do things, want revolution". As he openly said:

> While we stand for freedom with leadership under centralised guidance, in no sense do we mean that coercive measures should be taken to settle ideological matters and questions involving the distinction between right and wrong among the people. Any attempt to deal with ideological matters or questions involving right and wrong by administrative orders or coercive measures will be not only ineffective but harmful . . . Administrative orders issued for the maintenance of social order must be accompanied by persuasion and education . . . Contradictions in a socialist society are fundamentally different from contradictions in old societies, such as a capitalist society. Contradictions in a capitalist society find expression in acute antagonisms and conflicts, in sharp class struggle, which cannot be resolved by the capitalist system itself, but only by socialist revolution. But contradictions in a socialist society are not antagonistic and can be resolved one after another by the socialist system. Such contradictions are those between the relations of production and the productive forces, and between the superstructure and the economic base.

Contained in this statement is the basic difference of outlook between Mao Zedong and Liu Shaoqi, whom the Red Guards were to brand as China's "number one capitalist-roader"; Deng Xiaoping (born 1904) was called "number two capitalist-roader". What Mao Zedong was saying essentially touched upon the authority of the Chinese Communist Party itself. Neither blind obedience nor uncomprehending support could be enough; only through the correct handling of the contradictions within Chinese society would a socialist culture come into existence. Party leaders could not assume that they were the sole repository of wisdom, as the catalogue of Comintern-inspired errors prior to Yan'an had revealed. Only an effective dialogue with the people (which in China meant the peasantry) would secure the revolution.

No matter how disruptive the various campaigns were later recognised to have been by the Chinese themselves, there can be no denying that Mao Zedong's calls for action evoked immense support from the mass of the population. In the Great Leap Forward he proposed that with bare hands China should build its future. By late 1958 the rural cooperatives had been merged into 25,000 communes, each with around 20,000 members, as compared with 3000 in the average cooperative. The basic aim of the commune movement was to provide investment funds for industrial development by making use of economies of scale, by obtaining greater agricultural output through improved rural organisation, and by producing low-grade steel in "backyard furnaces". Because the area of a commune was often coincidental with a county it was hoped that any contradiction between economic and administrative functions would disappear. Apart from better communal facilities such as canteens, nurseries and homes for the aged, which freed women for productive tasks, enlarged resources and manpower ought to have given the commune an advantage over the cooperative in handling schemes for water conservation, irrigation and afforestation.

The initial surge of production in 1958 was excellent, with foodstuffs 5 million tonnes up on the 1957 total and steel production almost doubling in volume. Reports of output records being broken throughout the provinces became commonplace, and in consequence targets were raised for 1959. Overlooked in the excitement of the campaign was the very poor quality of the backyard steel (much of it was unusable) and the exaggeration of many local officials on making agricultural returns. When the 1959 cereal harvest finally became known, the total was 30 million tonnes down on the 1958 figure of 200 million tonnes. Bad weather had played its part as well as the dispersion of labour into too many projects. Instead of taking note of these warning signs and revising economic strategy accordingly, Mao Zedong pressed on with the Great Leap Forward until famine forced a halt. Food shortages probably accounted for an extra 10 million deaths in 1960 and, though this figure is low in comparison with any of the bitter years of the 1920s and 1930s, it was the first occasion since the founding of the People's Republic that so many people had died from diseases caused by malnutrition.

So in late 1960 the Great Leap Forward was abandoned and peasants engaged in industrial production or large-scale projects were sent back to the fields, in a desperate effort to alleviate the food shortage. Communes were reduced in size and rewards given according to the performance of a family or a team: also private plots, which had been largely eliminated during the campaign, were restored.

Mao Zedong was unable to prevent this reversal of policy. Although he was still chairman of the Chinese Communist Party and consulted on policy matters, he found that he was often overruled by other senior members, usually at the behest of Liu Shaoqi or Deng Xiaoping. Later Mao Zedong said that he felt like a revered ancestor to whom only polite gestures were made. Perhaps he ought to have compared himself to a temporarily neglected grandfather, for his method of regaining power was to urge on his seventy-third birthday a rebellion of the young. Sensing the frustration of young people in 1966, Mao Zedong guided their revolt into an attack on the complacency of the Chinese Communist Party itself.

The Great Proletarian Cultural Revolution started in the spring of that year with what was ostensibly an academic debate in newspapers and magazines about a historical play by Wu Han entitled *Hai Rui Dismissed from*

Office. The argument had arisen when an article, published in November 1965, alleged that the dramatist, who was deputy mayor of Beijing, intended a defence of the retired Peng Dehuai because, like the official in the play, the ex-minister had not hesitated to say what was wrong with government policy. Underneath such an interpretation lay a knotty theoretical question; namely, could a former member of the privileged classes have been a true friend of the people. In December 1963 Mao Zedong had already felt constrained to rebuke university lecturers who discussed the social teachings of Confucius. He told them that there should be less talk about personalities of the past and more about the contemporary situation. A year later, he advised a Nepalese delegation that China's education system was "fraught with problems, the most important of which is dogmatism. . . .The school years are too long, courses too many, and various methods of teaching unsatisfactory. The children learn textbooks and concepts which merely remain textbooks and concepts: they know nothing else." Educational reverence of the past was Mao Zedong's prime target, not least when an emphasis was placed on the art of calligraphy, since this must inevitably depress the social standing of the people. China was a poor country without even universal primary education. Strenuous efforts were being made to train teachers and expand provision, but the in-built advantages enjoyed by the children of well-educated parents were very apparent; and a worrying phenomenon when graduation from a secondary school or a college was virtually the guarantee of a responsible position in Chinese society.

So as to forestall the growth of a Communist bureaucracy cut off from the realities of daily life Mao Zedong persuaded the Chinese Communist Party in 1963 that its members should take part in manual labour. Moreover, he had already introduced a "socialist education" campaign replete with antihierarchic slogans and encouraged criticism of the education system. At the same time Lin Biao was planning a similar programme within the People's Liberation Army that led in 1966 to the publication of a selection of Mao Zedong's thoughts as the famous "little red book".

At first Mao Zedong may have considered Wu Han's play as yet another instance of "bourgeois mentality" rather than a direct threat to his developing line on education. He seems to have changed his mind on finding that he could not even arrange for the publication of an attack on the play in Beijing. He had to use the connections of his third wife Jiang Qing (born 1914) in Shanghai to get an adverse review published. A Shanghai actress whom Mao Zedong married in Yan'an, Jiang Qing had until this time obeyed the prohibition on political activity imposed when the Chinese Communist Party gave permission for the marriage. Ill-health in the 1950s had involved Jiang Qing undergoing prolonged periods of treatment in the Soviet Union, but she was sufficiently recovered by the mid-1960s not only to take a leading role in the Great Proletarian Cultural Revolution but to exercise even greater power in the last few years of Mao Zedong's life. Under her ruthless direction the campaign broadened from an attack on "bourgeois" influences in art and literature to an assault on unacceptable thought amongst intellectuals in general. On 5 April 1975 a certain Zhang Zhixin, a minor official from Liaoning province, was executed as "an active counter-revolutionary" for challenging Jiang Qing's right to speak on behalf of Mao Zedong. It was as much a tragedy for Mao Zedong as it was for China that the Great Proletarian Cultural Revolution appealed so strongly to Jiang Qing's thwarted theatrical talents.

Although Liu Shaoqi tried initially to control the campaign by putting advisory teams of party members into the main universities and colleges, the students of Beijing University reacted against this supervision and in a wall poster *(tazibao)*, put up during May 1966, they demanded that it should be a vigorous mass movement. Once Mao Zedong had the poster reprinted in the *People's Daily,* the challenge to Liu Shaoqi's handling of events was obvious and Beijing students responded in a manner worthy of the May Four Movement. Student agitation increased, wall posters attacking professors and administrators appeared, links were made with factories and farms, and the first Red Guard organisation was formed. Within a fortnight of the display of Mao Zedong's own big-character wall poster, "Bombard the Headquarters", Jiang Qing staged on 18 August in Tiananmen square the first of the eight gigantic gatherings that brought, within three months, 11 million Red Guards to Beijing in order to exchange experiences.

"Bombard the Headquarters" charged that there were people in the Chinese Communist Party at all levels up to the very top who were following reactionary policies. Mao Zedong did not name the chief culprits, but it soon became clear that they included Liu Shaoqi (head of the government) and Deng Xiaoping (party secretary). Lin Biao then joined in the attack and both Liu Shaoqi and Deng Xiaoping were stigmatised as followers of "the capitalist road". Deprived of their freedom in Beijing, they were not transferred until 1969 to provincial prisons, where Liu Shaoqi died in Kaifeng, the site of the Northern Song capital. Somewhat younger, Deng Xiaoping fared better with his family in the disused primary school to which he was exiled farther south in Nanchang, Jiangxi province. Recalled to Beijing in 1973 at Zhou Enlai's request, Deng Xiaoping managed to survive further attacks by Jiang Qing and ended in 1978 as the effective leader of the Chinese Communist Party. Commenting on the whole sequence of events in 1980, as the numerous portraits and statues of Mao Zedong put up during 1960s were coming down, Deng Xiaoping pointed squarely at the mishandling of the Great Leap Forward as the source of trouble. He said:

In the first half of 1959 we were correcting 'Left' mistakes . . . But Peng Dehuai's letter of criticism caused a change of direction. His views were correct, and it was normal for him as a member of the Political Bureau to write to Chairman Mao Zedong. Although he had his shortcomings, the way the case was handled was totally wrong.

From this dispute had come the extension of the Great Leap Forward, the economic consequences of which Liu Shaoqi and Deng Xiaoping had been incarcerated by the Red Guards for overcoming; and significantly for the power struggle initiated by Mao Zedong, the elevation of Lin Biao. The "little red book" that Lin Biao collected together from the *Quotations of Chairman Mao* which he published in the army newspaper *Liberation Daily* provided a handbook for the Red Guards as well as the military forces under his command. It made certain of the acquiescence of the People's Liberation Army.

In February 1967 the Red Guards were ordered home. The mass movement of the young was being slowed down, although millions still remained on the roads visiting famous revolutionary sites or participating in local drives against "feudalism, capitalism and revisionism". In moments of excessive enthusiasm they destroyed traditional cultural objects and harassed persons with Western-style clothes or possessions, a xenophobia reminiscent of the Boxers. They called upon party officials to acknowledge their aims, and make self-criticism (*ziwo piping*). Although formal higher education had come to a virtual standstill, colleges and universities stayed open as centres of discussion and political activity. Even in secondary schools there was unprecedented confusion as rivalry between contending youth groups took on a social complexion. In many cases this led to serious injury or death. The school movement had at first been dominated by the children of revolutionary veterans, but other groups were quick to challenge their leadership, not least where they comprised the children from educated families who resented the privileges accorded to the offspring of party members. Just as discontented with the selection system used for entry to secondary schools were the children of urban workers and peasants who also had to meet somewhat higher standards to win admission. Since their parents were poorly educated, few of them managed to find places.

The peasants were better off than before 1949: there was peace in the countryside and more protection against natural calamity, even with the temporary dip in agricultural output caused by the Great Leap Forward. The interest taken by the Chinese Communist Party in their welfare had been evident from the Yan'an era onwards, but for Mao Zedong this solicitous attitude was as reactionary as Guan Zhong's concern for the people's livelihood unless it went hand in hand with real opportunities to shape political events. Was there not a danger that China would revert to its traditional social pattern and Communist officials become another educated upper class? Duke Huan's famous minister had argued in the seventh century BC that prosperity in the villages made the common people easy to control. His policies were aimed at securing obedience, not promoting social revolution. In contrast Mao Zedong was prepared to risk disorder on a national scale during the Great Proletarian Cultural Revolution so as to galvanise thought about Communist goals.

The judgement of Deng Xiaoping and his followers was that the period from 1966 to 1976 had been a "Tenyear Catastrophe". Their strictures were given dramatic form at the trial of Jiang Qing in November 1980, when along with others she was convicted of hounding 34,274 people to their deaths. The total number of casualties remains unknown, although the nature of the cultural conflict never remotely reached to the extremes of Stalin's terrorism. Yet it has to be accepted that the experience of the last decade of Mao Zedong's life was very unpleasant indeed for many Chinese, peasants and urban workers alike.

An insight into the vanity of certain bearers of the cultural revolutionary flag during this traumatic time is offered in *A Small Town Called Hibiscus (Furong Zhen)*, a novel published in 1981. With strokes as devastating as Lu Xun's humour, its author Gu Hwa (born 1942) exposes the domineering pretensions of a party secretary who has visited Dazhai, the commune in Shaanxi province that was credited with remarkable success through the correct application of Mao Zedong's thought. A scene which touched many readers in China, and made the novel an overnight success, depicts the spreading of the

Dazhai gospel at a meeting in the village market-place. To his horror, the returned party secretary Wang Quishe finds in the middle of the address he is making to the Hibiscus production brigade that the obligatory portrait of Chairman Mao is not on the wall behind him. A subordinate official immediately rushes to fetch "a glorious image" from the local primary school, whence he returns covered in sweat and dust, a portrait of Mao Zedong in his hands. As they have no paste or drawing pins at hand, Wang Quishe orders his subordinate to hold up the portrait carefully and reverently in front of the assembled peasants, while at inordinate length he demonstrates the correct posture to adopt in "facing the red sun". Standing to attention, chest out and head thrown back, he gazes into the distance, his left arm at his side, his right elbow bent to clasp the "little red book" to his heart. Then waving the book above his head and looking sideways at the portrait, Wang Quishe leads the villagers in praising Lin Biao as well as Mao Zedong. The establishment of this ceremony as a part of the daily routine of Hisbiscus commune so impresses the provincial authorities that Wang Quishe is sent around the various communes in a jeep, to pass on this newest innovation of the Great Proletarian Cultural Revolution.

The achievements of the Dazhai production brigade were ridiculed publicly in the early 1980s as part of a government programme to reduce the importance of communes. Whilst the enterprise of the brigade in transforming barren hillsides into terraced fields was still acknowledged as a tremendous feat, it was revealed that Dazhai's supposed spirit of self-reliance had in fact been subsidised with government aid. It is a point that Wang Quishe misses when a young man of "impeccable class origins" queries the use of chemical fertiliser at Dazhai. "If 10,000 people go there every day and even spend only a single night," he is asked, "think of all that human waste! With that much manure, why should they need to use government fertiliser as well?"

But *A Small Town Called Hibiscus* is notable for being the first Chinese book to put into perspective the absurd lengths to which admiration for Mao Zedong was taken. "Holding high the banner of Mao Zedong Thought" came close to veneration at the height of Red Guard activities in 1966-7. Many of the trappings of a religion were discernible and the worship of Mao paralleled the treatment accorded Hong Xiuquan by the nineteenth-century Taibing Christians. Once again an inspired leader was about to found a perfect state among men. Besides the ritual of carrying and raising aloft the "little red book", the emphasis placed on self-criticism as a way of avoiding bourgeois attitudes was akin to the practice of conversion.

As early as July 1966 Mao Zedong seems to have been taken aback at the intensity of popular feeling. He wrote that month to Jiang Qing saying how he would "never have imagined that my little books could have such magical powers". But with Lin Biao intent on pushing his collection of sayings as gospel truth and Jiang Qing throwing her energies into organising mass rallies, Mao Zedong may have thought that he could usefully ride the revolutionary tidal wave. Following an instance of Red Guard violence in Hunan province, however, he decided to allow Zhou Enlai to draw up a list of officials, party members and senior citizens who were to be protected from harassment. One of these was the widow of Dr Sun Yatsen, whose hairstyle had become an object of cultural contempt. The problem for the authorities was that the factions into which the young revolutionaries inevitably formed had different ideas as to whom they should direct their socialist zeal against, a circumstance affording ample scope for anyone who wished to manipulate them for their own ends. Mao Zedong tried to qualify his initial call for rebellion by reminding the Red Guards that it was only justified "against reactionaries", but once aroused to the task of purifying ideological goals they were not readily held back—even after the decision in early 1967 to send them back home.

The summer of 1967 was the high-water mark of cultural agitation, although comparative calm returned to China only after the intervention of the People's Liberation Army between 1969 and 1970. The burning of diplomatic offices in Beijing may have alerted Mao Zedong to the growing influence of the "ultra-Leftists", who urged the destruction of a section of the British embassy in August as a response to the imprisonment of "patriotic" Chinese journalists in Hong Kong. This was no part of his strategy and later an official apology was made to Britain over the incident. Nor did he approve of the Red Guard siege of the Foreign Ministry, where veteran commander Chen Yi (1901–72) made no secret of his distaste for their methods of interrogating supposed reactionaries. "In the Party's history there have been people who have used their position to frame loyal members and abuse them in the most abominable way," Chen Yi told his young accusers. "But in later years these types ended up going over to the counter-revolutionary camp. Here are people trying to do the same thing. Let me tell you they will come to no good." When Mao Zedong was asked about what the head of the Ministry of Foreign Affairs had said, he answered that "Chen Yi made fewer mistakes in forty years than his critics have made in forty days." His unease must have been deepened by a conversation with Zhou Enlai, who not only recounted the threatened violence at a meeting held to criticise Chen Yi, which he had attended in order to see fair play, but also told Mao Zedong of his own gruelling forty-eight hours of questioning by Red Guards. That a consummate politician—who had managed to arrange compromise administrations in the provinces, save officials from unjust attack and maintain production in the factories—felt that a crisis was at hand must have given Mao Zedong reason to pause.

Although he believed firmly that the Great Proletarian Cultural Revolution had placed the People's Republic at "the centre of world revolution", Mao Zedong could not be unaware that its progress was being endangered by factionalism. At the beginning of October, he issued a long report on what had been achieved in the provinces, where "Revolutionary Committees" with a membership based on a "three-in-one combination" of Red Guards and revolutionary workers, party officials and members and the People's Liberation Army had assumed control. In conclusion he cautioned prudence because "we are at the very moment when the little Red Guard generals run the risk of making mistakes; they must learn from the experiences of those among them who have made errors in the past." It was a point he hammered home a year later, when he told the Red Guards to accept the leadership of the peasants. In December 1968 Mao Zedong stated: "It is necessary for educated people to go to the countryside to be re-educated by the poor and lower-middle peasants. Party members and other people in the cities should be persuaded to send their sons and daughters who have finished junior or senior middle school, college or university to the countryside." Going to the rural areas is estimated to have involved 17 million youngsters between 1968 and 1978, and one of the pressing demands Deng Xiaoping has had to deal with in the 1980s is requests for the return of individuals and institutions from the countryside, where they were sent prior to Mao Zedong's death.

The attempt to curb the worst manifestations of violence in autumn 1967 compelled Jiang Qing to modify her combative slogan, "Attack with words, but defend yourself with weapons". She had to admit her support for Mao Zedong's call for a peaceful, not an armed, struggle. Captured weapons were to be surrendered and the People's Liberation Army authorised to deal with any breakdown of law and order. Getting rival factions of Red Guards to sink their differences was far from easy; the street fighting which occurred in several cities in the spring of 1968 and involved tanks and casualties were still reported as late as the summer, at the time when the movement to the countryside started in earnest. The confusion served only to increase the influence of the People's Liberation Army and strengthen the position of Lin Biao, who in 1969 was designated Mao Zedong's "close comrade-in-arms and successor".

The canonisation of "Marxism—Leninism—Mao Zedong Thought" by means of the "little red book" undoubtedly raised Lin Biao to this exalted role. Mao Zedong later claimed that the cult under which he became almost a sacred object, had in fact been something that the commander-in-chief of the People's Liberation Army had propagated in order to further his own ambitions. Surprised though he may have been at the popular response to his ideological wishes, Mao Zedong did China a disservice by not renouncing the cult altogether. Only with the greatest difficulty have the "practical" men who today support Deng Xiaoping's plans for modernising the country managed to separate daily reality from dogma. At the height of the Great Proletarian Cultural Revolution a reference to one of Mao Zedong's sayings was enough to justify any action. How ridiculous this was became apparent in one of Chen Yi's confrontations with the Red Guards. At the Beijing Foreign Languages Institute he caused wonderful disarray when, on being asked to recite a quotation, Chen Yi intoned: "Chairman Mao says, 'Comrade Chen Yi is a fine comrade.' " It took a frantic search of the "little red book" before the penny dropped— he had made the saying up himself.

Lin Biao's eminence so impressed Wang Quishe that all the way back from the railway station to Hibiscus, after the visit to Dazhai, he kept shouting "Long live the red sun! Long live the red sun!", until he caught a chill and his voice was hoarse. Waving the "little red book" and chanting slogans was something everyone knew the party secretary had learned from a film about Mao Zedong's successor. For Lin Biao basked in the reflected glory of "the red sun" to such an extent that he seemed to be inseparable from its revolutionary power. Besides this carefully stage-managed and widely broadcast association, it is now believed that Lin Biao instigated many of the Red Guard campaigns against senior party members whom he feared, such as Chen Yi and Zhou Enlai. The latter somehow kept himself at a distance from Lin Biao's utter commitment to the aims of the Great Proletarian Cultural Revolution without either offending Mao Zedong or opening the way to a sustained Red Guard attack. Speaking affectionately of Zhou Enlai to an Italian journalist in 1980, Deng Xiaoping said that the former premier "had to say and do many things he would have wished not to do. But people forgave him because had he not done and said those things, he himself would not have been able to survive and play the neutralising role he did, which reduced losses. He succeeded in protecting quite a number of people." Deng Xiaoping added that the turbulence of the 1966–9 period was not the sole responsibility of Mao Zedong, since institutional factors were as much to blame as personal ones.

But Lin Biao's use of the Red Guards, and afterwards the People's Liberation Army, to "sanitise" the Chinese Communist Party and remove potential rivals proved of no avail. As soon as public order was restored in 1970 Mao Zedong began to reduce the role of the armed forces in the running of the country and, possibly to lower their importance in the eyes of the people following the clashes with Soviet troops the previous year at Zhenbao, he also indicated a willingness for better relations with the United States. President Nixon was to make a historic state visit to China in 1972 and reverse the whole of American post-war policy, for in a joint communiqué issued at Shanghai the United States accepted in principle the future withdrawal of its forces from Taiwan. Neither of these moves suited Lin Biao, who tried to flee the country in September 1971, according to official sources, after his plans to kill Mao Zedong and usurp the chairmanship were uncovered. The Trident in which he sought to escape crashed and burst into flames at Ondor Huan, just inside the borders of Mongolia. The cause of the crash is still not known.

Although the fall of Lin Biao was not announced straightaway and a series of denunciations occurred before the news broke in November, Mao Zedong felt pleased enough with the educational results of the Great Proletarian Cultural Revolution to relax the "antibourgeois" line that Jiang Qing wished to maintain. The whole spirit of learning had been altered to reduce the gap between those who used their brains and those who used their hands. Educational opportunities were widened at primary and secondary levels, while the number of students enrolled in higher studies was initially kept below the 1965 total; and the duration of schooling had been reduced so that equal emphasis could be placed on the experience to be gained by young people in class and at work. Examinations as a method of selection for further study also remained out of favour. "Teachers tackle students as enemies", Mao Zedong remarked, "and launch surprise attacks against them." A mathematics lesson cited as a proletarian model under the new dispensation was conducted by an old peasant; it was called "A Debt of Blood and Tears" and brought home to a class the onerous method of calculating the rate of interest paid to a landlord over a number of years.

So government office and senior responsibilities were once again opened to a wide range of party members, even those who had taken "the capitalist road". The crucial rehabilitation took place in 1973 and restored Deng Xiaoping to his former position in the Political Bureau. He was lucky enough to be untouched by the anti-Confucius campaign of 1974 as well as the attack Jiang Qing launched in the last year of Mao Zedong's life. "It is contrary to the will of the people to revise verdicts," she alleged Mao Zedong to have said. But it was already too late for the "Gang of Four", as Jiang Qing and her closest associates were later called. First Zhou Enlai died in January, then Mao Zedong in September, leaving the reins of government in the comparatively inexperienced hands of Hua Guofeng (born 1920), an administrator from Hunan province upon whom the succession had been settled.

CHINA AFTER CHAIRMAN MAO

The death of Mao Zedong, who was eighty-two years old, on 10 September 1976 was an event of world-wide interest. As the tributes flowed into Beijing from foreign heads of government and internationally known politicians, it was clear perhaps for the first time how significant he had been for China, and how far his revolutionary ideas had penetrated the consciousness of the world. Few people indeed were ignorant of his name, an accolade shared previously by no Chinese person. Only from Taibei came a discordant note when an official statement denounced Mao Zedong as a "despotic leader". Yet Hua Guofeng, the successor of Zhou Enlai as well as Mao Zedong, might have adopted the words spoken in 960 by the first Song emperor and in reply asked of Macao, Hong Kong and Taiwan: "What wrong have your people done to be excluded from China?" For the Chinese view of the world has not fundamentally changed: it has adjusted to take account of the modern world, but only so far as to permit China to retain its central place. Although the technically inclined supporters of Deng Xiaoping would not today laud "Marxism—Leninism—Mao Zedong Thought" as the only yardstick for measuring revolutionary progress, there can be few doubts in their minds as to the universal value of Chinese socialism. China, not the Soviet Union, is the Middle Kingdom of the Communist bloc.

The re-emergence of China as a major power was the work of Mao Zedong, who gave his country what it had longed for after a century of chaos and uncertainty—the revolutionary leadership, the strategy, the institutional framework and, above all else, the ideology that could inspire its regeneration. Unlike other revolutionary leaders, including his loyal assistant Zhou Enlai, he did not venture abroad and his origins within the peasant life of the provinces were not even grasped by his Chinese comrades at first. The rebellious son of a "rich peasant", he was unique in his understanding of the land problem which had so worried Dr Sun Yatsen. Once Mao Zedong discovered Marxist theory he was able to use it, and transform it, in his analysis of the contradictions of China and the outside world. His great accomplishment, said Liu Shaoqi in 1946, "has been to change Marxism from a European to an Asian form . . . The basic principles of Marxism are undoubtedly adaptable to all countries, but to apply their general truth to concrete revolutionary practice in China is a difficult task. He is the first that has succeeded in doing so." Eight years earlier Mao Zedong had talked of "the Sinification of Marxism" and laid stress on the need to avoid dogmatism by the discussion of politics in a manner of speech accessible to the average Chinese. His acute sense of the learning capabilities of the peasantry never left him: he remained at bottom a teacher, yet as he had told Edgar Snow, "one must be a pupil of the masses before one can become their teacher."

In observing the events in the People's Republic after the death of Mao Zedong, it is necessary to recall not only the errors of judgement he himself made but also his own keen awareness of the limitations of what had been achieved. The triumph of 1949, which united the country as it had not been since the early nineteenth century, was perceived as but the beginning of revolutionary development, for as soon as China had room to manoeuvre Mao Zedong resumed the search begun in Yan'an for a distinctly Chinese path to socialism. Just as the Great Leap Forward shook up the countryside through the commune movement, so the impact on the cities of the Great Proletarian Cultural Revolution was intended to liberate revolutionary energies and purify official dogma. According to Mao Zedong, there had been eleven important struggles against "enemies" within the Chinese Communist Party, since the 1935 conference at Zunyi on the Long March.

For Jiang Qing the last struggle arose during April 1976, ironically in Tiananmen square, where she had organised the Red Guard rallies. At the time of the *Qingming* festival—the occasion on which filial duty used to be demonstrated by sweeping the ancestral graves but remembrance of one's forbears is now shown through flowers—wreaths in memory of Zhou Enlai started to appear on the Monument to the People's Heroes, an unheard-of event. Within a matter of days thousands of tributes were placed there, many of whose inscriptions implied dissatisfaction with the policies of Mao Zedong's faction. That the citizens of Beijing should have chosen the largest memorial ever built in the People's Republic to reveal their gratitude for the moderation that Zhou Enlai had always championed is not altogether surprising. As it was Zhou Enlai's final wish to have his ashes scattered in the countryside, the monument offered a convenient substitute for the traditional memorial column, not least because on its northern face a long inscription composed by Mao Zedong is written in Zhou Enlai's own calligraphy. The final sentence aptly recalls the "people's heroes who from 1840 laid down their lives in the many struggles against internal and external enemies, for national independence and the freedom and welfare of the people".

Overreaching themselves in dealing with this demonstration of public feeling, Jiang Qing and her close associates arranged for the police to arrest mourners and cordon off Tiananmen square. They blamed Deng Xiaoping for the disorder which erupted after these measures were taken, and he was relegated to the background for a couple of months. But not everyone in the Political Bureau was content with his exclusion for "instigating counter-revolutionary riots". Marshal Ye Jiangyang (1897–1986) stalked out of the disciplinary hearing and made no secret of the fact that other senior members of the People's Liberation Army shared his impatience with Jiang Qing's actions. Deng Xiaoping seems to have already obtained the backing of several powerful military figures prior to the death of Mao Zedong so that he could afford to bide his time. He did not have to wait long, however. In the second week of September, Hua Guofeng and Ye Jiangyang agreed that Jiang Qing and her associates should be detained, which they were in less than one month. The exact circumstances of Jiang Qing's capture are unknown, despite rumours that her bodyguard resisted the government troops sent to her country residence near Beijing.

The "Gang of Four", Mao Zedong's most fervent disciples, did not go on trial until the winter of 1980–1, along with some followers of Lin Biao. When the case opened, the government announced that the defendants were not on trial for having lost a power struggle, but for having used illegal means in trying to win it. The guilty verdicts handed down were intended to show that the

People's Republic had returned to the rule of law and had rejected their "ultra-Left" policies. The delay in bringing charges against Jiang Qing is explained in the time it took Deng Xiaoping to establish effective control, which he had won by the close of 1978.

As rehabilitated "rightists" Deng Xiaoping's supporters were initially obliged to regard the Great Proletarian Cultural Revolution as a worthwhile exercise, whose purposes had been distorted by Lin Biao and Mao Zedong. The gradual swing of the political pendulum towards Deng Xiaoping's position allowed only a slow build-up of comment upon the strife of 1966–9, but not until 1979 was it possible for Ye Jiangyang to declare publicly how disastrous the cultural revolution had been. Complete condemnation still needed to wait another two years: then the people were informed that unless the country was freed from such "ultra-Left" movements China could never expect to modernise itself.

Deng Xiaoping has not been able to carry out a total purge of party members or officials who believe Mao Zedong's launching and direction of the Great Proletarian Cultural Revolution was correct, just as he has been unable to deny entirely the spirit of the educational reforms that accompanied it. Although his remarks on wasted scientific talent have a telling ring about them (he said that the Academy of Sciences "is not an academy of cabbage cultivation; it is not an academy of beans"), the fact remains that educational opportunities were widened as schools and colleges reopened in the early 1970s. The authority of the party bureaucrat or the technical expert in his field has not passed away as Mao Zedong may have wished, but peasants and workers are now politically more aware than ever before. Examinations and qualifications have been gradually brought back, while selection to college has once again become primarily the result of a written test. In July 1985 free higher education was abolished, except for those who are studying to be teachers, those who are very poor, or those who expect particularly tough job assignments after graduation. The repeal of this "ultra-Left" principle, and the linking of income with academic performance, was announced as a move aimed at raising standards in order to prepare a generation of experts to push through the government's modernisation plans. This ambitious programme is called the "Four Modernisations" *(sihua)* and covers agriculture, industry, science, and defence.

Competition for entrance to colleges and universities remains fierce, with less than 6 per cent of those who successfully completed secondary education going on to higher studies in 1986. Pressures in this bottleneck—through which must flow the upwardly mobile—probably accounts for some of the demands made during recent student protests. The demonstrations of December 1986 in Beijing, Wuhan, Shanghai and other cities took the Political Bureau by surprise, even though it has been suggested that Deng Xiaoping was at first pleased with student urgings of further reform. He seems to have recognised the dangers of their call for "democracy" *(minzhu)* when 20,000 workers also came out on strike in Luoyang, capital of Henan province. Deng Xiaoping reacted by sacrificing his heir-apparent Hu Yaobang (1915–89), who resigned as premier in 1987 for permitting the "bourgeois liberalism" which had stirred up the students. As his successor Zhao Ziyang (b. 1919) said, the "weak and lax leadership" of the former minister had encouraged a false belief that it was possible to "break away from the party . . . and negate socialism".

Senior members of the Chinese Communist Party are concerned about the effect that rapid modernisation is likely to have on the attitudes of the young. In May 1985 Beijing had its first taste of soccer hooliganism, when foreigners' cars were stoned, buses wrecked and taxis overturned after a Hong Kong side used time-wasting tactics to protect a 2–1 lead over China in a World Cup qualifying match. Although the violence of this incident pales in comparison with the riot started on the same day by English supporters in Brussels, an event which left nearly 500 people dead or injured, the Chinese authorities felt the need to deal severely with the culprits and heavy sentences were handed down. They were embarrassed as much by the outburst of xenophobia as the ill-will directed at the Hong Kong players, who in the agreement then being signed with Britain were due to become citizens of the People's Republic in 1997, the year fixed for the colony's return to China.

The current attacks on "bourgeois liberalism" are to be seen therefore in the context of a perennial worry about the importation of foreign ideas into China. It is essentially the dilemma that faced reformers in the final years of the Qing dynasty. How can the country modernise itself through borrowing foreign equipment and ideas without losing its own character? In the late nineteenth century the loss was perceived in terms of the Confucian empire, today it is Chinese socialism. Deng Xiaoping thus finds himself wresting with the paradox of "Marxism—Leninism—Mao Zedong Thought", the Chinese character of which has been the basis for its unique contribution to the development of Communist theory. He has had to repudiate the Great Proletarian Cultural Revolution without undermining the prestige of China's modern sage. Towards the end of his life, it is said today, Mao Zedong was responsible for implementing policies which have slowed down the country's progress. These misguided decisions, however, in no way diminish his contribution to the founding of the People's Republic; on the contrary, "the party and the people would have had to grope in the dark much longer had it not been for Mao Zedong": but this admission of error, no matter how face-saving, means that the infallibility of dogma has at last gone. Justification in future should come from facts, and not any equivalent of the "little red book".

As long as Deng Xiaoping is able to convince the Chinese Communist Party that his modernisation programme is working, the general drift of government policy will continue to be a dismantlement of Mao Zedong's cultural revolution. Having stripped the communes of their political and administrative functions, the government announced in 1984 that almost all land was to be allocated to peasants on fifteen-year contracts. In parallel with this abandonment of collective farming, a certain amount of free enterprise was allowed in industry, including bonus schemes and investment. Special investment zones were additionally established in which foreign capital could finance industrial projects and make a profit from the labour of Chinese workers. Most notable of these new zones is Shenzhen, which surrounds Hong Kong on the landward side and acts as an economic buffer between the colony and the People's Republic. Whilst the countryside has answered the relaxation of regulation with increased output—cereal production rose from 305 tonnes in 1978 to 407 million in 1984—there are signs that the economy as a whole is somewhat overheated, as complaints about inflation indicate. For a country that has been until very recently isolated from world-wide inflation, the advent of price rises came as a shock and a reminder of the monetary horrors of Jiang Jieshi's final years. In 1948 the retail price index in Shanghai had reached 287,700,000 from a 1937 base of 100.

Responding to criticisms in September 1985, Deng Xiaoping told senior party members that "utilisation of foreign investment funds in a planned way and the promotion of a degree of individual economy are both serving the development of the socialist economy". But he conceded that certain "evil things that had long been extinct after the liberation have come to life again" and these problems will need "firm steps to deal with them". By this public display of firmness, Deng Xiaoping was telling Chinese and foreigners alike that no one was going to undermine the almost miraculous recovery the economy had already achieved under the Chinese Communist Party. To many outsiders the speech appeared to be half-hearted capitalism, which it certainly was not. All that Deng Xiaoping meant to indicate was that there were limits to private enterprise—not an unusual notion in a country whose long experience under the imperial system had been a high degree of central control. Just in case the inhabitants of Hong Kong missed the message, or mistook student calls for popular reform, he reminded them in April 1987 that they would never be permitted to use "the cloak of democracy" to turn future discontent against China's interests. The decision to cut back on foreign borrowing in order to reduce the current deficit is but another example of the tough measures the government is ready to take when necessary.

That "number two capitalist roader", as the Red Guards once labelled Deng Xiaoping, was obliged to rebuke "rightists" following the student protests would have amused Jiang Qing, if her prison guards bothered to tell her. Yet the pace of change which he set in motion is bound to cause a radical realignment of the various groups making up the Chinese Communist Party. For some members Deng Xiaoping remains too conservative, just as for others he is too liberal.

This was indeed the uneasy position in which Deng Xiaoping found himself when protesting students again took to the streets of Beijing and other cities during the summer of 1989. Calls for democracy, a free press, and an investigation of official corruption left him with little room for manoeuvre, once it became obvious that neither the Political Bureau nor the student leaders were inclined to compromise.

Student protest in Beijing began with the announcement on 15 April of the death of Hu Yaobang, the disgraced ex-premier. Tributes to the would-be reformer showed discontent with government policy from the moment they were stuck up on notice boards at Beijing University. An early one read: "A true man has died, false men are living." The students who caused Hu Yaobang's fall two years before obviously felt the need to record their support for the modernisation programme he had dared to pioneer. They may even have had in mind his criticism of the education system, the only subject he continued to speak about. Despite his ill-health, Hu Yaobang attended an important Political Bureau meeting on 8 April to express his view that schools and colleges should serve the modernisation of China, and not abstract ideology. His collapse there was sufficiently worrying for an official denial of any direct link between the debate and the heart attack.

Recalling the precedent set by Zhou Enlai's mourners,

the Chinese Communist Party broadcast within four hours of the announcement of death a radio tribute to Hu Yaobang, the "great proletarian revolutionary and statesman". No mention was made of his ejection from office, however. For the students of Beijing University this was tantamount to an insult to Hu Yaobang's memory, and they swiftly demanded his full rehabilitation, a course of action that would have obliged the Political Bureau to acknowledge its mistake in sacking him. Wreaths were also placed on the Monument to the People's Heroes in Tiananmen square, although the first demonstration only occurred on 17 April.

Barely four hundred students took part in the demonstration, but the slogans they shouted in Tiananmen square that day formed the agenda for the mass movement of May and June. After placing their wreath on the monument, they chanted: "Long live Hu Yaobang. Long live democracy. Long live freedom. Down with corruption. Down with bureaucracy." For those who were caught up in the subsequent demonstrations, students and Beijing citizens alike, these slogans incorporated a general sense of grievance at the slowness of political change. If modernisation of agriculture, industry, science and defence had been the stimulus of the first decade after Mao Zedong, then political reform came to be seen as the critical issue of the late 1980s. Both within, and without, the Chinese Communist Party there were people who believed that material progress would not be achieved without political reform. In 1986 Deng Xiaoping had encouraged speculation, giving a welcome to comments from academic reformers outside the party establishment, and the licence to criticise was renewed under Zhao Ziyang, the successor of Hu Yaobang. That limits to discussion still existed became transparent in February 1989, when the scientist Fang Lizhi (b. 1936) was barred from attending a barbecue hosted by President Bush. Chinese police told the outspoken university teacher at the entrance of the Great Wall Sheraton Hotel that he was not permitted to be a guest. His error, according to official sources, was of "instigating trouble by saying that Chinese intellectuals . . . ought to constitute an independence force".

Though Fang Lizhi was eventually cast as the chief villain behind the "counter-revolutionary rebellion" of 1989, the Political Bureau cannot be unaware that he played no direct role in the protests once they had started. Probably his comments to foreign newspaper correspondents caused the greatest annoyance. "This is not just for Hu Yaobang," Fang Lizhi said. "This is a chance for students to let the government know they are unhappy with the present situation." His flight to the United States embassy, the day after the People's Liberation Army moved into Tiananmen square, merely confirmed suspicions of American manipulation of the student movement. As Deng Xiaoping told ex-President Nixon on a damage-limitation visit to Beijing in November, "Frankly speaking, the U.S. was involved too deeply in the turmoil. . . . China was the real victim and it is unjust to reprove China for it."

Such an explanation of the tragic events of June 1989 ignores the unpremeditated upsurge of protest that followed the announcement of Hu Yaobang's death. Furthermore, it discounts the widespread support shown for the student protestors in Beijing and other cities. Rallies and hunger strikes were reported from Guangdong, Hubei, Hunan, Shaanxi and Sichuan provinces, while in Shanghai protest ended with the firing of a train after it had ploughed into crowds blocking the railway tracks. In Beijing itself the ordinary population also suffered at the hands of the People's Liberation Army. The shooting-up of a crowd of pedestrians and cyclists outside the Beijing Hotel, on the main avenue leading to Tiananmen square, shocked even seasoned reporters. But it was the savagery of the attack of 3–4 June on the students in Tiananmen square that was immediately dubbed a massacre. Officially nobody was killed in the night clearance, but eyewitnesses say that they saw numerous corpses strewn across the flagstones. The total death toll for the city may have run into several thousands.

The tragedy was watched by millions outside China,

because foreign television crews were still in Beijing following the visit of Mikhail Gorbachev, President of the Soviet Union. His arrival in the middle of May, and the attention it received from world media, gave the students a unique opportunity to embarrass the Chinese authorities, already on the defensive through foreign reports about unrest in Tibet. A month earlier, the *People's Daily* had cautioned that "the Lhasa riots have their own particular background, but they show how we must value a stable environment. . . . Haste and impatience for progress on the question of democracy will only increase the sources of instability".

At first, viewers of the television coverage abroad were amazed at the restraint of both the Political Bureau and the student leaders. Zhao Ziyang, moreover, seemed to balance effectively the need to restore order with a fair hearing of the students' complaints. Conscious of the unpredictable forces which the author of *glasnost* could unleash in Beijing, Zhao Ziyang was anxious that the first visit by a Soviet leader for thirty years should be a diplomatic triumph equal to the coming of President Nixon in 1972. It was unfortunate that his efforts to diffuse the confrontation in Tiananmen square failed so miserably. The student leaders ignored his warnings of repressive measures, and the Political Bureau lost patience with his visits to hunger strikers and his public appeals. On 18 May Deng Xiaoping ordered soldiers to the capital. In one account of the decision, Deng Xiaoping shouted, "I have the army behind me." When Zhao Ziyang countered by shouting, "But I have the people behind me," he rudely was told, "You have nothing."

That power resided in the barrels of the People's Liberation Army proved to be quite correct. The military backers of Deng Xiaoping fearing perhaps a return to the chaos of cultural revolution, bloodily put down the student protest. At the same time Zhao Ziyang was relieved of all his posts, and Jiang Zemin (b. 1926), a senior official from Shanghai, became prime minister in his place.

A striking parallel of the reform debate in the 1980s has been the activities of writers and film-makers.

Novelists have turned their attention to forgotten corners, evoking the atmosphere of ordinary people's lives before and after 1949. Deng Youmei (born 1931) writes of impoverished retainers surviving on their wits in Beijing as Manchu power crumbled; Lu Wenfu (born 1928) tells of the tribulations of Tianjin street vendors, one of whom earns the dubious title of "profiteer" for daring to sell soup; and Gu Hwa, as we have seen, manages to shed new light on village manners. Their description of both human frailty and dignity is a welcome relief after the heavy-handed propaganda themes favoured by Jiang Qing. It is also a contribution to thinking about the way in which China should develop.

No less thoughtful are the films of Chen Kaige (b. 1952), a director who prefers to work in provincial studios. Controversy was stirred by his *Yellow Earth (Huang Tu)*, because the young cadre in the story fails to save an intelligent young girl from an arranged marriage. What the superb camera work really shows, nonetheless, is the extent to which the impoverished peasants of Gansu province are at the mercy of their splendid but harsh homeland as well as the superstitious beliefs that appear to secure their survival in it. Just as controversial was *The Big Parade (Da Jianyue)* a film which looked at the appalling pressure on the individual soldier to perform well in the preparations leading up to a national celebration mounted by the People's Liberation Army.

The language itself, or at least the written script, is a part of the debate too. Throughout the empire there was an awareness of the difficulty involved in mastering characters, but the preference for calligraphy always stopped any transfer to a phonetic alphabet in spite of the invention of movable type. To deal with this hindrance to cultural aspirations, Mao Zedong had declared in 1951 that "the written language must be reformed; it should follow the common direction of phoneticisation which has been taken by the world's languages." In reality, adopting the Roman alphabet for a monosyllabic language that relies largely on tone for the differentiation of meaning proved far too complicated, so instead it was decided to simplify the number of strokes used to write 2000 of the most common characters. But a further series of more than 800 simplifications that the government tried to introduce in 1978 met so much resistance that they had to be scrapped. Compromise is now favoured, Deng Xiaoping in 1980 forbidding the proliferation of do-it-yourself simplifications on advertisements and shop signs. Most successful of all is Pinyin, a phonetic romanised script developed to overcome the confusion which invariably arises through the transcribing of Chinese words into different foreign languages. This allows the same form for Mao Zedong to appear in French, Swedish, German, Spanish, Italian and English. Pinyin is not intended for use in China, where in 1987 it was officially admitted that "characters will continue to be the nation's written language for a long time to come".

A reluctance to jettison the achievements of the past can be observed, too, in the care with which archaeologists explore sites dating from all periods. One motive behind the current spate of excavation may be a lingering determination to bury once and for all the scepticism of Western scholars at the beginning of the twentieth century towards Chinese historical traditions. The discovery of Peking Man in the 1920s and the Shang capital at Anyang in the 1930s forced a change of attitude, but it is a tribute to the work of present-day Chinese archaeologists that so much of the ancient chronology of the Histories is now accepted as fact. Of central importance to our understanding of the emergence of China's civilisation are the excavations in progress at Erlitou, in Henan province: this site could be authenticated as the first Shang capital, whose traditional foundation date of 1766 BC is close to that suggested by radio-carbon analysis. Even the Red Guards failed to slow down the number of archaeological discoveries, although they damaged many relics during their rampage, and therefore we may confidently anticipate a further stream of fascinating finds. At the very least the prestige that archaeology now enjoys in the People's Republic ensures that there will be no repetition of the tomb robbery and destruction of ancient sites which occurred prior to 1949, when road and railway construction did more to enrich the antique trade than the economy.

The beginning of a tourist industry must also encourage further preservation of the only continuous cultural heritage in the world today. President Nixon's visit marked the end of China's international isolation, and the opening up of the country to tourists under Deng Xiaoping is a sign that the Chinese are confident of what they have on display. Not even the tragedy of Tiananmen square can reverse permanently the changes that Deng Xiaoping has overseen. The settlements regarding the future of both Hong Kong and Macao permit a more relaxed approach to the world at large, just as improved relations with Taiwan clear away an unnecessary obstacle to mutually beneficial trade and investment. The Guomindang response to the events of June 1989 was unusually muted. A spokesman in Taibei let it be known the chief mistake of the Beijing students was that they wanted revolution not evolution. They went too far in criticising Deng Xiaoping.

This restrained comment indicates the extent to which the People's Republic has become accepted as a world power, even on Taiwan. But if the siege of China has been lifted by the Chinese people themselves, then the People's Liberation Army deserves credit since 1949 for its ability to deter new enemies. Border disputes with India (1962) and Vietnam (1979) are unlikely to become major conflicts, since modern China has exactly the strategic aims as the empire from which it grew: deterrence of invaders. Providing the People's Liberation Army is not weakened by its involvement with political conflict at home, there is little reason to suppose that country will endure another period of disunity.

Another internal problem the People's Republic has still to solve is population growth. In the early 1980s, when the total number of Chinese passed the 1000 million mark, it contained a high proportion of people just approaching marriageable age, but only a small proportion of very old people. To tackle this imbalance and halt the rate of increase a national birth-control campaign was launched in which one-child families and late marriage played key roles. Reports indicate that this is already having an effect, although the government finds it easier to limit births in urban areas than in the countryside, where the traditional family structure is much stronger and where children are often an economic asset on contract plots. Informed estimates predict a levelling out of China's population at about 1200 million in the year 2000. Another 20 million who reside at the moment outside the People's Republic, mainly in South-East Asia, should remain overseas Chinese and citizens of the countries they inhabit. At the Bandung conference of Asian states in 1955 Zhou Enlai reversed what had been Guomindang policy towards them by declaring that no longer would all persons of Chinese descent be automatically regarded as citizens of the People's Republic.

This gesture was intended to assure delegates of China's lack of territorial ambitions beyond its borders. Not unlike the Ming admiral Zheng He, Zhou Enlai would have been prepared to accept token recognition of the place his country occupied in East Asia, but this was the era of Washington's "domino theory" when any concession to the Communist threat seemed a dangerous move. So instead Zhou Enlai chose to remind those at the conference of their common experience of colonialism. "If we seek common ground", he said, "and remove the misfortune and suffering imposed on us by colonialism, then it is easy for us to understand and respect each other, to be sympathetic and helpful to each other." His words can stand for the experience of China itself in the last hundred years—the Chinese have come through untold woes to reclaim their membership of the society of great nations.

CHRONOLOGY

(showing key periods and dynasties)

Sui dynasty 589–618
Tang dynasty 618–906
Five dynasties 907–960
Song dynasty 960–1279:   Northern Song 960—1126
                               Southern Song 1127–1279

The Late Empire

Yuan dynasty 1279–1368
Ming dynasty 1368–1644
Qing dynasty 1644–1911

POST-IMPERIAL CHINA

Republic 1912–49
People's Republic 1949 onwards

NOTES AND REFERENCES

The following notes and references are intended to assist the reader in pursuing topics of special interest. They draw attention to publications that may provide greater detail themselves or suggest ways in which further investigation can take place. It has to be said, however, that coverage of Chinese history is scant in English, although there are encouraging signs that this deficiency will soon be less serious. Two series of books in particular are doing much to round out our view of China. The first is Joseph Needham's *Science and Civilization in China*, begun in 1954: sixteen of the twenty-five volumes planned are now available. The most recent is subtitled *Military Technology: the Gunpowder Ethic* and deals with the invention of the gun. Secondly, there is *The Cambridge History of China*, edited by D. Twitchett and J. K. Fairbank, several volumes of which have appeared since 1978. While the best atlas remains A. Herrmann's *Historical and Commercial Atlas of China*, reissued in Chicago and Edinburgh in 1966, a lot of background information can be obtained from a *Cultural Atlas of China*, C. Blunden and M. Elvin, Oxford, 1983. Other useful references are *Key Economic Areas in Chinese History, as revealed in the Development of Public Works for Water Control*, Chi Chao-ting, London, 1936, reissued New York, 1970, and *The Pattern of the Chinese Past*, M. Elvin, London, 1973. Many of the quotations from the Histories may be located, in one form or another, in *The Imperial History of China,* J. MacGowan. London, 1897, reissued 1973.

CHAPTER 1: THE EMERGENCE OF CIVILISATION

The best analysis of early finds appears in *Archaeology of Ancient China,* Chang Kwang-chih, revised and enlarged edition, New Haven, 1977. *The Cradle of the East,* Ho Ping-ti, Hong Kong and Chicago, 1975, is also a stimulating inquiry into the origins of Chinese culture between 5000 and 1000 BC. It includes a lengthy discussion of both religion and thought down to the Early Zhou period. Full treatment of the Shang era is to be found in *Shang Civilization,* Chang Kwang-chih, New Haven, 1980. For a translation of *The Book of Songs* see A. Waley, London, 1937, and of the *Book of History,* J. Legge, new edition, London, 1972.

CHAPTER 2: THE CLASSICAL AGE

An excellent way into the political intrigues and wars that bedevilled the feudal states is J. I. Crump's *Chan-kuo T'se,* Oxford, 1979, a large collection of historical anecdotes covering the period from *c.* 300 to 221 BC. Although the translation of Sun Zi's *Art of War* by S. G. Griffith, Oxford, 1963, has an excellent introduction, the detailed commentary alongside the text and translation made earlier by L. Giles, London, 1910, deserves study for anyone who wishes to read properly what is the oldest military treatise known in the world. An overview of political thought in general, including the use of armed force, is available in *A Political History of Chinese Political Thought, Volume I: From the Beginnings to the Sixth Century* AD, Hsiao Kung-chuan, translated by F. W. Mote, Princeton, 1979. Books on individual philosophers are *Confucius and the Chinese Way,* H. G. Creel, New York, 1960; *Confucius,* D. H. Smith, London, 1973; (Lao Zi) *The Way and its Power: A study of the Tao Teh Ching and its*

Place in Chinese Thought, A. Waley, London, 1934; (Mo Zi) *Mao Tzu: The Neglected Rival of Confucius*, Y. P. Mei, London, 1934; (Shang Yang) *The Book of Lord Shang: A Classic of Chinese Law*, J. J. L. Duyvendak, London, 1928, reprinted 1963; (Zhuang Zi) *Chuang Tzu: Taoist Philosopher and Mystic*, H. A. Giles, London, 1889, reissued 1961; *Mencius*, D. C. Lau, Harmondsworth, 1970; (Xun Zi) *Hsuntze: The Moulder of Ancient Confucianism*, H. H. Dubs, London, 1927; and finally, a more recent comparison of the main contending schools of philosophy, *Individual and State in Ancient China*, V. A. Rubin, translated by S. I. Levine, New York, 1976. The social turmoil that prevailed during the Classical Age is analysed by Hsu Cho-yun in *Ancient China in Transition: An Analysis of Social Mobility, 722–222 BC*, Stamford, 1965.

CHAPTER 3: THE EARLY EMPIRE

For the Qin dynasty there is *China's First Unifier*, D. Bodde, Leiden, 1938, reprinted Hong Kong, 1967, as well as his *Statesman, Patriot and General in Ancient China*, New Haven, 1940. The latter is a translation of three lives from Sima Qian's history. I have also drawn on my own *The First Emperor of China*, London and New York, 1981. Translations of Sima Qian include B. Watson's *Record of the Grand Historian of China* (two volumes) New York, 1961, and *Records of the Historian*, New York, 1965, as well as *Records of the Historian written by Szuma Chien*, Gladys and Hsienyi Yang, Hong Kong, 1974.

Recently the Han dynasty has begun to receive more thorough attention in the West. There are *The Han Civilization of China*, M. Pirazzoti-t' Serstevens, translated by J. Seligman, Oxford, 1982; *Han Social Structure*, Chu T'ung-tsu, translated by J. L. Dull, Seattle, 1972; *Han Agriculture*, Hsu Cho-yun, Seattle, 1980; *Crisis and Conflict in Han China*, M. Loewe, London, 1974, as well as his *Ways to Paradise: The Chinese Quest for Immortality*,

London, 1979. An informative study of Sino-barbarian economic relations is contained in *Trade and Expansion in Han China*, Yu Ying-shih, Berkeley, 1967.

For the period following the dissolution of the Han empire there are *Inner Asian Frontiers of China*, O. Lattimore, New York, 1951, and *A History of China*, W. Eberhard, revised and enlarged edition, London, 1971. The arrival of Buddhism, and its subsequent metamorphosis is chronicled in K. Chen's *Buddhism in China*, Princeton, 1964, and his *The Chinese Transformation of Buddhism*, Princeton, 1973, as well as E. Zurcher's *The Buddhist Conquest of China*, Leiden, 1959.

An excellent introduction to the revolution in communications caused by the invention of paper is contained in D. Twitchett's *Printing and Publishing in Medieval China*, New York, 1983.

CHAPTER 4: THE MIDDLE EMPIRE

Studies of eminent figures include (Tang Tai Zong) *Son of Heaven*, C. P. Fitzgerald, Cambridge, 1933, reissued New York, 1971, as well as his *The Empress Wu*, London, 1956; (Wei Zheng) *Mirror to the Son of Heaven*, H. J. Wechsler, New Haven, 1974; and (Bai Juyi) *The Life and Times of Po Chu-I*, A. Waley, London, 1949. For a general appreciation of Tang poetry S. Owen's translations and commentary are recommended in *The Great Age of Chinese Poetry*, New Haven, 1981. A selection of the Song poet Su Shi's work can be found in *Su Tung-P'o*, translated by B. Watson, New Haven, 1965.

Although many books are now available on ceramics and painting, a well-illustrated and up-to-date guide is W. Watson's *The Art of Dynastic China*, London, 1979. James Cahill's *Hills Beyond a River*, New York, 1976, covers painting in the Yuan dynasty, while his *Parting at the Shore*, New York, 1978, and *The Distant Mountains*, New York, 1982, deal with most of the Ming dynasty. The Chinese garden and its relation to landscape painting are sensitively explored in O. Sirén, *Gardens of China*, New York, 1949.

CHAPTER 5: THE LATE EMPIRE

Interesting perspectives on the Mongol imperium are offered in I. De Rachewiltz's *Papal Envoys to the Great Khans*, London, 1971, and *The Secret History of the Mongols*, translated by A. Waley, London, 1963. The victory of Zhu Yuanzhang at Boyang lake is recounted in *Chinese Ways in Warfare*, F. A. Kierman and J. K. Fairbank, Cambridge, Massachusetts, 1974, along with the campaigns of the Han emperor Wu Di and the capture of the Ming emperor Ying Zhong by Mongol tribesmen at Tumubao in 1449. The early Qing period is perhaps best represented by J. D. Spence's *Emperor of China, K'ang Hsi*, London, 1974, which comprises historical documents including writings by Kangxi; the middle period by *Shantung Rebellion: The Wang Lun Uprising of 1774*, S. Naquin, New Haven, 1981, and *An Embassy to China: being the journal kept by Lord Macartney during his embassy to Emperor Ch'ienlung 1793–94* (Qianlong), edited by J. L. Cranmer-Byng, London, 1962; and the later period by *The Opium War Through Chinese Eyes*, A. Waley, London, 1958, and *The Taiping Revolutionary Movement*, Jen Yu-wen, New Haven, 1973. For a biography of Kang Youwei see *A Modern China and A New World*, Hsiao Kung-chuan, Seattle, 1975.

CHAPTERS 6 AND 7: THE REPUBLIC AND THE PEOPLE'S REPUBLIC

Since most studies of modern China start just after the end of the imperial system, these chapters for bibliographical purposes need to be treated as a single period. Sino-Japanese relations can be approached through S. Kato's *The Japan-China Phenomenon: Conflict or Compatibility?*, London, 1974. J. Ch'en's *Yuan Shik-k'ai* (Yuan Shikai), Stanford, 1972, is a good introduction to the early republic, just as his *Mao and the Chinese Revolution*, Oxford, 1965, remains an excellent account of the Chinese Communist Party before 1949. The Communist defeat of the

Guomindang receives detailed military attention in *The Communist Conquest of China*, L. M. Chassin, translated by T. Osato and L. Gelas, London, 1965, while J. F. Melby's diary *The Mandate of Heaven*, Toronto, 1968, and London, 1969, provides a graphic account of US involvement. A personal account of Communist resistance to the Imperial Japanese Army is also contained in *The Unknown War: North China 1937–1945*, M. Lindsay, London, 1975. Recommended for post–1949 developments are *The Political Thought of Mao Tse-tung*, (Mao Zedong), S. R. Schram, New York, 1963, as well as R. MacFarquhar's monumental study of cultural revolution, two volumes of which have been published so far: *The Origins of the Cultural Revolution: Contradictions Among the People, 1956–57* and *The Great Leap Forward, 1958–60*, Oxford, 1974 and 1983 respectively. However. *The Second Chinese Revolution*, K. S. Karol, translated by M. Jones, London, 1975, is still a readable, though uncritical, narrative of the Great Proletarian Cultural Revolution. For a Chinese viewpoint on the last two decades the relevant chapters of *Zhou Enlai: A Profile*, P. J. and L. G. J. Fang, Beijing, 1986, are illuminating. Foreign policy and international relations in general are covered in *The World and China, 1922–72*, J. Gittings, London, 1974, and *Defending China*, G. Segal, Oxford, 1985. *Tiananmen: The Rape of Peking*, M. Fathers and A. Higgins, London and New York, 1989, offers a vivid account of the June 1989 tragedy.

INDEX

Macartney, Lord, 228–230, 235
Malindi, 204–205
Manchuria and the Manchus, 7, 149, 202, 246, 248, 250, 259, 262, 266, 267, 273–274, 286, 287, 288, 293, 294, 295
see also Qing dynasty and Manzhouguo
Mandate of Heaven, xvi, 28, 33, 73, 124, 290
Manzhouguo (puppet state), 253–254, 262, 271–272
Mao Zedong, xviii, xxiv, 210, 237, 255, 259, 263–264, 266, 268–273, 275, 278–279, 280, 281–283, 286, 287, 290, 291, 292–297, 298–299, 300–301, 302, 303–322, 324, 327, 330, 331
personality cult, 313, 315–316
understanding of the countryside, xviii, 264, 268, 269, 270, 319–320
Marshall, George (general), 291–292
Mawangdui (tomb site), 97–98, 99, 127
May Fourth Movement (1919), 254–255, 256, 308
medicine, 4–5, 127, 129, 174–175, 216, 217
Mei Fei (painter), 180
Mencius (philosopher), xxi, 9, 30, 72–76, 165
metallurgy, xviii, 15, 16, 20, 25, 31–33, 63–64, 124, 125
see also iron and steel

Miao (peoples), 225, 234
Min (river), 50–51
Ming (dynasty), 99, 127, 152, 192–222, 225, 226, 229, 233, 333
Ming Chong Zhen (emperor), 221
Ming Hong Wu (emperor), 99, 192–195, 197
Ming Hui Di (emperor), 195
Ming Ying Zong (emperor), 194, 212–213
Ming Yong Le (emperor), xix, 195, 196, 197, 199, 202–203, 204–205, 206, 207, 210, 211, 212, 216
Ming Wu Zong (emperor), 213
Mo Zi and Moism, 68, 73, 76–77
money: coinage, 11, 66, 88, 89, 112, 176
paper notes, 176, 183
Mongols and Mongolia, 61, 99, 110, 166, 172, 186–193, 194, 197, 199, 200, 202, 203–204, 207, 212, 217, 218–219, 224, 287
monopolies see nationalisation
Mount Li (First Emperor's tomb), xxiv, 49, 65, 86, 94
Mukden Incident (1931), 266, 268, 274
music, 99–100, 101
Mycenaeans, 23